Ultra. It saved [] S0-AWU-922 e
Luftwaffe in the skies over England, turned the
tide at El Alamein, destroyed the Nazi U-boat
fleet, outfoxed Rommel in the desert, and
kept Normandy from turning into a disaster. It
allowed the Americans to win the vital battles of
Midway and the Coral Sea, and to shoot down
the plane carrying the great Japanese Admiral
Yamamoto. It made some Allied generals look
like super-geniuses, and others like bloody fools.
And it placed a soul-crushing burden on both
Churchill and Roosevelt.

Now for the first time we can know what Ultra
was and what it did.

**"Heady reading. It casts a whole new light on
World War II. We will have to rewrite all our
books."**

—The New Republic

**"The ruthless decisions to let men and cities die
rather than expose the secret was justified in
history."**

—The New York Times

**"FASCINATING, COMPELLING
READING . . . GREAT HISTORICAL
IMPORTANCE!"**

—Hartford Times

**"THE GREATEST INTELLIGENCE
TRIUMPH THE WORLD HAS EVER
KNOWN!"**

—Washington Post

THE
ULTRA
SECRET

F. W. Winterbotham, CBE

A DELL BOOK

Published by
DELL PUBLISHING CO., INC.
1 Dag Hammarskjold Plaza
New York, New York 10017

Dell ® TM 681510, Dell Publishing Co., Inc.
Reprinted by arrangement with Harper & Row, Publishers, Inc.
Printed in the United States of America
First Dell printing—December 1975
Second Dell printing—February 1976
Third Dell printing—March 1976
Fourth Dell printing—March 1976

To my wife Petrea
and our daughter Sally,
without whose encouragement
this book would not have been written.

Acknowledgements

I should like to thank the Marshal of the Royal Air Force, Sir John Slessor GCB, not only for his decisive Foreword, but also for the help he gave me; Ronald Lewin, who jogged my memory and put me right on numerous dates and places from his profound knowledge of World War II events; Professor R. V. Jones, my old colleague, who recalled for me some of his triumphs in the Scientific field of the Secret Service; Venetia Pollock who pulled the book together, and Nancy Neiman of Weidenfeld and Nicolson who so carefully edited the manuscript.

Preface

This is primarily the story of how, during World War II, the highest form of intelligence, obtained from the 'breaking' of the supposedly 'unbreakable' German machine cyphers, was 'processed' and distributed with complete security to President Roosevelt, Winston Churchill and all the principal Chiefs of Staff and commanders in the field throughout the war.

It also tells what the most important signals contained and how the various commanders reacted to and used the information and, finally, illustrates the decisive part it played in the Allied Victories.

I have given some of the background of the cypher breaking operation which was accomplished by a team of brilliant mathematicians and cryptographers at Bletchley Park near London, but both for security reasons and because I am not a cryptographer I have not given details of this near miracle.

Since virtually all the signals quoted or referred to in this book were in the Enigma Cypher I have thought it unncessary to label each one and have therefore included them all under the 'umbrella' of the code name *Ultra* which was given to this particular intelligence.

This code word will be repeated from time to time to remind the reader that this narrative is about intelligence available at the time, and not a history based on hindsight.

Unfortunately I have had no access to official records, and the book is written from my own recollections of the events described and of the hundreds of signals which I left locked in the vaults of Whitehall. If therefore I have made any errors on the cryptographic side they will, I hope, be forgiven; they might in any case add to the security of cryptography.

It has not been my intention in this book to magnify the part I played in the war effort. Rather it is my hope to add a necessary contribution to the history of World War II, a contribution resulting from the job I was given to do by the Chief of the British Secret Service.

The laurels for the Enigma Operation belong to the Code-breakers of Bletchley.

F.W.W.

Contents

Foreword 11

1   Introduction 15
2   Science to the Rescue: The Birth of Ultra 23
3   The Plan 37
4   The Battle of France 49
5   Interlude 63
6   The Battle of Britain 67
7   Operation Sea Lion 89
8   The African Campaign 99
9   Alamein 111
10 Naval Affairs and Briefing the Americans 125
11 'Torch' 139
12 'Husky' 155
13 'Avalanche' 161
14 Preparation for 'Overlord' 175
15 The Battle of Normandy 191
16 Hitler's Miracles 211
17 The Beginning of the End 229
18 Arnhem 235
19 The Japanese War 241
20 Hitler's Ardennes Offensive 253
21 Götterdammerung 261
22 Conclusion 267

Index 275

Foreword

by Marshal of the Royal Air Force Sir John Slessor
GCB, KCB, CB, DSO, MC, DL

It will probably occur to some readers of this book to wonder whether it is wise to make public so much about the supremely important source of Intelligence information which General Eisenhower described, just after the end of the Second World War, as a decisive factor in the Allied victory, and as having saved thousands of British and American lives. What has been known during the past thirty-four years to relatively very few people, even in the fighting Services, as *Ultra*, was indeed an almost incredibly valuable source of Intelligence—more even than the other British triumph in that field when we controlled and actively ran the German espionage system in Great Britain, described by its leading spirit, Sir John Masterman, in his enthralling book *The Double Cross System*. There is something especially thrilling about any really authentic story about Intelligence in war.

When the lights went out in 1939 Fred Winterbotham had been the senior Air Staff representative in the Secret Intelligence Service for ten years. In the early days of the war he was largely responsible, in co-operation with people like R. V. Jones and with Denniston, Knox and other excellent 'back-room boys' at Bletch-

ley, for the inception of *Ultra* and subsequently for its
working, through the Special Liaison units, throughout
the war. I don't suppose anyone had a more interesting
time of it during those years, dealing direct as he did
with virtually all the leaders on the highest levels, British and American, from the Prime Minister down-
wards on this incomparably useful and entirely reliable
means of informing them about what was going on 'on
the other side of the hill'. It will be seen from this book
that no one was more conscious than the author of the
vitally essential need for the complete security of the
system at the time. Incidentally it is a curious reflection
on our system of Honours and Awards that he should
have finished up after the war as a retired Group Captain with a CBE on a quiet farm in Devon.

There was nothing very new about the art of crack-
ing enemy cyphers as such—see for instance Kahn's
The Codebreakers and Roberta Wohlstetter's *Pearl
Harbour*. But with the secret abstraction from Poland
of the theoretically unbreakable German cypher machine *Enigma*, which gave birth eventually to *Ultra*,
that art took on a completely new dimension; and surely no other act in history of officially sponsored skul-
duggery ever had comparably fruitful results.

The official ban on any reference to Ultra until the
Spring of this year 1974 has certainly had an inhibiting
effect on the writing of military history in every field. I
have myself made several unsuccessful attempts, on the
highest levels, during the past twenty years to get that
ban lifted. And I am sure that this long-deferred disclo-
sure of *Ultra* and of its almost fabulous influence on
Allied strategy—and even sometimes on tactics—in the
last of the great conventional wars will not be a danger
in any great, and hence inevitably nuclear, war of the
future.

As Director of Plans in the Air Staff I was, of

course, aware of *Ultra* from its inception. On the fall of France I well remember the deep anxiety of dear Archie Boyle (for years the link between the Air Staff and the Secret Service) lest this gift from the Gods should fall into enemy hands which, thanks to the gallant and loyal Colonel Joubert, in the event it did not. It is a pity that the author has felt unable to deal more fully with the influence of *Ultra* on the Maritime side where (characteristically and not always with happy results) the Admiralty were allowed to keep these Signal Intelligence matters in their own hands. But I have the best reason to know that in the Battle of the Atlantic *Ultra*, in conjunction with HF/DF, was a real war-winner. As Commander-in-Chief Coastal Command in 1943 I made a habit, at specially critical times, of attending the regular morning conference over the scrambler telephones, referred to in this book, between Roger Wynn at the Admiralty, Max Horton's Headquarters in Liverpool and my own at Northwood—by the end of which there was little or nothing we did not know about what the U-boats were up to in the Atlantic at the time.

To me an interesting feature of this book is the light it throws on the character and methods of some great leaders—Churchill, Montgomery, George Patton and 'Stuffy' Dowding, for instance. It may detract a bit from the glamour surrounding some of them to know that they might not have done quite so well, had they not so often held in their hands pretty full details of the enemy's strength and dispositions, logistic situation and operational plans, before and throughout their battles. I am glad the author gives Dowding the credit that is his due for never letting on, in the course of that unhappy (and wholly unnecessary) Air Staff conference in October 1940, that he had known so much from *Ultra* of the Luftwaffe's plans throughout the Battle of Britain.

I was present on that occasion, and was not aware—
though I ought to have taken it for granted—that
Dowding was 'in on' *Ultra;* but I know that in his place
I should have been sorely tempted to use my knowledge of it to confute his more junior critics who, unfortunately but quite rightly had, for security reasons, not
been admitted to this priceless secret.

The word 'fascinating' tends to be overdone in fore-
words and reviews of books; but I feel sure that readers
of this book will agree that it amply merits that descrip-
tion.

J. C. SLESSOR
MRAF

9 April 1974

CHAPTER ONE

Introduction

On 25 May 1945, at the request of the Prime Minister, I sent a signal message to all the Allied Commanders and their staffs in the European theatre of war who had been in receipt of Intelligence from what Winston Churchill called 'my most secret source'.

It asked them not to divulge the nature of the source or the information they had received from it, in order that there might be neither damage to the future operations of the Secret Service nor any cause for our enemies to blame it for their defeat. After thirty years, time has changed both these conditions of secrecy. The techniques employed by the Secret Service and the code breakers have been widely published and, indeed, have long been known to governments and Intelligence services around the world, whilst our war-time enemies are now our allies.

It is, however, the privilege of the victor in war not to disclose just how or how often he broke his enemy's cyphers, and in this book the privilege will be maintained. At the height of hostilities the German war machine was sending well over two thousand signals a day on the air. It can be recognized therefore, that when, from time to time, we were able to intercept a number of signals and break the cypher, their contents covered a very wide field.

The enemy signals referred to in this book are those

which in my view played a decisive part in our conduct of World War II. They are only a part of those which passed through my hands and bear little relation either to the number which were broken or to those periods during which we were able to break them.

Nevertheless, I would go so far as to say that no history of World War II is complete which does not take into account our knowledge of our enemy's intentions, disclosed by our 'most secret source'.

Winston Churchill's appreciation of this Intelligence is not available for publication, but that of General Dwight D. Eisenhower, sent to the Chief of the British Secret Service, is amongst his papers in his Presidential Library at Abilene, Kansas, for all the world to see:

July 1945

Dear General Menzies,

I had hoped to be able to pay a visit to Bletchley Park in order to thank you, Sir Edward Travis,* and the members of the staff personally for the magnificent services which have been rendered to the Allied cause.

I am very well aware of the immense amount of work and effort which has been involved in the production of the material with which you have supplied us. I fully realize also the numerous setbacks and difficulties with which you have had to contend and how you have always, by your supreme efforts, overcome them.

The intelligence which has emanated from you before and during this campaign has been of priceless value to me. It has simplified my task as a

---

* Commander Edward Travis, knighted in 1942, was, during the 1930s, head of the Naval Section of the Government Code and Cypher School and also No. 2 to its Chief, Commander Alastair Denniston.

commander enormously. It has saved thousands of British and American lives and, in no small way, contributed to the speed with which the enemy was routed and eventually forced to surrender. I should be very grateful, therefore, if you would express to each and every one of those engaged in this work from me personally my heartfelt admiration and sincere thanks for their very decisive contribution to the Allied war effort.

Sincerely,

(Sgd) Dwight D. Eisenhower

The dramatic part that this special Intelligence played in the war created for me, and those top Allied commanders who received it, the unique experience of knowing not only the precise composition, strength and location of the enemy's forces, but also, with few exceptions, of knowing beforehand exactly what he intended to do in the many operations and battles of World War II.

No doubt future historians will continue to argue the pros and cons of the value of secret information. I am only concerned here in telling the story of how this topmost secret Intelligence was received and processed by a brilliant team of men and women, of how it was safely distributed to commanders in the field and how, in my first-hand and personal opinion, it played a vital part in our survival in 1940 and 1941, and in our later victories. Our ability to read, at most of the important periods of the war, secret signals between the topmost enemy commands, including Hitler himself, was obviously not only of unparalleled positive strategic value, but it also had a valuable negative use in telling us what the enemy did not know about our own operations.

As I was lucky enough to get to know most of the top Allied commanders personally, it was interesting and sometimes frustrating to find the different attitudes the varying personalities adopted towards the information—those with rigid ideas on orthodox methods of fighting an enemy seemed to think it was not quite right to know what he was going to do; those, on the other hand, with more flexible minds were ready to take every advantage the information offered them.

In due course, if the full British secret documents are made available for comment, history may change its assessment of some of the generals and personalities of World War II, but the fact that the commander in the field knew that all the information he received was also received by the chiefs of staff and principal political ministers at home must be taken into consideration, for it was this fact which might well have accounted for undue caution by some, while others would 'have a go', and usually succeed.

As many of the situations are sufficiently bizarre to raise doubts in some minds as to their authenticity, before proceeding with this book I have thought it advisable to give my own credentials and explain how I came to be responsible for much of the organization which handled this 'sensitive' subject.

I started World War I as a seventeen-year-old subaltern in the Royal Gloucester Hussars Yeomanry, but in 1916 our beloved horses were taken from us and we were supplied with bicycles or finally drafted to the infantry. Flying was to me the obvious alternative, so I became a fighter or 'scout' pilot in the RFC and finally got to France to join No. 29 Squadron early in April 1917. Alas, I was shot down in a 'dog fight' over Belgium on 13 July 1917 by the famous Richtofen Geschwader and the unfortunate odds of ten-to-one against. I was then taken prisoner and spent the next eighteen months in a POW camp where I passed the time learning German. On my return home, on the strength of the back pay that had accumulated, I went to Christ Church, Oxford, where I took a law degree. However, I never followed the profession but instead decided to repair the damage done to my health by life in the POW camp by doing some farming. As a teenager I had learnt fluent French and travelled round the world: I had lumbered in Canada and been a Jackaroo in the Australian outback. Once again in 1929 I set out on safari, travelling through Sudan, Kenya and Rhodesia. But depression was in the air everywhere and so I decided to return to London to get a job.

During the 1920s the Royal Air Force had been fighting for its independence, but by 1929 it was fully established as the third arm of the nation. The Air Staff had set up its own Intelligence Branch and now required its own representative with the Secret Service, alongside those of the Navy and Army. In December 1929 I got the job; my task to find out from secret sources what foreign air forces were up to.

By 1933 Nazi euphoria had closed down most of the secret agents I had managed to get hold of in Germany, and Nazi rearmament had begun. I decided to do something about it personally and upset the protocol and tradition of the Head Office of the Secret Service by going to Germany myself.

By 1934 I had obtained personal contact with the Head of State, Hitler, and with Alfred Rosenberg, the official Nationalist Party philosopher and Foreign Affairs expert, Rudolph Hess, Hitler's Deputy, Erich Koch and some of the senior serving officers of the Army and Air Force, and by working on their intense desire to keep Britain out of their coming wars of expansion and a belief that the RAF would respond both to persuasion and threats, I got them to disgorge from the 'horse's mouth' much of what we wanted to know.

From my personal meetings with Hitler I learned

about his basic belief that the only hope for an ordered world was that it should be ruled by three super powers, the British Empire, the Greater Americas and the new Greater German Reich. He gave me an assurance that the Germans themselves would destroy the Communists by the conquest of Russia. He admitted that in 1934 the generals had too much to say and told me he had had 'to sell them half his birthright'. He totally rejected the Versailles Treaty and gave me the figures and plans for his great new Air Force. Conversations with him inadvertently also revealed to me that he had some sort of dual personality which he could switch on and off at will. Later, I have no doubt, the unreasonable one took over.

From General Walther von Reichenau, Hitler's favourite general, I learned, in 1934, details of the German plans against Russia, and the strategy of the blitzkrieg, the massive tank spearheads supported by their mobile artillery, the dive bomber. From Air Force General Albert Kesselring I discovered the composition of the air fleets and how the operation of dive bombing had finally been perfected. It all came true in the battle of France.

From the many days and weeks I spent in the company of Rosenberg I learned of all the hopes and fears and plans of the Nazis for their thousand-year Reich. From Eric Koch, who showed me all over the great concrete preparations in East Prussia for Operation Otto, I found out the approximate date of the operation against all Russia. But perhaps more than anything else I gained some insight into the character and mentality of these top Nazis, their attitude and thought patterns, figures of speech and mental images, which was to prove most useful during the war.

Ever since I had joined the Secret Service in 1929 I had realized that amongst those who trod the carpeted corridors of power in Whitehall it was fashionable to smile in tolerant disbelief at anything the Secret Service told them. It was frustrating to see the information on German rearmament being quietly ignored. As my efforts with Hitler and company had had the full backing of Admiral Sir Hugh Sinclair (Quex to his friends, 'C' to the establishment, to me the Chief), he complained to the Prime Minister when he saw no use was being made of my knowledge. In 1935 I was finally summoned to appear before a Cabinet Committee to substantiate my reports. They were accepted by the committee. Then Baldwin retired, Lord Swinton took over as Air Minister from Lord Londonderry, and I got all the help and backing I wanted.

Alas, by 1938 my real job was 'blown' to the Germans and I was warned by Rosenberg not to return to Germany, and warned too, for the last time, not to rely on the French Army. To fill the information gap I ordered a cabin-heated Lockheed aircraft from America through British Civil Airlines, with the approval of the Air Staff, and experimented with aerial photography. At this time no photo could be taken above eight thousand feet due to condensation fogging the lenses. With the Germans antagonistic, this height was now suicidal, so we found a way of passing warm air beneath the lens which enabled us to take pictures up to thirty thousand feet and continue to operate over Germany until September 1939. My Lockheed became the forerunner of all spy planes which were responsible for most of the accurate ground Intelligence both during and after the war.

After thirty years of somewhat smug propaganda on the subject of how the Allies routed the evil forces of Nazi Fascism, it is difficult to tell people now how very nearly it never happened. How those of us who knew the might of the German war machine, and the accurate facts of our fight for existence, wondered at the blind optimism of the Army Staff, and of Winston Churchill himself, that we could hold the Germans in France.

It took the fall of France and great pressure from the Air Staff to convince him that things had changed since World War I. It was at this critical moment that the greatest Intelligence triumph of all time came to our rescue, a secret that was kept throughout the war and after. That is what this book is all about.

CHAPTER TWO

Science to the Rescue:
The Birth of Ultra

In the almost static war of 1914–18 information about the enemy's operations was largely gleaned from low-level aerial photography and from trench raids, both of which proved highly dangerous and very expensive in manpower and aeroplanes. There was also the beginnings of a system of watching the volume of the enemy's wireless traffic which gave some indication of his activity, and on the naval side valuable intelligence was obtained by breaking and reading the German naval wireless signals, a triumph for the cryptographers in the famous Room 40 at the Admiralty.

Now, towards the end of 1938, the German security services had already cracked down on the cloak and dagger agents operating out of Germany. It is true they had not been of great use to my Air Section, but I had been able to balance this to some extent by my own visits to Germany and the flights of my spy plane.

Early in 1939 I set up the first Scientific Intelligence Unit in my Air Section of the Secret Intelligence Service [S.I.S.]. I had been getting queries from Robert Watson-Watt, the inventor of the British radar system, on German radar progress and other scientific devices which might be used by the Luftwaffe, and so with the help of Sir Henry Tizard, the Scientific Adviser to the Air Ministry, and Robert Watson-Watt, I was supplied with a young scientist, Dr R. V. Jones, whom I set up in an office close to my own in Broadway, near Victoria, to begin his training in the art of spotting the difference between good and bad information and evaluating such Intelligence as we could get hold of. Jones was a good choice; his early reports on enemy radar development and later on beam bombing, jet-engine experiments and Hitler's secret weapons, the V1 and V2, were classic examples of the vital role science was to play in our wartime Intelligence.

Despite our secret success with high altitude photography, I soon realized that in a war of rapid movement, such as General Reichenau had described to me back in 1934, rapid and accurate information about the enemy's intentions might well mean the difference between swift defeat and eventual victory.

Two floors below the one on which I worked were the cryptographers of the Government Code and Cypher School. I had from time to time been able to help them with aviation terms and names of aircraft types in the signals they were busy decyphering. These backroom boys were a dedicated team of highly intellectual individuals under the control of Commander Alastair Denniston who had been one of the original cryptographers in Room 40 at the Admiralty during World War I. He was a quiet, rather reserved man of about fifty, somewhat short of stature but certainly not of intellect. He had organized the present set-up, and it was from talking to him that I began to learn the enormous possibilities of the broken enemy cypher. He told me about the failures and successes of the inter-war years, the hopes and possibilities of the future and, one single fact which was to serve me in good stead later, that the only really secure cypher at that time was the one that is used only once.

Denniston explained to me that there were a number

of methods used to encypher messages, mostly based on the use of books of numerals held only by the sender and the recipient, but that machines had also been tried out. The basis of encyphering was that each service up to now had used its own particular code book in which a multitude of words and phrases likely to be used by that particular service had opposite each phrase or word a numerical group. Thus 'To the Commanding Officer' might read 5473, 'The Division will move' 0842, 'on Monday' 4593. Most code books are not considered to be completely secret since they get lost or stolen or because in time the meaning of the groups becomes generally known.

In order to make the message secret, therefore, additional groups of figures known only to the sender and receiver must be added so as to make the final groups in the signal untranslatable by any third party.

The safest way to do this is for both the sender and receiver to have a sort of tear-off writing pad, on each sheet of which are columns of four digit groups printed absolutely at random.

The sender indicates the page, the column and the line where the message is to start in the first group of the signal, thus 1348 would mean page 13, column 4, line 8. Now if the next three groups on the pad are 4431, 7628 and 5016 and these are added to the ones already quoted, we find that the message reads 1348.9904.8470.9609 which means 'To the Commanding Officer, the Division will move on Monday'.

Once used the whole page of the pad is torn off and destroyed. This is known as the one-time pad system and was at that time the only known absolutely safe cypher. If, for instance, the cypher groups are in a nondestructible book form and are used over and over again, in time an enemy will work out where the groups occur in the book and be able to read the signals. This unfortunately occurred in our own naval cyphers during the war.

The one-time pad method is, however, a long and very cumbersome method to use on any very large scale. All the printing presses in Germany could hardly have coped with the numbers of tear-off pads required. It was therefore thought likely that Germany would turn to a mechanical system which could be quick and easy to operate, a system of so changing the letters of the words in the signal by progressive proliferation that only the receiver who knew the key to the system could set his own machine to unscramble the letters back to their original meaning.

I will not try to enlarge on the subject of codes and cyphers, a subject which has been so excellently covered by David Kahn in his book *The Codebreakers*, but from my talks with Denniston, it was obvious that we ought to get to know all we could about the Germans' signals set-up. It seemed evident that the great German war machine dedicated to the rapid blitzkrieg must have a secure and quick wireless signalling organization, since the laying of land lines would hardly be possible, and that the one-time cypher would be far too cumbersome and out of the question for such a volume of traffic. So enquiries had already been sent out to our agents in Europe to try to find out just what the Germans were going to do about it. What sort of cypher system would they use?

In 1938 a Polish mechanic had been employed in a factory in Eastern Germany which was making what the young man rightly judged to be some sort of secret signalling machine. As a Pole, he was not very fond of the Germans anyway and, being an intelligent observer, he took careful note of the various parts that he and his fellow workmen were making. I expect it was after one of the security checks which were made by the Gestapo on all high security factories that they discovered his nationality. He was sacked and sent back to Poland. His keen observation had done him some good, and he got in touch with our man in Warsaw. The Gestapo in Poland were active, and so he was told to lie low. Meantime, we received the information in London. It was obviously a very delicate matter, and our Chief, Admiral Sinclair, decided that the fewer people, even in our office, that knew about it, the better. He therefore put the development of the concept in the hands of his Deputy, Colonel Stewart Menzies, and it was decided that only the departmental heads were to be kept in the picture.

In due course the young Pole was persuaded to leave Warsaw and was secretly smuggled out under a false passport with the help of the Polish Secret Service; he was then installed in Paris where, with the aid of the Deuxième Bureau, he was given a workshop. With the help of a carpenter to look after him, he began to make a wooden mock-up of the machine he had been working on in Germany.

There had been a number of cypher machines invented over the years and our own backroom boys had records and drawings of most of them. It didn't take them long to identify the mock-up as some sort of improved mechanical cypher machine called Enigma. The name Enigma was given to the machine by the German manufacturers. The Pole had been told not to attempt to make his wooden model to scale. In fact, the bigger the better, because he could then more easily incorporate any details he could remember. The result was rather like the top half of an upright piano, but it was enough to tell us that it would be essential to get hold of an actual machine if we were to stand any chance of trying to break into its method of operation. So, while the Pole was carefully looked after in Paris, we set about working out a scheme with our friends in Poland, who were just as keen as we were to try and grab a complete machine from Germany. We knew where the factory was and all about its security methods, and that there were still some Poles working there under German names. However, the Polish Secret Service thought the scheme might stand more chance of success if we gave them the money and they did the job. They knew the terrain and the people much better than we did, so we gladly agreed.

It was Denniston himself who went to Poland and triumphantly, but in the utmost secrecy, brought back the complete, new, electrically operated Enigma cypher machine which we now knew was being produced in its thousands and was destined to carry all the secret signal traffic of the great war machine.

It is difficult to explain this cypher machine in a few words so I do not intend to try to describe the working of the complicated system of electrically connected revolving drums around which were placed letters of the alphabet. A typewriter fed the letters of the message into the machine, where they were so proliferated by the drums that it was estimated a team of top mathematicians might take a month or more to work out all the permutations necessary to find the right answer for a single cypher setting; the setting of the drums in relation to each other was the key which both the sender and receiver would no doubt keep very closely guarded.

No wonder the Germans considered that their cypher was completely safe.

Despite the fact that we had an actual machine, were we now faced with an impossible problem? By August 1939 Denniston and his Government Code and Cypher School had moved to Bletchley Park, a secluded country house which the Chief had previously acquired as a wartime hideout; with them went the machine.

Alas, at the end of the year only months before Bletchley became fully operational, Sinclair died. To me personally it was a sad loss. He had fought the government of the day for the recognition of my 'Nazi' information; he had no need or intention of allowing anyone to corrode the absolute independence of the Secret Service, the last Chief to do so. Over the years we had had many a quiet chuckle over my visits to Hitler and Co.

He seemed the only person to understand how and why I had become a confidante of the Nazi hierarchy. Somehow the Nazis seemed unable to communicate with the career diplomats, and Rosenberg, himself an amateur, preferred to explain Nazi policy to another amateur.

In my case as a 'supposed' admirer of the regime, they believed I could influence my friends in high places in London in their favour and achieve the neutrality of Britain in their coming wars.

I never attempted to conceal my association with the Foreign Office, and copies of the reports I was supposed to have submitted to the FO were described by Rosenberg as 'glowing' in a memo to Hitler.

The weeks I spent each year from 1934–8 travelling freely about Germany with Rosenberg, Rudolf Hess, Erich Koch or the ADC Rosenberg supplied me with, gave me an almost unique insight into the Nazi plans for the future and perhaps more important into the mentalities of these men, including Hitler.

If I expressed a desire to know more about any subject, then either Hitler or Rosenberg would give some expert the green light to talk to me.

It had not been an easy part to play, especially when associating with such cold sadistic characters as Himmler, but I had got away with it for four years without disaster to myself or embarrassment to my Chief. He and Sir Robert Vansittart, the head of the Foreign Office, were close friends, but even together they had been unable to dent the shield of disbelief that Neville Chamberlain and Lord Halifax had erected to protect them.

Had the admiral lived to serve Churchill, he might well have helped him to better understand what we were up against in those hectic first months in office as Prime Minister.

To be Chief of the Secret Service, a post which by long tradition had been a gift of the Monarch, was, of course, a plum job. In recent years it had been a perquisite of the Navy and now the admirals were lining up. However, Colonel Stewart Menzies had other ideas. I had worked with Stewart as a colleague for the past nine years and I think all of us in the office were anxious that he should take over rather than that we should have a new broom at this critical stage. Our only misgivings were whether he carried the weight to hold on to his chair. He had been educated at Eton, and, like so many sons of wealthy parents, he had gone into the Household Cavalry. He won the DSO and served on Haig's staff during World War I. He was a member of the exclusive White's Club and had personal contacts with the highest in the land. He was a Scot, he had a ready smile and the assurance which had come down with the profit from the millions of gallons of whisky distilled by his ancestors. His family owned the lovely Dorchester House set on an island in Park Lane, soon to become the great yellow-white edifice of the hotel, and, back in my own home county of Gloucestershire, his family estate sat quietly in secluded elegance next to that of the Duke of Beaufort. He wouldn't give in easily and, by the end of 1939, realization that something very big might come out of the Enigma cypher operation made him doubly determined to hold on. He had kept his word and personally informed me of the progress being made. But there were tremendous problems to be overcome.

In September 1939 the SIS were also evacuated to Bletchley Park, some fifty miles north of London near the main road and railway to the north-west. It was one of those large and rather ornate houses of red brick with timbered gables in the prosperous late Victorian style, probably built by one of the wealthy owners of the many brickworks which abound in this rich clay area. There must have been twenty or more rooms in the house, which was a long two-storey building, entered through a pretentious porch. There were spacious green lawns with the regulation cedar trees, a croquet lawn and a ha-ha, a sunken boundary fence that was invisible from the house and gave the idea of unbroken space. This was a favourite place later on to sit and eat one's sandwich lunch.

Bletchley was only a small town. It was not beautiful; five miles away was Woburn Park and Abbey where the Duke of Bedford lived. A number of wooden huts had been erected on the wide lawns at Bletchley and it was in Hut No. 3 that I and my small staff set up office. We lived, however, in billets in the surrounding country, and it was in another big house, which belonged to a man who owned a near-by glucose factory, that I found I had a number of backroom boys as fellow boarders. They were a cheerful lot, even if the conversation was at times well over the top of my head. I had known several of them when we all worked in the same building in London. Between them there was little they did not know about cyphers, and now that we had actually got one of Hitler's latest Enigma cypher machines, it was possible to understand with some accuracy its function and complexity. Enigma, the ancient Greek word for a puzzle, was certainly a good name for it. We could now at least get the machine accurately duplicated.

In the absence of a grey-stone quadrangle of an old university college, what remained of the green tree-studded lawns of the English country house was as good a place as any for the assembly of a pride of intellectual lions. There had come to Bletchley some of the most distinguished mathematicians of the day. Alexander, Babbage, Milner Barry, Gordon Welchman, names to whisper in the world of chess. They had been persuaded by Denniston to leave their comfortable universities and join with our own backroom boys to try to prove or disprove the theory that if man could design a machine to create a mathematical problem, then man could equally design a machine to solve it.

It was, I think, generally accepted that of our own backroom boys 'Dilly' Knox was the mastermind behind the Enigma affair. He was quite young, tall, with a rather gangling figure, unruly black hair, his eyes, behind glasses, some miles away in thought. Like Mitchell, the designer of the Spitfire fighter aeroplane which tipped the scales in our favour during the Battle of Britain, who worked himself to his death at the moment of his triumph, Knox too, knowing he was a sick man, pushed himself to the utmost to overcome the problems of Enigma variations (introduced by the Germans to further complicate their cyphers between 1940 and 1942). He, too, died with his job completed. J. H. Tiltman, another brilliant brain, had been borrowed from the Army. He was tall and dark with a short, clipped, military moustache, and his regimental tartan trousers eventually gave way to green corduroy slacks which were thought slightly way out in 1939. Oliver Strachey was an individualist, tall though a little stooped, with greying hair, broad forehead; his eyes, behind his glasses, always had a smile in them, as if he found life intensely amusing, except when our billetor used to stand at the foot of the stairs on Saturday mornings collecting our cheques. Oliver was also extremely musical. I believe he played several instruments, but he most enjoyed playing duets with Benjamin Britten on the grand piano in his rather untidy London flat. Then there was 'Josh' Cooper whom I saw fairly often, as he was primarily concerned with Air Force matters. He was another brilliant mathematician. Still in his thirties, he had to use powerful glasses which often seemed to get in the way of his straight black hair. Dick Pritchard, young, tall, clean-shaven, rather round of face, with a quiet voice, could talk on any subject with witty penetration. He, too, was deeply musical. It struck me at the time how often the art of undoing other people's cyphers was closely allied to a brain which could excel both in mathematics and music. It was rather frightening playing one's evening bridge with these men. It all came easily to them and the conversation was ever interesting. I could well have spent longer in our country retreat than I did, but it soon became apparent that the phoney war would last over the winter of 1939–40, so I took my small staff back to London in order to be near the Air Ministry. I missed the professorial atmosphere of Bletchley.

It is no longer a secret that the backroom boys of Bletchley used the new science of electronics to help them solve the puzzle of Enigma. I am not of the computer age nor do I attempt to understand them, but early in 1940 I was ushered with great solemnity into the

shrine where stood a bronze-coloured column sur-
mounted by a larger circular bronze-coloured face, like
some Eastern Goddess who was destined to become the
oracle of Bletchley, at least when she felt like it. She
was an awesome piece of magic. We were, of course,
all wondering whether the great experiment could really become operational, and if so, would it be in time for
the hot war which we now felt was bound to break out
in the spring? Hitler had given us six months' respite.
Each day had, I think, been used to the full by every
branch of the nation's defences. We all knew it was too
little, too late, but at least in this one vital concept the
possibilities were prodigiously exciting, for we had in
our hands the very encyphering machine the Germans
would be using in their wartime communications.

It must have been about the end of February 1940
that the Luftwaffe, the German Air Force, had evidently received enough Enigma machines to train their
operators sufficiently well for them to start putting
some practice messages on the air. The signals were
quite short but must have contained the ingredients the
bronze goddess had been waiting for. Menzies had giv-
en instructions that any successful results were to be
sent immediately to him, and it was just as the bitter
cold days of that frozen winter were giving way to the
first days of April sunshine that the oracle of Bletchley
spoke and Menzies handed me four little slips of paper,
each with a short Luftwaffe message dealing with personnel postings to units. From the Intelligence point of
view they were of little value, except as a small bit of
administrative inventory, but to the backroom boys at
Bletchley Park and to Menzies, and indeed to me, they
were like the magic in the pot of gold at the end of the
rainbow.

The miracle had arrived.

NOTE

Since this book was completed, Polish officers now living in Britain have stated that the Poles constructed a number of Enigma machines from information extracted from the factory in Germany coupled with the help of their own cryptographers, and that it was presumably one of these which they supplied to us. This may very well be true and certainly the Polish mathematicians and technicians displayed brilliance and great courage, but the story I have given is the one told to me at the time.

CHAPTER THREE

The Plan

Stewart Menzies had asked me to take the precious 'first results' over to Charles Medhurst, who was Director of Air Intelligence at the Air Ministry, a post which was soon upgraded to that of Assistant Chief of Air Staff Intelligence. Charles was short, thick set and dark, with a quick brain and a quiet voice and a very nice sense of humour. He was my Air Ministry boss. I knew him well and had, during the 1930s, done tours with him in the Middle East on Intelligence inspections. As I came into his office that morning, he gave me his usual smile and, though he had a lot of papers on his desk, I could see that he had made time to see me. I handed him the bits of paper. He looked at them, but had obviously got something else on his mind, because he just handed them back and said: 'You will have to do better than that.' He had evidently taken them on their face value as rather unimportant scraps of information and not as the pieces of magic they were, despite the fact that Menzies had told him all about the Enigma and our hopes of being able to solve some of the signals.

I had been turning over in my mind the whole subject of how best to deal with this new Intelligence before I even went to see Charles. In fact I had thought of little else ever since I had got the signals. It was, I think, Charles's lack of interest which prompted me that

evening to get down to working out a plan to handle
this new material, if, as we hoped, it would mushroom
into a vital source of information. I don't think I slept
that night, but I now knew what I wanted, and the following morning I went in to see Stewart as soon as I
got the all clear from his secretary. Miss Pettigrew, as
usual, looked as if she had just stepped out of a Rolls-
Royce; she was never flustered, but quite impossible to
get by unless one had a good reason to see her boss—it
was advisable to enter via her own office. Fortunately,
the old Chief had always made time if I wanted to see
him, and Miss Pettigrew and I were on good terms. She
looked up and smiled. I suppose a bit of suppressed excitement was running round the office that morning.
Stewart himself was almost excited, for the imperturba-
ble Scot that he was, and his first question was, 'What
did Charles think about it?' I told him what had taken
place at the Air Ministry and then I quickly led into all
the arguments I had prepared to get his approval for
my plan.

In the normal course of events, information from
such a top secret source as this one would be distributed only to the directors of Intelligence of the service
ministries. Thereafter, it was up to the directors to
make whatever distribution they thought fit. This
worked quite well where there were but a few items of
Intelligence in this category, but it seemed obvious that,
if we were lucky enough to break the code on just one
day, a mass of hundreds of signals would have to be
dealt with separately by all three Services, and not only
might translation differ, but the number of people involved in such work, and in any subsequent distribution,
would be immense. And if, as one could anticipate,
each director wished to inform one or more commands overseas of vital and urgent information, the
same material would probably be going out on the air

in several different cyphers which was, cryptographically, an extremely dangerous procedure.

There would be no control over its use and, in addition, just the extent of traffic alone would arouse enemy suspicions. It would, in my opinion, only be a question of time before the enemy tumbled to what had happened and the source would be blown. He might disbelieve that we were unbuttoning his cypher ourselves, but would certainly believe that there was a leakage serious enough either to stop using the Enigma machine or complicate its operation so as to nullify our success.

I could see that Stewart was so far in agreement regarding the dangers, and with the fact that, although he and the Bletchley boys were primarily responsible for the breakthrough, under the present system he might well lose control of the results and weaken his own position as sitting candidate for 'C's' chair. I waited for what I hoped and expected he would say. After a few moments he asked me what I had to suggest. I was glad that I had got my ideas cut and dried.

I proposed that as a first step, since so far only Luftwaffe signals had been received, I should ask the Air Ministry to let me have three or four non-flying, German-speaking, RAF officers whom I would install in my own Intelligence hut—No. 3 at Bletchley. They would be virtually next door to Hut 6 where the signals would be decyphered in the original German. I suggested the signals should then be passed over to Hut 3 for translation, and further action as directed by me.

I should naturally have to vet the young officers for security and I proposed to attach to them one of my own Intelligence staff, who would brief them with all the known details of the German Air Force in order to help them get names, addresses and such details as squadrons and other formations correct. Since it could only be a matter of days before the German Army started up its signalling, I could then make a similar request to the War Office.

The Director of Military Intelligence, General Davidson, was a good friend and always co-operative. I felt sure that a small joint Army and Royal Air Force Intelligence Unit would appeal to him. But Admiral John Godfrey, the Director of Naval Intelligence (DNI), could be much more difficult. By tradition the Navy kept itself to itself and the idea of co-operating with members of the two junior Services to produce a single translation would probably be unacceptable. However, I felt that if the unit became operational, there would be more chance of the DNI joining in if, and when, naval Enigma became available, and so, as I told Stewart, I wanted to go ahead with the Army and Air Force unit for a start.

This was the first phase of the plan to get a single and correct translation of the signals. There was also another equally important angle to a combined Services unit, and that was to decide the necessary priority of any given signal and who most needed to know its contents. Those of us who had worked for the three different Services inside the SIS had for long hoped that one day there would be a combined Intelligence department for all three service ministries. There was so much more than the bare bones of information which could be extracted by inter-Service discussion. After examining the 1934 German War Office List of Officers with my military colleagues, for instance, I had noticed some names which rang a bell as German fighter pilots in World War I, and further research had revealed a complete secret air staff which at that time was illegal —obviously under training and hidden in the various departments of the German War Office. Now, if I had my way, a single translation, along with its priority and distribution, would be agreed between a combined Services unit at Bletchley.

Stewart Menzies, I could see, was beginning to like the idea. I reminded him of the time in mid-1939 when I had landed on the Air Ministry lap a series of some one thousand sharp, clear photographs taken by the spy plane and showing every detail of the Italian aerodromes and installations, naval bases, dockyards, fortifications, ships and aeroplanes along the North African and Italian coasts. Archie Boyle, who was then the Deputy Director of Air Intelligence at the Air Ministry, had acted as swiftly as the machinery of expansion would allow. But it was not until a year later that the Interpretation Centre for Aerial Photographs at Medmenham was in full swing. Three individual Services would not, I think, have been able to set up the necessary machinery to deal with the possible Enigma output in the weeks that were now available before the hot war started, quite apart from the question of security.

Stewart agreed that so far I had made my case, but there still remained the security risk of wide dissemination of the material to commanders in the field, if it was to be used to the best advantage. This was covered by the second part of my plan which I feared might run up against opposition from the directors of Intelligence. We already had our own highly efficient Secret Service short-wave radio network and through it we could communicate direct with our organizations in most parts of the world. I suggested that if this could be expanded to include encyphering and transmission to the main overseas commands in the field, I should then be allowed to form small units of trained cypher and radio personnel and attach these to the commands in question, with the double purpose of providing an immediate link for the information and having an officer on the spot charged with seeing that all the necessary precautions were carried out for its security.

I pointed out that there would have to be very strict rules as to the number of people who could know the existence of this information and perhaps, on a more delicate footing, rules for those in receipt of the information, to ensure that they did not take any action which would either arouse enemy suspicions or confirm his fears that the Allied commander had any preknowledge of his plans. This one, I knew, was a hard one to put over to a commander-in-chief. In some circumstances it might be very tempting to make a quick but tell-tale *coup*. I thought that such security measures as I could devise should have behind them the Chief's full authority, with even higher backing if necessary. In this way the officer in charge of what I proposed to call the 'Special Liaison Units' (SLU) in the field, would tactfully be able to ensure that no risks were taken.

In view of our own success with the Enigma machine, I proposed that all transmissions put on the air should be in what was known as 'one-time pad' cypher which I have already described. It was at this time, as far as I knew, the only absolutely safe cypher in existence, although the Germans obviously thought otherwise. I also proposed that if any of the government departments which received this material wished to put it on the air for any reason, it should be done through the Special Liaison Unit organization. This, I hoped, would tie up our own cypher security without too much opposition—the exception being the Admiralty which had their special problems and used their own cyphers. Later on, we were able to use the new RAF Type X machine cypher which had been developed with all the knowledge of our success against the German Enigma. These machines were installed at most of the main headquarters which served two or all three of the Services, such as Malta, Cairo, Algiers, and later Caserta and Colombo. They were never 'read' by the enemy.

This was the complete plan which I put before my Chief the day after the backroom boys' first success. No one as yet knew how many hours, or even days, would elapse between the interception of the message and the answer to the Enigma keys being found, or how many messages would have to be read, sorted for priority and distribution, translated and dispatched. But the scheme did allow for expansion and, above all, for security. Copies of all signals would, of course, still be sent to the directors of Intelligence whose responsibility it would be to keep their chiefs of staff fully informed and to co-ordinate the logistical information of the various enemy units, which we call the order of battle.

I suppose it had taken me the best part of an hour to put the whole plan forward, it took another five minutes of careful weighing up by Stewart before I got my answer. 'All right,' he said, 'you can go ahead if you can get the approval of the directors of Intelligence.' I saw his point, it would not look such a major decision on his part if I made the arrangements. If it came off, it would leave the power of this almost unbelievable triumph in his own hands.

When I went to see Charles Medhurst, he was in an excellent mood and took the whole thing in his stride. 'It seems a good way of getting the translations done,' he said, but he still did not seem to grasp the immense potential of the source.

The next day three junior German-speaking flying officers reported to me. Charles had kept his word, a search had been made through the Air Ministry Intelligence Branch, so that they had already been screened for security. They were all young men who had recently joined up and were obviously the right type and keen. I myself took them up to Bletchley and installed them in Hut 3, together with one of my own Intelligence officers, armed with maps and the Luftwaffe order of battle with as many details of the various units and their commanders as we could get together.

As luck would have it, the next signals to be caught and unbuttoned were from the German Army, once again unimportant and probably practice ones, so the following morning I went to the War Office and explained my proposals to General Davidson, the DMI. I told him that they had the approval of Stewart and that I had already got my RAF officers and I hoped he would give me his co-operation. Two Army officers and a sergeant arrived at Bletchley the next day, bringing with them all they knew about the German Army.

I spent the next few days with them, getting them settled into suitable billets and initiating them into the work that I wanted them to do, together with all the priority and security angles of the whole business, though until I got my Special Liaison Units operational, obviously the messages would go only to the directors of Intelligence and myself in London. Fortunately they were able to settle themselves in slowly: there was no rush of signals being broken. Sometimes it was taking as much as twenty-four hours to get a result; later on, with some luck, we got the answer in three or four. Prime Minister Chamberlain had been told of the success so far, also the chiefs of staff who had now given Menzies backing for additional money.

After several weeks of rather slow and relatively unimportant progress, Charles Medhurst rang me up on the phone one day and told me that he had got a very good German-speaking officer who had just joined up —would I like him. Wing Commander Humphreys, 'Humph' as he was called, was a godsend. A commercial salesman in Germany, (I never did discover whether it was watches or motor-cars, but he must, I think, have been successful whatever the hardware was) he knew the country like his clean-shaven chin. I don't think there was a dialect that he could not speak perfectly. About five feet ten, around forty years of age with slightly greying hair brushed back from his clean features and blue eyes, he was never still. A bundle of energy, it was all the more to his credit that he stuck the desk job I gave him and worked all hours of the day and night. He was a good talker—I suppose it stemmed from his sales job—but when required he could put his ideas in a nutshell. He seemed to me the obvious leader for Hut 3. I made him a wing-commander and put him in charge. He quickly won the confidence of the team which was destined in a very short while to grow from six to sixty.

It was only a little while after I had got the Army and RAF components operational that the German naval Enigma was broken. I knew it would not have been any good trying to get John Godfrey, the DNI, to come in earlier. He wasn't at all keen even now. I knew Godfrey personally after he became DNI and throughout the war. He was not a dynamic character but organized his department well, and NID was efficient except for their lapse over naval cyphers.

Whether it was he or the First Sea Lord, Admiral Pound, who insisted on going their own way over Ultra, I don't know. Having lost the post of 'C' to Menzies I think the Navy was determined not to join, but I managed to persuade him to send one naval officer to join the party at Bletchley. Despite the fact that Lieutenant-Commander Saunders was a brilliant German scholar, the DNI insisted that naval signals should still go to Admiralty in the original German, notwithstanding the fact that those that concerned the U-boat traffic or German ship movements were already being translated by Humphreys and being sent to Coastal Command of the RAF.

The Admiralty could not use the SLU system as they had to send their orders and instructions to so many ships and convoys at sea (but instead used their own naval cyphers) except where they shared a SLU with the Army and the RAF at main base headquarters.

I felt it was necessary at this point to distinguish our particular Enigma Intelligence completely from other types which came under the headings of Secret or Most Secret (the American category of Top Secret had not yet arrived on the scene), so I had a talk with each of the directors to see if we could decide on a name by which it would be known to all those persons on the list I kept of authorized recipients. The title of Ultra Secret was suggested, but the final agreement was just to call it Ultra. Having been in at the birth, I had now conducted the christening of a source of Intelligence which was so deeply to affect our conduct of the war. As our successes in breaking Ultra increased, it became obvious that these signals carried the very highest command traffic, from Hitler and his Ober Kommando Wehrmacht (OKW) High Command, from the Chiefs of the Army, Air and Navy Staffs, and from Army, Airfleet and Armoured Group Commanders. The German Abwehr, which dealt with spies and counter-espionage, used a different cypher of their own which was also broken. It was widely used by our own security services and was responsible for the picking up and neutralization of German agents. It has been referred to by Professor Hugh Trevor Roper, Kim Philby and others.

To that vast majority of people who were either too young to realize what was going on in World War II and who have been nurtured on the Allied victory over the Nazis, the story which follows may well provoke the question why, if we knew so much about the enemy's strength and intentions, did we not finish him off more quickly. It is perhaps difficult for those younger generations to realize that in 1940 we were totally defeated in France, and that all that stood between us and total surrender was the disarmed remains of the British Army evacuated from Dunkirk, and the Royal Air Force, pitifully small compared with the vast air fleets of the Luftwaffe. To those of us who knew the score, the total surrender of Britain depended on whether the RAF could prevent the Luftwaffe wiping out or grounding our air squadrons. If they had done so, no Royal Navy ship could have survived in, or under, the waters of the English Channel whilst the Luftwaffe held control of the air. The decisive part that Ultra played in saving us from defeat will become apparent in the chapters that follow.

Invasion, however incompetently mounted and carried out, would have been invincible with all the airborne and seaborne troops and armament the Germans could have sent against our thinly held coast. For two long years we were virtually fighting the great German war machine with our wits. It was our wits and brains which produced the Ultra intelligence that provided the key to Air Marshal Dowding's strategy of keeping the Luftwaffe at bay and saving the RAF from the knockout blows aimed at it by Goering during the Battle of Britain. It was Ultra which told us of all the preparations which were going on for Operation Sea Lion, the invasion of Britain. Later on it was the same Intelligence which enabled General Auchinleck in North Africa to fight Rommel and his Afrika Korps like an elusive boxer, bobbing up where Rommel least expected him, delivering a hard punch, then away again to mount a swift attack somewhere else. It was Auchinleck's skill that brought Rommel to a standstill at the very gateway to Egypt. Had he not done so, the whole of the Mediterranean would have been lost to us, together with our scattered Imperial Forces in the Middle East, our oil, our naval bases and our route to India.

Even when, after Alamein, the pendulum at last began to swing our way a little, the advance knowledge of the enemy's movements, strength and likely behaviour gained through Ultra still did not enable us to achieve any quick results: we just did not have the men, machines and resources. Let no one be fooled by the spate of television films and propaganda which has made the war seem like some great triumphant epic. It was, in fact, a very narrow shave, and the reader may like to ponder, whilst reading this book, whether or not we might have won had we not had Ultra.

CHAPTER FOUR

The Battle of France

As this is the first published account of the use of Ultra under operational conditions, I have tried initially to give an overall picture of events, made up not only from the knowledge of our own Allied operations and Ultra forecast enemy operations, but also from the German Armed Forces documents captured and made available after the war. I have done this purposely in order to give a general lead in to the war as seen from the Intelligence side and to show that even the very limited amount of Ultra we were able to obtain during the Battle of France served some purpose, if only to bring home to Winston Churchill and the General Staff in London the true magnitude of the French collapse, and hasten the decision to get out as quickly as possible. I cannot, however, emphasize too strongly that this book is not a short history of World War II, and, as the story of our operations in the months and years ahead unfolds, the emphasis will be almost entirely on the Ultra information which was put at the disposal of the Allied commanders, rather than on the way in which they conducted operations.

In 1936 Hitler had re-occupied the Rhineland and had correctly guessed that neither France nor Great Britain would do anything about it. In September 1939, following the seizures of Austria and Czechoslovakia, he had declared war on Poland and, by moving the bulk of his army to the East, had virtually denuded the western frontier. Once again he had correctly guessed that France and Great Britain, beyond declaring war, would do nothing about it.

There had been ample Intelligence available in the 1930s as to the build up of the great Nazi war machine but it was not until midsummer of 1939 that Intelligence from all our sources correctly pointed to the end of August as the time for the attack on Poland. We know now, from documents, that on 27 September 1939, Hitler told his generals that he also intended to attack in the West that autumn, since the French and British armies were as yet quite unprepared. He named November the twelfth as D-Day, and on October the tenth he issued his war directive No. 6 containing specific orders for the attack, but there were inevitable postponements, and we also know now that the original plan of attack in the West, known as the Yellow Plan and which envisaged a main frontal attack through Belgium, Holland and Luxemburg, was to undergo considerable alteration as the weeks went by. In January 1940 a German aircraft carrying two German officers made a forced landing in Belgium. They were carrying the revised operational orders of the Yellow Plan for the Army Group B's assault on the West. After the war we learned that soon after this the proposals of Field-Marshal Gerd von Rundstedt, Commander of German Army Group 'A' and of his chief of staff General Erich von Manstein to transfer the weight of the German attack to the German left wing was approved by Hitler. A massive armoured thrust, the Blitzkrieg was made on the German left flank just north of the Maginot line and through the Ardennes forest, which the Germans knew the French believed to be impassable for tanks. Then, with a scything movement, the armour would make for the coast and push the encircled Allied armies in Belgium into the sea.

With the capture of the documents aboard the German aeroplane, the Allies had at least had definite proof that Hitler meant business in the West. We now know that the orders for the final version of the plan of attack were only issued as late as 24 February 1940 and that it was still left open to the Germans to switch back to the main Belgian front if the Ardennes thrust did not succeed. This much is now history, but the German High Command had played their hand very close to the chest. The Belgians had anticipated that after the January warning the Franco-British Army would at once move up into Belgium, but no action was forthcoming from either. As a result, the Belgians, fearful of a let down, began to push their neutrality to the utmost, and, amongst other things, refused to give the British any details of their available aerodromes.

About the beginning of April 1940 Ultra signals began to increase. However in the earlier days of the war the Bronze Goddess was still somewhat immature and intermittent in operation, and, I believe, it was our good fortune in obtaining an Enigma machine complete with operational keys from a shot down German aircraft off Norway. Later the same useful material was captured from a German Tank Signals unit which had got too far ahead in the Battle of France, and again in May of 1941 the Navy's capture of a German U boat, complete with its Enigma and chart of operating keys intact, not only gave us direct access to much of the naval military and air Enigma traffic but was also invaluable in helping the brains of Bletchley to bring the Bronze Goddess to maturity. They kept up a small but steady flow of Ultra until early in 1942, by which time a bevy of newly sophisticated Goddesses, now established in their new brick temple and attended by some thousands of secret people, probed with their dainty fingers the secrets of the Enigma machine and attained complete mastery over all the German signals.

But now in April 1940 a good many of the Ultra signals dealt purely with logistics. The General Staffs of the German Army and Air Force kept careful track of the state of readiness of every unit of the armed forces. It included the actual strength in men and machines: aeroplanes, tanks, guns, fuel, or any other resources. Also run on the same lines was a regular system for indenting for supplies, such as ammunition, spare parts and replacements, including casualty replacements. The German Army and Air Force General Staffs could probably have told at a glance exactly what was at their disposal, anywhere at any time. It was fortunate for us that many of these logistical returns were sent by Ultra signals over the air. In fact, it seemed as if the various quartermasters had been told to use the air when there was free time for them to do so, rather than block up the land telephone lines with non-operational traffic. It enabled our own service ministries to complete very accurate enemy orders of battle for their chiefs of staff. The order of battle is that master document prepared by the Intelligence staffs of the fighting Services which shows the strength, disposition and equipment of all the fighting formations and units involved in operations. It is this information which formed the basis for the plans we had to make for all our operations during the war. Ultra was responsible for almost all of this accurate information.

For a start there was to be one SLU with the Commander-in-Chief in France, Lord Gort, and which would also serve Charles Blount in command of the air component of the BEF (the British Expeditionary Force in France). Another would serve Air Vice-Mar-

shal Barratt commanding the British Advanced Air
Striking Force stationed a good deal further south than
Gort's Headquarters at Wachines. Major Humphrey
Plowden, who had been a colleague in the London office since I first joined, was sent to the Commander-in-
Chief with a wireless unit and a couple of cypher sergeants, while I put a unit of three cypher sergeants and
wireless unit under Squadron-Leader 'Tubby' Long,
also an old personal friend, at the aerodrome at
Meaux, close to Barratt's RAF Headquarters. I had
chosen this spot as it was next to the spy plane unit
which had now been taken over by the Air Ministry and
made an official part of the RAF, and where my old
faithful Lockheed aircraft was always standing by for a
quick get away. It was from this aerodrome that in
April 1940 the Spitfire spy planes, now cruising at thirty thousand feet, unseen in their pale eggshell blue
camouflage, actually photographed every aerodrome in
Belgium. Protocol had required that no one was told
about it until it was completed, which gives some idea
of the nonsense that was going on between the French,
British and Belgians at that time.

I had chosen two trusted personal friends, both of
whom had strong enough characters to guide their
commanders on the correct use of the Ultra material,
if, as we hoped, it would provide them with the enemy's
operational orders. It was absolutely vital to the whole
Ultra project that no mistakes should occur at this first
operational tryout. I also felt that the physical security
of the material might well need some quick thinking.

Throughout the 1930s it was my responsibility to
keep in touch with the French Secret Service in Paris.
Georges Ronin of the French Air Force was my opposite number in the French Deuxième Bureau (SIS). In
April I had made what was to be my last visit to Paris
and had found my old friend and colleague completely

depressed. He told me the morale of the Army was low and that in the back of people's minds was a belief that they'd been sold-out by the politicians; everyone was very jittery. Over the years I had worked very closely with Georges in all Intelligence matters against Germany and by 1940 neither of us had any illusions as to the peril in which the Allies stood. In May 1940 Georges returned to active service and flew until bombs and fuel were no longer available.

After the fall of France, at my suggestion, he joined the Vichy Government as Chef de Cabinet of the Vichy French Air Minister and until we met again in Algiers on Christmas Day 1942 he kept in touch with me by special wireless link, a very dangerous job.

He was accused of 'collaboration' after the war, but my personal intervention with General de Gaulle resulted in his complete vindication and reinstatement as General of Air Force. He died in 1956, a very gallant Frenchman.

Whilst I was in Paris I decided to visit Air Marshal Barratt and my SLU at the headquarters of the Advanced Air Striking Force near Meaux, to the east of Paris, but to do so I had to go through the French zone and relations were not too good. Permits, I was told, would take a week and then one couldn't be sure. Tubby Long had come down to Paris to meet me and was to drive me up in his Citröen, so he and I eventually resorted to providing ourselves with a pass on a very important looking piece of paper with the red seal of a 'Vat 69' whisky bottle, a piece of red tape and a few signatures which worked like a charm. Right up to the middle of April we had been co-operating on the Enigma problem with one of the chief French backroom boys, Colonel Philip Joubert. He alone, I think, knew of our success. He was a brilliant and loyal officer and after the fall of France not a murmur of what he knew escaped him.

Over and over again the role of the dive bomber in the armoured blitzkrieg had been submitted to the War Office and the Air Ministry on Intelligence reports. General von Reichenau had explained to me how the blitzkrieg would work against Russia, way back in Berlin in 1935. He and I both knew that he was referring to a Western war as well. It had been a small but purposeful straw in the wind which the Nazis were blowing towards Britain in their twin endeavours to frighten and persuade us into neutrality. Whether it was because none of the high echelons of military staff could ever imagine the experience of being on the receiving end of a screaming, dive-bombing demon I do not know, but the new form of war, with massed tanks backed up by a completely mobile and very effective air artillery was, I believe, never taken seriously enough by either the French or the British Staffs. They were to learn the hard way.

In the last two weeks of April 1940, Ultra signals started to show movement orders, and we were, at last, getting concrete evidence that the German Army and Air Force was on the move to the western frontier. At the time we still had no knowledge of the modification to the captured Yellow Plan foreshadowing the attack through Holland and Belgium. However, the formidable group of armoured units now moving westward, supported by dive-bomber squadrons, left little doubt that the blitzkrieg tactics would soon be applied. One couldn't help having doubts as to how that mixture of the Dutch, Belgian, French and British armies would stand up to the highly co-ordinated operations which had surely, over months of training, been practised by the Germans. I was interested to learn from one of the signals that Reichenau himself was in command of the sixth Army which was assembling opposite the British sector of the line of defence in Belgium. At least Lord Gort by this time had some good idea of what was going to bump into him. One thing which came across clearly on Ultra was the extent of the German Air Forces to be employed in the coming operation. The two Air Fleets, Luftflotte 2, under the command of my old acquaintance Kesselring, and Luftflotte 3, under Sperrle, together mustered over a thousand fighters and nearly four hundred dive-bombers, in addition to eighteen hundred long-range bombers and other communications aircraft. It was about double the French and British air strengths, and Kesselring would, I knew, use it with the same ruthlessness he had used in his climb to his top command. There was going to be no mercy in the air.

Tension began to build up in Whitehall and in my own office, and, at Hut 3 at Bletchley, excitement as well. I was in constant touch with Humphreys and we were putting the finishing touches to the small but efficient outfit that we hoped would play a vital role in the hot war, though no one knew exactly what would go on the air or how often we should be able to read the cypher.

On May the first, eight days before the German invasion began, the French military attaché in Switzerland reported back to French General Headquarters that the Germans would open their offensive between the eighth and the tenth of the month and that the main attack would come at Sedan. Whether this information was ever passed on to the commanders-in-chief or whether it got lost in the General Staff, I do not know. I never heard of it at the time and I was very much concerned with Intelligence. Ultra was, of course, quite silent regarding operational orders at this stage. There was obviously no need for them to be put on the air, each divisional commander must have known exactly what he had got to do and no doubt their field telephones were in full use. Besides, the Germans were very well aware of the necessity of keeping wireless traffic as near normal as possible in order not to give anything away simply on the volume count. There doesn't seem to have been any French air reconnaissance, despite the military attaché's warning.

Eventually it was one of our Spitfire spy planes flying over the French sector which saw the vast armada of German tanks assembling in the Ardennes on May the eighth. Barratt told me that he had suggested a bombing operation from Britain on the massed armour. It never came off for various reasons, one of which was the lack of bombs large enough to do any real damage. Despite all the information available, the full appreciation of where the armoured thrust was to come appears to have been ignored by the French High Command, and even when the French tank patrols finally met the German tanks in the forest of Ardennes, there was still no air reconnaissance ordered. It seems almost impossible to believe that General Gamelin, the French Commander-in-Chief, had so staked his reputation on his assessment that the Germans could not and would not attack through the Ardennes that he refused to change his mind or his strategy. It is difficult to say more without accusing Gamelin of treason. To the intelligent onlooker it appeared that he was deliberately allowing the Germans a quick victory, whilst making some show of resistance in the North.

On May the tenth came the opening of the offensive through Holland and Belgium. Reichenau was doing extremely well and I could picture his smiling face, his duelling scars flushed with triumph, writing out his story for his friend and protector, Hitler. He reported the destruction of fifty of Belgium's operational aircraft on the ground and the capture of two bridges over the Albert Canal, which was supposed to be the Allied forward defence line. His airborne troops had captured the vital fort of Eben Emael, which had been constructed much on the lines of the forts on the Maginot Line.

There were reports from the German Eighteenth Army of their advance in Holland. Luftflotte 2 was well satisfied at the destruction of aircraft on Rotterdam airfield. The River Meuse had been crossed. Already it looked bad for the Dutch. On that day Winston Churchill took command of the nation.

That fateful tenth of May, which saw the sheer weight of the attack by German Army Group B under the command of General von Bock pushing back the Allies in Belgium, was also to see the start of a movement of von Kleist's tank armada through the Ardennes. By the eleventh, the Allies had fallen back to their pre-arranged line of defence in Belgium. On the thirteenth, Army Group B reported a victory in a large tank battle against French forces, but there was no breakthrough. It looked as if the Allied line was now holding, but the trap was about to be sprung. It was on the fourteenth that General Walter von Brauchitsch sent an Ultra signal to Reichenau to keep up his attack on the sixth Army front. But on the fifteenth came the news that the great armoured thrust at Sedan had resulted in a breakthrough.

To those of us sitting weary-eyed in our London offices, with St Jame's Park already decked out in greenery and flowers, it wasn't a great surprise. After the sightings of the mass armour by our spy planes, we were just about waiting for it. On the strength of the armoured breakthrough, the French General Alphonse Georges, commanding the Allied forces in the North, ordered a general withdrawal, but the order for some reason never reached Lord Gort until the following morning, the sixteenth, and it was no doubt this situation which decided Churchill to fly to Paris on the sixteenth, to try to stop the rot that seemed to be settling in amongst the French commanders. We had at that time a direct telephone line from our office in London to Bill Dunderdale, our man in Paris, and I promised Downing Street that I would send any vital Ultra information to Churchill while he was there. In the event he got so little joy from the French General Staff that he flew back at once. To add to our troubles we got an Ultra signal on the sixteenth giving orders for a full Panzer (Tank) Corps to move south from the Belgian front and join in the Sedan breakthrough. This certainly relieved the pressure on the British front but it gave no consolation for the future of Allied resistance further south.

The situation was now tense and it was not helped by a signal from General Halder, Chief of the German Army General Staff to von Bock, who commanded the Army Group opposite the British, ordering him to 'exercise restraint' against the retiring Allies. The signal was puzzling, it looked all wrong in the light of previous orders to Reichenau.

From a purely Intelligence view it looked as if the Germans wanted to keep the British Army well up in Belgium. This proved to be the case, because as we were soon to learn, they wanted to surround them. On the nineteenth the Germans crossed the Scheldt at Antwerp and on that same day General Gamelin was dismissed as Commander-in-Chief of the French Army, and replaced by General Maxime Weygand.

It was on the morning of the twenty-third that the vital Ultra signal from General von Brauchitsch at the German Army High Command (OKH) was intercepted and decoded. Brauchitsch himself, able to see the

broad picture of Allied disarray, put out a signal ordering the two Army Groups 'to continue the encircling
movement with the utmost vigour'. Rundstedt's Army
Group was to swing rapidly northwards towards Os-
tende, whilst Army Group B was to swing round in line
with Army Group A facing north. So here it was at
last, the fulfilment of the scythe plan finally accepted by
Hitler three months earlier. This was the signal that decided both Gort and Churchill that the time had come
to get out of France. Rundstedt didn't seem to have
quite the same confidence as Brauchitsch and fortunately for us he wasn't playing. Instead he evidently decided to stop a while and regroup his Panzer Divisions.
Presumably he did not immediately inform Brauchitsch
of what he was doing so that later that day Brauchitsch
issued a further order for General Gunther von Kluge's
Fourth Army to be transferred from Rundstedt's command to Army Group B further north. This Ultra signal was not of great significance to us as it was a command move obviously made for the better co-ordination of the encircling movement. But the result of
Brauchitsch's orders, both of which we had received,
was more dramatic. However, it was only after the war
that we learned that Hitler was at Rundstedt's headquarters at the time and, not only cancelled Brauchitsch's order about the transfer of Kluge's Army but
also gave an order to halt all the panzers until he himself decided they should proceed.

Lord Gort later told me that it was the first of
Brauchitsch's signals which influenced his decision to
make for the sea as quickly as possible. He knew that if
the BEF were destroyed and captured, there would be
nothing to stop a Nazi occupation of Britain, if they
could get across the Channel. He was the complete soldier determined to save his men and possibly his country from the danger threatening the whole Western

world. To Churchill, too, the Brauchitsch signals were the sign for the speed-up of Operation Dynamo and the mustering of the little ships for Dunkirk. We knew from Ultra that Brauchitsch had not been 'bluffing', and the fact that others, through Ultra, were now convinced of the danger was an extremely important new factor in the conduct of the war.

Whatever Weygand's true motives were at this juncture in telling the British that the re-formed French Seventh Army was going to attack northwards to cut off the panzers, and asking for a British attack southwards, one can at best presume that he was totally in the dark as to the real situation. There are those who say that it was a move to blame the British for France's defeat, since quite obviously Gort could not risk trying to mount an attack from the North at this late date; if he had done so, the BEF would undoubtedly have been surrounded.

Rundstedt was a wise old bird; he had got the British and the Belgian armies where he wanted them and he knew that he could deal with the disorganized French Army later. He had, without doubt on Hitler's orders, stopped Brauchitsch's all-out drive to the sea to destroy the British Army and instead had re-grouped his armour so that he could meet any unlikely French attack on his flank from the south whilst he quietly isolated the British on the channel coast. Gort was well aware that the French armies were in no position to carry out Weygand's dreamed-up attack, but those who were not in the Ultra picture in London seemed to be in a state of 1914 'Miracle-of-the-Marne' euphoria. Those who could read the truth knew what had to be done with all speed.

The failure of the German Army to press home their advantage did not seem to fit in with Hitler's character. There seemed to be something more behind it. At the time I believed I knew what the 'little man' was after; ever since I had met Hitler for the first time in 1934 I had felt that his desperate desire for peace with Britain was no bluff. I knew that above all he genuinely feared the British as an enemy, and now that France was virtually finished, he obviously wanted peace in the West before he set out on the great mission that possessed his soul—if he had one—the destruction of Communist Russia. I believed he was deliberately letting the BEF go home. As far as we know, Hitler never issued any further orders for his tanks to advance. War against England had swung for the moment from the military to the political arena. I felt sure myself that Hitler had argued that if he bottled up the BEF in prisoner-of-war camps, they would be running sore and might well jeopardize the peace which he believed he could now get from Britain. Lord Gort had been given the breather he needed and resolutely brought the BEF to the beaches of Dunkirk. Without in any way detracting from the epic of Dunkirk, I believe that if Hitler had let his victory-drunk armies and air forces loose there would have been little for the small boats to pick up. Did Hitler let the BEF go home, having stripped them of all their armour? We now know that soon after Hitler ordered his tanks to stop closing in, he addressed his military staffs in France. According to one German general who was present, Hitler told them exactly what he had told me in 1934: it was necessary that the great civilization Britain had brought to the world should continue to exist and that all he wanted from Britain was that she should acknowledge Germany's position on the continent. He went on to say that his aim was to make peace with Britain on a basis which she would regard as compatible with her honour to accept. All his efforts, as we know, were rejected. This time he had totally misjudged the mood of the British people.

CHAPTER FIVE

Interlude

I believe that during the period between 1934 and the collapse of France the use of Intelligence by both the politicians and the General Staff was minimal. Fortunately, in the Battle of France, Ultra had passed its first test with merit. It had shown us that, as we suspected, it was going to be the link between Hitler and his higher commands in the armed forces. Hut 3 had got their teeth into the job with tremendous enthusiasm and it now looked as if they were going to be at the very heart of the war. As the war progressed, 'Humph', who had studied Hitler's endless speeches in Germany in the thirties, came to know his phraseology so well that the translations of his vitally important signals were extremely accurate. I christened his outfit the Shadow OKW.

I, too, felt rather as if I was getting a letter from someone I knew and, from the signals, I was able to glean a little of the thoughts behind the words. I cannot refer here to more than a very small fraction of those high-value Ultra signals which passed through my office during the war, and many of which came back to me bearing the neat red-ink remarks of Winston Churchill. Nor can I quote the long, sometimes rambling, orders which Hitler himself indulged in, for they have remained locked in the vaults of Whitehall. But I have tried to include signals which were imprinted on my memory and to recall the moments when we succeeded in breaking a signal which might change the course of the war.

It was during the Battle of France that the pattern of Ultra signalling began to emerge. There was evidently a rule that all Army and Army Group commanders should render a situation report back to the OKH or to the OKW each day. These situation reports often confirmed what we already knew. They did, however, enable our commanders in the field to check up their own information and also, as the war developed, allowed the Prime Minister and the chiefs of staff in London to assess the overall situation.

It was about the beginning of August, when the Battle of Britain was starting to warm up, that Winston Churchill, obviously impressed by the signals he had received during the Battle of France, now requested that any important signals we had been able to break should be sent over to Downing Street and that each message should bear a note as to its significance and why. Menzies advised me that this would be my responsibility. It was one I very gladly took on. After all, I had organized the Shadow OKW in Hut 3 and now I was to look after the needs of the top man.

I realized I should have to have an efficient communications set-up with Hut 3. Hitherto they had sent the Ultra signals down by road, or telephoned the more important ones. Now I had a teleprinter line put in and was able to get signals direct from Hut 3 as soon as they had been edited: annotating them or headlining them, as I called it, was a more difficult job. I had to bear in mind that the chiefs of staff would be getting the signals and would advise the Prime Minister on their contents. Nevertheless, I think I managed to indicate their degree of importance and urgency without treading on anybody's toes. In any case the Prime Min-

ister very soon learned to read the correct meaning into
them. When he was in London I used to send the selected signals over to him in a red box to No. 10
Downing Street; then, as the Battle of Britain developed, to the underground war rooms below Storey's
Gate; if there was something very urgent I would phone
his private secretary and send the signal over at once. If
Bletchley was in good form I would sleep in the office
so that I could send overnight material to him around
7.30 a.m., when he liked to have his papers brought to
his bedroom. This was usually the job of General Sir
Hastings Ismay, so I would phone and forewarn him
also. I found it a wise precaution to follow the advice
of the late Admiral Sir Hugh Sinclair, 'Royalty and
Prime Ministers must never be taken by surprise.'

Churchill usually went to Chequers at weekends, so
if there was anything which I thought he should know,
I would ring through and read it to him on the scrambler telephone. I was nervous the first time I had to do
it but I soon got used to the routine. The voice of his
private secretary would come on; he knew me and
would tell me if the Prime Minister was immediately
available; then there would be a pause until I heard
heavy breathing at the other end and I knew it was
time to identify myself by name and begin to read. Saturday evenings were difficult because after dinner (like
Hitler) he always used to watch a film and this usually
lasted until around 2 a.m. It was his one form of relax-
ation, so it was no good ringing him before the film
ended. I would go to sleep on my camp bed in my office and get the WAAF officer on duty in the teleprinter room to wake me at 1.30 a.m. with any late evening
signals. This gave me time to read them over carefully,
select those I wanted to phone and then get them word
perfect before I did so. There was no room for mistakes in this business.

Sometimes, as the war progressed, there would be long political despatches from Hitler to his governors in his new empire; these intrigued Churchill, and I would be asked to read them all over again to some other Cabinet Minister who was spending the weekend at Chequers. At other times there would just be a 'thank you', but one always had to wait for it because often the Prime Minister would mull the signal over in his mind and then come back with an order to take some action with the Ministry concerned. That well-known voice was always courteous. There would be times when he had been away for a conference overseas, and then I had to go round to Storey's Gate and bring him up to date on certain aspects of Ultra information.

By August 1940 all Churchill's preconceived ideas based on the 1914–18 war had been swept away. Whether he was not wholly in agreement with his chiefs of staff I do not know, but I do know that, with Ultra in his hand, he now began to run the war himself, and did not cease to do so until the end of 1942.

CHAPTER SIX

The Battle of Britain

Hitler hated the sea; I don't know whether it was because he was afraid of being seen sea-sick or whether he had real hydrophobia. When I was in Lubeck in 1936, Rosenberg took me as his guest on a short exercise by two new destroyers of the new German Navy; he had had to deputize for Hitler who found some. excuse not to have to go to sea. I believe this may well have been one of the reasons why he never really had any enthusiasm for the invasion of Britain. The German generals too had never been trained in the art of invading across the sea; they spent their lives training and learning how to defend or to cross rivers, but it wasn't the same thing. When, in July 1940, Britain showed no signs of responding to the overtures of peace that Hitler had felt sure would be accepted, invasion and occupation must have looked like the only solution if we were to be eliminated from the war and Germany was to be allowed to concentrate all her energies on the conquest of Russia. We were to learn after the war that the only real enthusiast for the conquest was Goering, who argued that the Luftwaffe alone could force Britain to capitulate. This would make invasion by sea unnecessary. While Britain waited, we in Intelligence believed that the German High Command wouldn't attempt the sea crossing so long as the Royal Air Force was still operational. The Germans needed total con-

trol of the air, not only for their massive air-lift operations and the defence of their seaborne armada, but
also to ensure that no British ships could operate in the
English Channel.

Once France had fallen there was, for a short time, a
lull in the signals picked up. Those which were broken
mostly concerned the disposition of troops and headquarters for occupational purposes in France and were
not of very much interest to us at the moment. It was
not long, however, before the Luftwaffe signals started
to increase again, and now it began to look more serious for us. In the middle of July Ultra produced the
signal we had all been waiting for. It had evidently
been delivered in great secrecy from Hitler's headquarters to the Army, Navy and Air Force commanders-in-
chief. Goering, however, then put the gist of it on the
air to the generals commanding his air fleets. In his signal he stated that despite her hopeless military situation, England showed no signs of willingness to make
peace. Hitler had therefore decided to prepare and, if
necessary, to carry out a landing operation against her.
The aim of the operation was to eliminate England as a
base from which war against Germany could be continued and, if necessary, to occupy it completely. The
operation was to be called Sea Lion. I sent the signal
over to the Prime Minister immediately. It was the first
time the words Sea Lion had been used and it now
made it much easier for us to identify any activities
connected with the invasion plan. It was certainly this
signal that gave Churchill the idea of making his famous speech telling the Germans that we would fight
them on the beaches and everywhere else.

By now my teleprinter line from Hut 3 to my office
was working well. No longer were there scraps of paper
of all shapes and sizes, they were now neat sheets about

seven by nine inches, and in bold red letters across the top the word Ultra.

In Germany, Goering was the man of the hour and he lost no time in throwing his considerable weight about. One result was that he became prolific in his signals. We soon learned from him that the whole of the Luftflotte 2 and Luftflotte 3 were being redeployed right along the channel coast. Luftflotte 5 was being divided between Norway and Denmark. Ultra was giving us the main framework and, indeed, much of the detail as well. It was possible now for the Air Ministry to get virtually an exact order of battle of these air fleets, including the aerodromes where their various units were being stationed. They were of course helped by the whole lot of low-level signals sent by the various squadrons from which, now that the units were not far away, we could get cross-bearing fixes on their precise positions. We also knew from Ultra that feverish activities had been made to try and bring the squadrons up to full strength but that due to the poor operation of their repair and supply organization, the numbers of serviceable aircraft were still only about seventy-five per cent of their full strength. It was therefore possible to estimate that although Britain was facing a paper force of nearly three thousand aircraft, some eighteen hundred of which were bombers, probably only three-quarters of this figure would be serviceable at any one time, and if losses exceeded replacements, their serviceability percentage would obviously decrease. From many secret sources of information, including my personal information from Erich Koch, it seemed certain that Hitler would attack Russia in the East in the spring of 1941 and if he wanted the Sea Lion affair mopped up in time to redeploy his main forces in the East, he must start his invasion by around mid-September at the latest. It didn't give him much time.

One of Goering's orders was for his troop carriers to practise landing on narrow runways which would simulate roads. The Air Ministry got to work on constructing barriers which were kept ready along all the long straight roads in the south. I was in constant touch with Air Commodore Gerry Blackford in the Directorate of Plans at the Air Ministry, who was organizing the counter measures that could be taken against any airborne tricks. There had been a good number of stories of the Fifth Column disguises worn by the Germans parachuted into France so we kept a keen eye on all Luftwaffe signals.

The main parachute troops were beginning to be stationed near the larger aerodromes in Belgium and Holland, and an important signal told us of Hitler's order to the German Army and Air Force to co-operate in setting up special terminals for the quick loading and turn-around of aircraft. This, of course, confirmed our view that as well as parachute troops, they envisaged a rapid air-lift of supplies and arms across the channel. A high-ranking Luftwaffe officer was put in charge of all the air-loading operations. Towards the end of July there were signals showing disagreement between the Army and the Navy as to how the vast requirement of ships for the seaborne transport was to be met, but, from the Ultra signals we were now receiving, it was obvious that the main emphasis was still on the operations of the Luftwaffe. We could only guess, from the vast air fleets being ranged against us, and an apparent lack of urgency coupled with the inability of the German Army and Navy to co-operate, that the air battle was going to be the decisive factor. It was a hopeful sign and I think everyone, including the Prime Minister, felt that if we could withstand Goering's efforts to eliminate the Royal Air Force, Hitler would probably give up the idea altogether.

Goering's next important signal to his Luftwaffe was on 1 August 1940 and it confirmed this view, because he ordered the Luftwaffe to overcome the British Air Force with all means at its disposal as soon as possible. The great Goering had come into his own at last. Now his dreams of becoming the next Fuehrer of a mighty German Empire must surely come true. His air fleets would be feared throughout the world. Unlike Hitler he had no admiration or fear of the British. He had always put on a swash-buckling arrogance on the few occasions that I had met him, except the one time when his bulk had got stuck in the entrance to a small bar at Nuremberg and only the presence of mind of my companion in opening the other half of the double door had saved the day, though not Goering's embarrassment. I knew that Goering did not get on with Rosenberg whom he considered to be a useless dreamer. Now Goering was to have his chance to get his own back for the defeat of World War I when he had been Second-in-Command of the crack Richthofen Fighter Squadron.

Sea Lion was obviously going to be the crunch. Hut 3 had been strengthened both on the RAF side and also by civilian translators. It will be remembered that Enigma was the top-grade cypher and Hut 3, therefore, was not involved in the mass of lower level cypher traffic or the German Security Service cypher used by the German spy network in Britain and which now began to get busy on wireless transmitters.

With August, too, came the swarming of the barges. It was evident that if the sea invasion was to follow up the air battle, then a vast quantity of sea-going transport would be required. It was evident, too, from Ultra that the German Army had scant ideas of what was really involved in a large amphibious operation. The German Navy had settled for the great barges which ply on the rivers of the continent, from the big self-pro-

pelled ones of the Rhine, right down to the smaller
ones usually towed in threes and fours by a powerful
tug, mostly on French and Belgian rivers and canals.
But they soon found that the barges available were not
going to be enough, and Ultra signals revealed a frantic
search for ships of all sorts in Germany, Holland, Belgium and France. As the barges began to assemble, it
was found that not enough of these were self-propelled,
so there was another panic instruction sent out on Ultra
to find suitable engines, but these too were evidently
scarce, and in some cases aeroplane engines were being
fitted. Signals became acrimonious and the whole picture began to show how very hastily the invasion arrangements had been put together. One can imagine that the
confusion, which was apparent even to us, must have
raised a question in Hitler's mind as to whether his invasion would ever take place. I knew from General Ismay that there was a suspicion of this in Churchill's
mind, though he could not, of course, say so in public.
He had, however, informed the Cabinet as far back as
July the tenth that he considered the invasion by sea
would be unlikely to take place because 'it would be a
most hazardous and suicidal operation to commit a
large army to the accidents of the sea in the teeth of
our very numerous armed patrolling forces'. Churchill's
conclusions were right but for the wrong reasons. He
thought that Hitler's invasion would fail because the
Royal Navy would stop it, not because it was ineffi-
ciently organized. Churchill had still not understood
that naval forces cannot operate in confined waters
against land-based enemy aircraft. He and the naval
staff had not yet had the experiences of Crete and Singapore which were to bring the lesson right home and, in
fact, change the whole structure of the Royal Navy.
The days of the battleship were numbered. Had the
RAF been eliminated in the Battle of Britain, no ship

of the Royal Navy, however courageous, could have lived under the weight of the air attack the Luftwaffe could have mounted from France, Belgium and Holland.

Early in August I had suggested to the Director of Air Intelligence that as time would be precious in the coming air battles, a small unit at Fighter Command would save the Air Ministry having to send the Ultra signals on to Air Marshal Dowding at Stanmore, Headquarters Fighter Command. 'D of I' was quite willing, and we both agreed that it would also preserve security and ensure that only signals which really helped him were sent to Dowding and his controllers, so as not to overload them. The officer-in-charge could also make sure that only those people authorized to handle the signals would in fact receive them and that nothing would be left lying about. It worked very well. The SLU were given a sound-proof cubicle 'down the hole', as the deep underground operations room at Stanmore was called, and I had a direct teleprinter line installed from Hut 3. I also put Air Vice-Marshal Keith Park, the Officer Commanding No. 11 Group, and his controllers in the Ultra picture, so that they would know what Dowding was talking about if and when we began to get prior information of raids. No. 11 Group, which directly commanded all the fighter squadrons in the south of England, was to take the brunt of the great attacks.

Meantime, Goering himself was indefatigable. The Reich-Marshal toured his units, obviously working up enthusiasm for the coming battle. He would send signals to his commanders advising them which units he proposed to visit on the following day. These signals shed an interesting light on the absence of spit and polish in the German squadrons. Goering was fastidious and he had obviously found some of the pilots, to whom he was lavishly handing out decorations, not quite to his liking. As a result his signals now instructed the commanding officers to make quite sure that the men whom he was going to decorate were properly deloused; he had obviously had an unfortunate experience. We used to call these signals 'Goering's funnies' and I would sometimes include one in my telephone conversations to Churchill at the weekend just to hear the deep chuckle at the other end.

I wonder if the Reich-Marshal, as he now toured his Luftwaffe units in France, would have been quite so cocksure of the coming victory if he had known that, in addition to his own units, we would be recipients of his signals as well.

It had been part of my job to try and understand what was going on under Sir Robert Watson-Watt's tender care in those wooden huts near the sea at Orfordness in Suffolk in the 1930s—the evolution of radar. It was vital for us to know whether the Germans had any form of radar themselves or had any idea about what we were doing. This had been one of the first jobs I had given to the young scientist, R. V. Jones. I had watched, too, the complex organization being set up by 'Stuffy' Dowding, Commander-in-Chief of Fighter Command, and Jack Slessor, Director of Plans at the Air Ministry, to co-ordinate all the aircraft detection systems and channel them on to the table of the operations room both at Fighter Command headquarters and those of its Groups, so that the speed, direction, height and size of enemy formations approaching Britain could be plotted even before the formations left the French coast and the fighters sent up to meet them before they arrived over the English side of the channel. All the information collected by R. V. Jones had gone to show that the Germans had developed a short-range radar themselves, which no doubt led them to try to knock out our own coastal radar stations at the beginning of the battle, but there was no indication from any source, including Ultra, that they knew how far and how accurately our radar operated. To us, facing an enemy with perhaps a three-to-one balance in their favour, radar was the first key to our survival. Ultra was to be the second. Goering's signals as he toured his squadrons were, of course, invaluable in filling in any gaps in our information as to the whereabouts of the bomber and fighter units that our pilots were about to meet, in the most famous air battle in history.

As I have said, the strength of three air fleets, now ranged against us, were of a size that, back in 1935, Baldwin had refused to believe possible and, later, Chamberlain had preferred not to. We learned that Luftflotte 2 was to operate from aerodromes in Holland and Belgium and the north coast of France against our south-east coast. It was commanded by Kesselring. Luftflotte 3, commanded by Sperrle, was to operate from Normandy and Brittany and would be ranged against the western half of our south coast. Luftflotte 5, which was smaller, was split between Norway and Denmark and was destined to operate against our north-eastern coast. Fighter Command had a bare seven hundred aircraft, despite the fact we had made wonderful use of the months since Dunkirk and had more than made up for the losses of aircraft in France.

Now, as August started to move on, the number of German signals began to boil over. They mounted to one, two and three hundred a day; when we could break them each one had to be scanned, sorted, translated and edited. We had been very lucky to find a number of WAAF officers who spoke German who were pressed into service at Hut 3, and they proved highly efficient at the job. In addition, a lot of wives and friends of Bletchley people were involved, including, for instance, Dorothy Denniston who had met the head of Bletchley in Room 40 in 1916, in the early days of interception and de-coding. Where total security is vital, family ties prove more reliable than the most elaborate form of screening.

On August the eighth Goering issued his order of the day, Operation Eagle. Within the hour it was in the hands of the chiefs of staff and the Prime Minister. Dowding had got his copy direct. Churchill wanted an extra copy and I believe took it over to the Palace. 'From Reich-Marshal Goering to all units of Luftflotte 2, 3 and 5. Operation Adler (Eagle). Within a short period you will wipe the British Air Force from the sky. Heil Hitler.' Though the signal had been given, the great mass raids expected on the eleventh did not materialize. The weather had clouded over and, although there were some fairly large formations which confined themselves to bombing shipping and coastal airfields, it was a bit of an anti-climax. Goering had apparently come up to the French coast to be with his squadrons and when the twelfth broke clear over the English Channel, there were a number of bombing operations against our radar stations and airfields. A few of the radar stations were hit but, surprisingly, they somehow managed to get going again. Although Goering's orders were now getting through to Dowding in good time, the actual targets were presumably only given at the local German briefings because they did not appear on Ultra signals. Nevertheless, it evidently helped Dowding to know the extent of the German effort for the day.

On the twelfth came the signal again designating August the thirteenth as 'Eagle Day' itself and the information that in the morning Luftflotte 2 was to attack airfields in the Kent and Thames area, Luftflotte 3 was to attack airfields further west. But early on the thirteenth Goering suddenly ordered the postponement of the attack until the afternoon. It may have had something to do with the bad weather, or possibly because he himself wanted to get right up to the coast in time to watch his air armada go over. Anyway, the result was chaotic because although we got his Ultra signal, apparently some of his units did not and the morning attack went off at half-cock. Nevertheless, by the end of that full day the RAF had had plenty to cope with.

The next day was quieter, but that evening Goering must have decided to have his really big show the following day. It had failed on the eleventh because of weather and on the thirteenth because of a mixed up order. Now he was evidently co-ordinating the operation himself, and this time he made sure that there would be no mistakes. The Ultra signal was precise. The attack would be made by Luftflotten 2, 3 and 5, and the orders sent to them warned us that their attacks were carefully timed so as to keep our defences fully stretched the whole day. The first raid was to be a formation of forty aircraft by Luftflotte 2, with fighter escort, in mid-morning, once again at airfields in Kent. Then, soon after mid-day, a larger formation of bombers with fighter escort from Luftflotte 5 was to attack airfields on the north-east coast. When it became clear that Luftflotte 5 would operate in this area, Dowding alerted Trafford Leigh-Mallory, commanding 12 Group, and Richard Saul, commanding 13 Group, on the north-east coast. A second raid by Luftflotte 5, operating from Denmark, was scheduled an hour after the first. The first raid by Luftflotte 5, which came from Norway, was, thanks to Ultra's early warning and good long-distance radar fixes, intercepted by 13 Group while well out to sea, and although some bombers got through, the formation lost fifteen of their hundred aircraft. The distance was too great for them to have their own fighters to protect them. The second raid by Luftflotte 5 from Denmark was met by 12 Group, again some damage was done by the enemy, but their losses were eight aircraft out of the fifty which came over. After all this, with no losses to the RAF, Luftflotte 5 did not try again. In the afternoon it was Luftflotte 2's turn again and two raids within an hour of each other duly came over Essex and Kent according to their scheduled orders. Teatime saw Luftflotte 3 join in. There was a big raid of up to eighty bombers, fully escorted, attacking the south coast, west of Portsmouth, and then, lastly, Luftflotte 2 had another go at around 6.30 p.m. at the Kent airfields. It was a massive effort and quite obviously intended to get as many RAF fighters into the air as possible. Goering wanted a quick kill. If Dowding had fallen for the bait, losses on both sides would have been higher than the RAF could afford. Dowding decided to meet each raid with a small number of fighters. This way he reckoned he could cause maximum confusion amongst the Luftwaffe formations with the minimum losses to the RAF. Radar and the Observer Corps gave no rest all day to the controllers and the apparently untirable WAAF plotters both at Fighter Command and Group Headquarters.

I managed occasionally to get down to Stanmore to watch the incredible speed and accuracy with which the WAAFs plotted the raids in the operations room. On one occasion I noticed a lovely girl who was working harder than most. She looked up and I saw a pair of laughing brown eyes. She became my wife.

The whole Fighter Command system, organized over several years, ran like a clockwork miracle and, as the speed, height and direction of the raids were plotted on the great table map below the balcony, Dowding would watch and give quiet orders to his controllers, who

were on the telephone to the AOCs at Group Headquarters. The numbers of enemy aircraft were so vast
that the plotters could only show such figures as eigh-
ty-plus or a hundred-plus which the radar stations
could calculate from their screens. It was then up to the
Observer Corps, in their sandbagged posts along the
cliffs, to try and give more accurate figures, as the
massed bombers and fighters swept towards the coast.
Dowding was counting his fighters now in penny numbers and would order them up as soon as the enemy
crossed the French coast; perhaps twenty of our Spit-
fires to harry and break up a formation of a hundred
bombers escorted by enemy fighters. At Group Headquarters the orders were passed on to the aerodromes
and the scramble was on. Then the Sector Aerodrome
Controllers took over, and from their own smaller operations room, once again with the help of radar, directed our fighters into battle.

Goering's strategy for destroying the RAF was two-
fold: first he wished to bomb all our aerodromes in the
south so as to make them unoperational, then he
wished to draw as many RAF fighters as possible into
battle where the Germans hoped to destroy them
quickly.

Fortunately we had a good number of aerodromes,
largely grass in those days, and the aircraft were so well
dispersed away from the aerodrome buildings and camouflaged and protected by high banks and camouflage
nets that it was difficult for the Luftwaffe either to put
an aerodrome out of action or to hit the aircraft on the
ground. Holes in the turf were easy to repair whilst accurate bombing of the camouflaged aircraft was prevent-
ed by anti-aircraft fire.

Goering replied with bigger formations of bombers
and the greater frequency of their attacks, believing
they would force Dowding to send up more and more

of our fighters to combat them; even if this caused heavier losses on both sides, Goering believed that the Luftwaffe could afford them whereas the RAF could not. Dowding, who was able to recognize Goering's strategy from his Ultra signals, was not to be drawn and continued to use the minimum of fighters to disrupt and confuse the bomber squadrons so as to make accurate bombing more difficult. At the same time, since the German fighter escorts dare not leave the massed bomber formations unprotected from above, it was much easier for our small units or even individual fighters to get amongst the bombers.

It was due to Dowding's tactics that we survived the onslaughts on our aerodromes as long as we did. No one had, of course, expected Ultra when the Fighter Command organization was being set up. Ultra was, therefore, a bonus Dowding had not counted on; now it gave him an invaluable overall picture of the enemy offensive and the strategy behind it. It also gave some indication of the enemy's true losses from the calls for replacement aircraft and crews by the various formations. The urgency of Operation Eagle was also evident. There could be no Operation Sea Lion until the Royal Air Force was eliminated. But the RAF kept coming up.

It was the radar and the Observer Corps who brought the whole battle alive, right into the operations room itself.

From time to time I also managed to get down to Biggin Hill, which was a sector aerodrome near London, in order to go round the dispersal points and once again get the smell and sound of aeroplanes. I would watch Wing-Commander 'Sailor' Malan scramble his Spitfire squadron and then I would go into the little sector operations room and watch his 'angels' guided up to do battle with the 'bandits' which outnumbered him ten to one. It was just a second-hand way of capturing some of the memories of those little dog-fights over France in 1917. Now our pilots were in massive battles two and three times a day. I found the Biggin Hill boys terribly curious about the remarkable accuracy of the warnings that Keith Park was able to give them. He was, of course, not allowed to tell them the facts revealed by Ultra, but experience soon taught them to put the right value on the orders they received. I was glad when the Prime Minister decided to stay in London for the weekend of August the nineteenth and not go down to Chequers. It saved me the 2 a.m. telephone calls at that time of little rest. I myself used my camp-bed in the office right through those hectic weeks.

Now that the Battle of Britain was at its height, the other German operations for Sea Lion were going ahead, but the German Ultra signals showed the continued lack of co-ordination and co-operation between the Army and Navy. They seemed unable to agree on the plans for the seaborne attack, whilst the Army was constantly finding snags in their large transport arrangements. The Ultra picture was one of muddle, which was encouraging for us.

Goering, evidently still convinced that he could do the job with his Luftwaffe, didn't appear to take much interest in the plans of the Army. Ultra gave us many bits of useful information—troops were moving to the coast, transport aircraft were being assembled for the great airlift, stores and supplies of all sorts were being lost on the railways, there was still difficulty in obtaining and fitting engines into the barges, there were still the constant appeals by the Navy to disperse the barges in order to save them from the hit and run attacks by the RAF. Goering was not happy. This was evident from an Ultra signal to his Luftwaffe commanders which asked for an explanation for their failure to destroy the RAF and summoned them to his headquarters. I have not doubt he was asking himself and his commanders why the RAF was still able to put up such opposition. At this time Goering advised Hitler and us that the RAF fighters had been reduced to some three hundred, in fact their Intelligence was about a hundred per cent wrong; we still had double that number thanks to the wonderful effort of our repair and production factories. But Goering was now also fighting for his reputation. He knew that from the point of view of the German officer corps, he was a political upstart with no staff training and only his experience as a World War I pilot. The gross underestimation of our defensive aircraft by Goering's Intelligence staff must have encouraged him to believe that he could still do the whole job with his Luftwaffe, or at least so reduce the RAF that Sea Lion could start on time, because early on August the eighteenth Ultra fore-shadowed a repetition of the immense raids of Eagle Day. Dowding was forewarned. Still the RAF came up and the Luftwaffe had one of the heaviest day's losses so far. Once again there was a lull and fortunately the weather turned sour.

There had been a 'dud day' in France in May 1917 when the commanding officer of my squadron had sent a dozen of us off to Amiens in one of the old Crossley tenders. There had been a nun who had given me a medallion of the Angel of Amiens when I had gone into the cathedral for a few moments' silence. Only a weary pilot knows how low clouds and rain are as much a godsend as they are to a drought-stricken Australian sheep farmer.

By now it must at last have become obvious to Goering that the strategy so far employed by the Luftwaffe had not achieved the desired results. Somehow Fighter Command was being too clever for them, so he now issued orders which we picked up on Ultra that 'the attacks were to go much farther inland in order to bring the RAF up to battle'. It was an important signal, primarily because it reiterated Goering's absolute need to bring the RAF fighters up in great numbers so that the Luftwaffe could destroy them. It was about this time that one of Dowding's subordinate commanders, Leigh-Mallory, commanding 12 Group, had been criticizing his Commander-in-Chief for not sending up large formations of RAF fighters to meet the German raids. Leigh-Mallory, as a Group Commander, did not get Goering's Ultra signals. The German raids were carried out in mass formations of bombers which, in themselves, were highly unmanœuvrable, and these were in turn protected by another mass formation of fighters. If, as Goering and Leigh-Mallory had wanted, Dowding had sent up mass formations of our own fighters, not only would they have been far less manœuvrable in attack on the German formations, but the balance of losses, which was in our favour when small formations of RAF fighters got in amongst the massed German aircraft, would have been lost.

From where I sat there was no adverse doubt at all about the way in which Dowding was fighting the battle, and his understanding and interpreting of Ultra was obviously an important contribution to our success during this part of the war. Security dictated that only a very few people should get Goering's signals, and no doubt some of the young pilots in the Midlands felt the other fellows in the south were getting the glory.

I watched Dowding and Keith Park handle the Ultra with supreme care, never hinting that the top secret alerts, which were given to the key sector aerodrome commanders, had come from intercepted signals.

Dowding's strategy of always having some fighters available to go up and meet every raid not only foxed the Germans as to our actual fighter strength, but also

gradually wore down the morale of the Luftwaffe and
finally made Goering change his tactics and send his
bombers further inland as stated in the second part of
the signal. Although Dowding must have been relieved
that there was to be some let-up on the bombing of the
aerodromes near the coast—which had taken a terrific
pounding and had seriously affected the operations of
11 Group's squadrons—nevertheless the aerodromes
further inland and nearer London which were now
threatened were the vital radar sector aerodromes
which directed our fighters up to and into contact with
the enemy. If these were knocked out it would ruin the
secret way in which our fighters could be guided to
their targets. However, a considerable point in our favour was that most of the German fighters could not
carry enough fuel to go the extra distance inland and
still be able to stay and protect the bombers. The attacks on the inland aerodromes began on August the
twenty-fourth and lasted with extreme intensity for a
fortnight. There was no set pattern from Ultra, but
when units from two different Luftflotten were employed, we sometimes got the signals co-ordinating
their efforts, thus giving us a good idea of the size and
timing of the larger raids. However, now that the German formations were coming further inland, the warnings from radar and the Observer Corps at the coast
gave our fighters a little more time to get up to them
before they reached their targets. Despite all Dowding's
efforts, Fighter Command was getting desperately short
of aircraft and pilots. The pilots were getting tired from
the endless sorties against the enemy formations. Our
main sector aerodromes, like Biggin Hill, were so badly
damaged that in some cases they were hardly able to
look after a single squadron in the air. To add to our
difficulties, the Luftwaffe had also turned their attention to some aircraft factories in the south of England,

the sources of our Spitfire and Hurricane supplies; but still the RAF came up.

On August the thirtieth and thirty-first Goering must have been getting really impatient; once again he took personal control of his air fleets and luckily for us on those two days gave us prior warning of the giant raids. The position of the RAF was now desperate. We knew that if the Luftwaffe was capable of keeping up the pace of the past fortnight for just another week or two, the result might very well be disaster. But the Luftwaffe, too, were licking their wounds; according to Ultra their replacement aircraft were no longer coming through. Their supply and repair organization had not been planned for this sort of a war. In Goering's view, the Battle of Britain should have been all over in a fortnight with but few losses to the Luftwaffe. Now they had scarcely fifty per cent of their aircraft serviceable. This was vital information. It showed that despite the appalling position of the RAF, the Luftwaffe were crippled; their morale too was suffering.

Then in a final effort to break the RAF Goering made his biggest mistake of the war. Had he kept up his blows at the aerodromes in southern England for another fortnight, he might well have grounded our remaining fighters, but at 11 a.m. on September the fifth Goering sent out an order on Ultra to Kesselring for a three-hundred-bomber raid on the London docks. There was to be massive fighter cover for the German bombers, the raid timed for late in the afternoon. This, at least, he thought, would bring up the last RAF fighters to be destroyed.

Thanks to Ultra, Goering's signal was in the hands of the Prime Minister and of Dowding within minutes of its despatch. There was tremendous speculation about this switch of targets from the battered airfields of Fighter Command to the capital city. Was this meant

to be the *coup de grâce?* Did Goering believe that the
RAF were nearly finished, or was the raid simply in revenge for a raid that the RAF had made on Berlin,
which had given the lie to Goering's boast that it could
never happen? Was he now preparing to kill two birds
with one stone, to finally liquidate the Royal Air Force
and take revenge for his bruised pride? Strategically,
his change of course was entirely wrong.

The Prime Minister was obviously determined to see
the raid himself; he rang to find if there was a more accurate time but I could only suggest between 4 and 5
p.m. It was one of those clear bright September days.
Churchill, I knew, was watching from the Air Ministry
roof in Whitehall not far from where I, too, was on the
high roof of our own offices. The afternoon sun shone
on the waves of enemy bombers as they came high
above the Thames to the docks, the target given in
Goering's orders. It was a daylight firework set-piece.
All the river fire-fighting units had been secretly gathered and every fire engine in the vicinity had been secretly alerted. But despite the RAF fighters weaving
their vapor trails high in the skies, the sheer weight of
the enemy gave them the chance to drop their bombs
where it hurt. Clouds of black and white smoke rose
from the docks, the deep boom of the bombs echoed
across the city. London was having its first taste of the
blitz. This was to be the kill and Goering was, without
doubt, in charge. It was always better for us when he
was on the spot, for he had complete faith in Enigma
signals which he used lavishly; in fact I often wondered
if he disliked using the telephone. The acrid smoke and
fumes of bombs and fires drifted slowly over London as
the bombers went home and we started to count the
cost.

Although the switch of bombing to the docks had
saved the remaining RAF fighters from being ground-

ed, it had barely saved the sector aerodromes. Some of the little operations rooms, such as that at Biggin Hill where I had watched the battles earlier on, had been hit and many of the girls had been killed, yet within hours an emergency room was again operational.

CHAPTER SEVEN

Operation Sea Lion

It is a curious character of the British that when a situation becomes really serious, all the fuss and excitement dies down and deadly calm prevails. The process was beginning now. My head WAAF officer, Mrs Owen, who kept her small flock of cypher officers in faultless order in my teleprinter room, took on a more formal and purposeful entrance when she brought me the urgent signals in the middle of the night. She was one of those completely capable woman, whose only apparent weakness was for Siamese cats. Later her quiet efficiency led me to send her as part of Churchill's staff when he went on his visits across the Atlantic to meet Roosevelt. She looked after all the Ultra for him.

Despite the fact that Goering had not achieved complete air superiority, it was feared that he still might feel that he had been sufficiently successful to give Hitler the green go-ahead light for the invasion, for the German invasion fleet appeared to be as ready as it was ever likely to be. The nests of barges along the Belgian and French coasts were becoming small armadas according to the daily count kept by the photographers of the spy plane unit, now officially named the Photographic Reconnaissance Unit. The standby alert for everyone in Britain was code-named Cromwell, and the hitherto silent bells of all the churches in Britain would tell the people when the invasion had begun.

On September the seventh Invasion Alert No. 1 was sent out which meant that the Germans might be expected within twelve hours and troops and Home Guard were brought to immediate readiness. The witch hunt for Fifth Column parachutists was eager. Nuns wisely kept to their convents. Sticky bombs were issued to the Army and the Home Guard—these were bombs which if stuck to the outside of a tank would put it out of action when they exploded. That night, once again, our bombers, such as they were, struck back at the massed barges, but that night, too, the German bombers struck again at London itself, the first of the real blitzes, purely against the civilian population. On September the ninth we got Goering's orders at 11 a.m. for an early evening raid by two hundred-plus bombers, again on London itself, but this time our fighters were able to meet them further south and few got through to the city. That night, however, they came again. Still the invasion barges remained in their ports; how many had at last got engines we did not know. On September the tenth came blessed rain and clouds; it lasted for four days.

To those of us scanning every signal of the German armed forces, the impression had been forming, ever since Goering's switch of attack away from our aerodromes, that time had run out for Sea Lion. Churchill I know felt this although he could not relax the mood of the nation in any way. That Hitler and his generals would not risk Sea Lion whilst the RAF still lived was evident, and Goering's last-minute efforts to break the morale of the civil population with bombs was having the opposite effect. The odds against invasion lengthened.

A month had now passed since the mass attacks of Eagle Day, a month of taut strung nerves, of hopes that someone, perhaps Goering, would put the invasion

plans on the air, though from the position of the barges
and the air-loading installations, the areas were not
hard to guess. It was obvious too that it must be now
or, we hoped, never. On the fourteenth the rains less-
ened but the weather was not good enough for any major effort. But, Sunday, the fifteenth of September,
dawned alas, an ideal day for the German planes,
cloudy but with sufficient gaps to find their way. Once
again the hand of Goering was guiding what he hoped
would be the final knockout. By mid-day, wave upon
wave of bombers were heading for London.

Dowding, correctly judging his moment, the low
morale of the German bomber crews, the lack of adequate fighter protection due to the size of their fuel
tanks, the desperate state of the RAF and the knowledge that it was now or never for Operation Sea Lion,
threw in everything we had. No. 11 Group fought them
from the coast, then 12 Group, operating now in
massed squadrons, took over near London. The unexpected strength of our fighters was too much for the Luftwaffe; they had been told we hadn't any left; they
turned and fled. Goering must obviously have been getting frantic by this time. He promptly ordered a second
raid, and this time it was to be pressed home. His signal
was duly picked up and this was an occasion when the
speed of the Ultra operation and the direct line to
Dowding made history. The fighters were refuelled,
rearmed and ready again to meet the second wave, and
once again the raiders dropped their bombs wherever
they could and fled. It was a tremendous day. There
was an unconfirmed rumour that the admirals were
prepared to guard Nelson's Column in Trafalgar
Square in case the statue on top should be replaced by
one of Dowding. He has never yet received the credit
that, not least in his understanding of Ultra, is his due.

We didn't, of course, know at that time when or

whether the mass air attacks would start again or whether the invasion was still a serious threat. Invasion alert Cromwell was still operative. But one of the main features of the German invasion plans had been the vast preparations that had been made on the Belgian and Dutch aerodromes for loading and quick turn-round of the supply and troop-carrying aircraft, which were by this time supposed to have an unopposed flight to England. On the morning of the seventeenth the officer-in-charge of these operations in Holland received a signal from the German General Staff to say that Hitler had authorized the dismantling of the air-loading equipment at the Dutch aerodromes. It was quite a short signal, but its significance was so great that 'Humph' had telephoned it down to me the moment it had been decyphered. It was obviously a signal which required some explanation if Churchill was to be able to grasp its meaning. I, therefore, indicated its full significance on my cover headline. If the loading equipment was being dismantled, the invasion could not take place, and I sent it over to the underground war room in its red box with another note to Winston's Principal Secretary John Martin asking him to see that the Prime Minister had it at once. I also explained the signal to Menzies, just in time, because the Prime Minister phoned Stewart immediately, asking him to go to a chiefs of staff meeting he had called for 7.30 p.m. and to take me along with him. I also phoned Charles Medhurst to ensure that the Chief of Air Staff was properly briefed.

Goering was hard to convince and was still determined to go on trying to bring Britain to her knees by bombing her cities, and that evening the banshee wails of sirens heralded the now nightly air-raids soon after dusk. There was already intermittent bombing and anti-aircraft fire as we left in Stewart's car for Storey's

Gate; it was drizzling, and ghostly forms moved about in the darkening streets. Underground, in Churchill's war room, Hastings Ismay was already welcoming the chiefs of staff and setting the conference in place. They had been briefed by their directors of Intelligence. Winston arrived. I was struck by the extraordinary change that had come over these men in the last few hours. It was as if someone had suddenly cut all the strings of the violins in the middle of a dreary concerto. There were controlled smiles on the faces of these men. Churchill read out the signal, his face beaming, then he rightly asked the Chief of the Air Staff Sir Cyril Newall to explain its significance. Cyril Newall had been well briefed; he gave it as his considered opinion that this marked the end of Sea Lion, at least for this year. Churchill asked Menzies if there was anything further to confirm the signal. He turned to me, but I was unable to give any further assurance as yet. But the conference knew that the dismantling of the air-loading equipment meant the end of the threat, and so it was accepted. There was a very broad smile on Churchill's face now as he lit up his massive cigar and suggested that we should all take a little fresh air. As we surfaced, the air raid was at its height. A little way outside the entrance to the underground war room at Storey's Gate was a massive wide concrete structure like a half folded screen some ten feet high, and despite the efforts of Ismay and Sir John Dill, then Chief of the Imperial General Staff, to stop the Prime Minister, he insisted on going round the screen and into the open. It was a wild scene. Standing with our backs to the concrete were ranged the three chiefs of staff, then General Ismay, Stewart and myself. Winston stood alone in front, his dark blue boiler suit undone at the neck, a tin hat on his head, his hands folded on his stout stick in front of him, his chin thrust out, the long cigar in his mouth, and just across the other side of St James's Park, Carlton House Terrace was ablaze: the boom of bombs exploding to the south, the crack and rattle of the AA guns and exploding shells, the red white glow of the fires silhouetting the tall black trunks of the great trees in the park. It was a moment in history to remember, and above the noise came the angry voice of Winston Churchill: 'By God, we will get the B's for this.'

The threat of invasion was past but there was much to do and night after night in the winter of 1940–41 came Goering's vengeance, the blitz. Somehow, he had to save face. He, and maybe some others, still held on to the view that they could reduce Britain to impotence by the nightly bombing of London. It was easy to get at; the river was a built-in compass, and no matter where the bombs dropped they were bound to do damage. There was no reference to the nightly bombing in Ultra. The raids came throughout the rest of September and October. One began to wait for the banshee's wail about half-past six in the evening. But in November, since the London raids didn't seem to be having the desired effect, Goering decided to start on some of the other big cities. Sometimes we would get warning of such a raid but the exact target was hidden by a code name which, of course, we did not know.

However, at about 3 p.m. on November the fourteenth someone must have made a slip-up and instead of a city with a code name, Coventry was spelt out. This was something we had not met before. Churchill was at a meeting so I spoke direct to his personal secretary and told him what had happened. I pointed out that whilst the signal had gone to Fighter Command, I had little doubt there would be reference back to the Prime Minister for a decision as to what to do and it would be an agonizing decision to have to make. There were, perhaps, four or five hours before the attack would arrive. It was a longish flight north and the enemy aircraft would not cross the coast before dark. I asked the personal secretary if he would be good enough to ring me back when the decision had been taken, because if Churchill decided to evacuate Coventry, the press, and indeed everybody, would know we had pre-knowledge of the raid and some counter-measure might be necessary to protect the source which would obviously become suspect. It also seemed to me, sitting in my office a little weary after the sleepless bomb-torn night before, that there would be absolute chaos if everyone tried to get out of the city in the few hours available and that if, for any reason, the raid was postponed by weather or for some other reason, we should have put the source of our information at risk to no purpose. I imagine that the Prime Minister must have consulted a number of people before making up his mind. In any case, the RAF had ample time to put their counter measures into action, such as jamming any of the aids to navigation that the Germans might be using. In the event, it was decided only to alert all the services, the fire, the ambulance, the police, the wardens, and to get everything ready to light the decoy fires. This is the sort of terrible decision that sometimes has to be made on the highest levels in war. It was unquestionably the right one, but I am glad it was not I who had to take it. Official history maintains that the Air Ministry had two days' notice of this raid. As far as Ultra is concerned it was now definite.

There was to be one other raid of which we got prior notice from Ultra, the second great fire of London in December of 1941. Goering made no bones about his demands for his bombers to burn the city. Here, there was no necessity to try to evacuate it; offices would be empty anyway, but the damage to property, if a great fire took hold, could be enormous. Once again every

fire chief for some miles around was secretly alerted, as
were once again the Thames fire-fighters and the other
services. The raid started early and I watched as the
great dome of St Paul's was silhouetted against a wall
of yellow flame.

It was some time after Dowding had left Fighter
Command that I had lunch with him at his club. Dowding had already, before the war, been longer in his job
as Commander-in-Chief of Fighter Command than was
normal in the RAF, but as it was he who, with the able
planners of the Air Staff, had set up the mechanism for
the air defence of Britain, the radar and the sector
aerodromes, the fighter aircraft and all that went to the
winning of the Battle of Britain, it obviously made
sense for Cyril Newall, the Chief of the Air Staff, to
keep him on to command the actual battle itself. Over
lunch we talked of the great air battles of August and
September and the part that Ultra had played in them.
He reminded me of the moment when he had received
the signal for the seven great raids on the big Eagle
Day and of how this information was vital in confirming his view that what Goering wanted was to get as
many RAF fighters into the air as possible in order to
try to make a quick killing, and confirming also his determination to conserve his slender forces so as to meet
all the raids, if only with a few aircraft each time. This
way he made Goering step up the size of his formations
in order to try and achieve his objective. Goering's tactics were clear from the Ultra signals, but the bigger
German formations had, in turn, as Dowding said, giv-
en us an even better chance to make a mess of the large
unmanoeuvrable masses of aircraft. How carefully
Dowding had worn down both the numbers and morale
of the Luftwaffe, and judged the time to let them have
it. Leigh-Mallory and others had been criticizing the
Commander-in-Chief for not using bigger fighter for-

mations against the Germans earlier. Leigh-Mallory's
criticisms were carried further at a high-level meeting,
held at his request at the Air Ministry in October. The
Battle of Britain had been won, but Leigh-Mallory
thought fit to bring one of his young pilots to argue his
case against Dowding and to criticize Keith Park whose
11 Group had borne the brunt of the fighting in the
south of England. In the words of one senior member
of Air Staff who later became its Chief, 'If I had been
the Commander-in-Chief and one of my Group Commanders had not carried out my wishes, he would have
had the chop.'

To those who knew him, Dowding had aged rapidly
during those critical six months of the war and it was
perhaps a measure of his tiredness and loss of grip over
his commanders that he allowed the argument to come
to the Air Staff at all, and it was a measure of Dowding's loyalty to the security of Ultra that forbade him to
use it to defend his conduct. It was also a measure of
the inherent courtesy and consideration of Sir Archibald
Sinclair, the Air Minister, when telling Dowding on
November the thirteenth that he would finally have to
relinquish his Command, to offer him a visit to America to help the war effort. When General Sir Edmund
Ironside was replaced as Chief of the General Staff after our defeat in France, Churchill had offered him a
Field-Marshal's baton or a Peerage. Ironside had asked
for one, then changed his mind and in the event got
both. When the victor of the Battle of Britain was replaced, he was offered neither. It wasn't a happy story,
but it is all now documented.

What, however, has not been told hitherto is the part
that Ultra played in it.

It has I think been rightly said that if we had lost the
Battle of Britain, we should have had to surrender, just as
later we should have had to have done so had we lost the

Battle of the Atlantic. To many it was a comforting
thought that we had Dowding at the controls during the
critical period. Over that lunch that he had given me I
had found nothing stuffy about this quiet elderly man.
One could sense no bitterness, but rather a failure to
understand the way in which he had been treated. I
think that those who knew him and saw him in action
during those days on the balcony above the ever-chang-
ing operations table down the hole at Stanmore, and who
experienced his real concern not only for his hard-pressed
pilots but for everybody who worked for him, whether
weary WAAF or tired-eyed controller, could not understand it either. It was *he* who had won the Battle of
Britain and it was *he* who had protected the security of
Ultra.

CHAPTER EIGHT

The African Campaign

From the Ultra point of view, the early part of 1941 was frustrating. Despite the information we were able to pick up, it didn't help us in our endeavour to stop the vast Axis forces. It did, however, provide Churchill with an accurate picture of the broad German strategy and gave us some of the details of their preparations for their attack on Russia, which evidently once again would include a south-easterly thrust to the much needed Russian oilfields. It is, I think, true to say that it was as a result of this information that Churchill was prepared to fight desperately to keep our hold on the Middle East. The Italian threat to Egypt was brilliantly countered and General R. N. O'Connor's victory at Sidi Barani where most of the Italian army was captured had given our morale a much needed stimulus. But there had been disquieting news from Berlin. Ultra signals had indicated a new build-up of German forces in southern Roumania. Hitler had already pressured both Roumania and Bulgaria into becoming subject states of the new Reich but signals had hitherto indicated the build-up of forces against Russia. Then the signals to and from the German general in Roumania and Berlin indicated that something else was afoot. The answer came in a directive from Hitler to the commander of the forces in southern Roumania, one of the few of Hitler's war directives which we were able to obtain, telling him to prepare to move southwards through Bulgaria for an attack on Greece.

It looked as if Hitler, no longer able to rely on the Italians in the Mediterranean, was himself going to secure his southern flank against the British in the Middle East for his Russian venture.

It was this Ultra information which prompted Churchill to send a mission to Greece to find out if the Greeks were going to fight. When they decided to do so, the Prime Minister, despite our already overstretched forces in the Middle East, considered that 'If on their own the Greeks resolved to fight, we must share their ordeal'. The chances of stopping the Germans getting into Greece were obviously slender, and for General Sir Archibald Wavell, Commander of the Middle East Command, it meant thinning out our forces in Cyrenaica even more. It was a political decision, which cost us dear. Early in February came the second blow. Hitler, seeing the low morale of what was left of the Italian Army, realized he must do something drastic if he was to keep them in the war. He had already sent the Xth German Fliegerkorps, under the command of Kesselring, down to Sicily in December 1940 in order to help the Italians harass our shipping in the Mediterranean, and now an Ultra signal to the Luftwaffe headquarters informed them, and us, that General Rommel would be taking command of the German Army units to be sent to North Africa. Was O'Connor's victory over the Italians on 7 February 1941 to be wiped out? By mid-February an Ultra signal to Berlin told us that Rommel had arrived in Tripoli. Up to now our only experience of Rommel had been when we panicked his tank force in a brief engagement in the Battle of France in 1940. Now we were going to get to know him better and Churchill, General Wavell and all those in the Ultra picture knew too that we should now have to fight the German war machine on two new fronts. In reply to Churchill's note to me as to how soon we could expect German forces in Cyrenaica, I was able to send over to him the OKW signals giving Rommel the approximate dates of the arrival in Tripoli of the units which were to constitute his Deutsches Afrika Korps, coming direct from Germany. The 5th Light Motorized Division was due in April and the 15th Panzer Division in May. It was to be armoured warfare in the desert.

A few days later a signal from Rommel to Berlin officially informed the OKW that he had assumed command of the troops in Tripoli, but it was the accurate knowledge which Wavell and O'Connor now had from Ultra, both of the build-up and strength of the Afrika Korps, that enabled the fighting withdrawal of the British and Imperial Forces to be carried through without complete disaster.

Early in March Ultra told us the 5th Light Motorized Division had arrived a month sooner than expected. Similarly, the 15th Panzer Division's arrival was signalled on the first of May. Wavell was now faced with two Armoured divisions much sooner than he had expected. Once Rommel had got his Afrika Korps operational, he took the bit between his teeth and began to drive our Imperial Army back towards the Egyptian border as quickly as they had come from it.

Meanwhile the Luftwaffe in Sicily was becoming a considerable nuisance to Admiral Sir Andrew Cunningham's Mediterranean Fleet which now had the extra commitment of looking after the convoys and the supplies to Greece, but in March the Germans induced the Italian fleet to leave its harbours and join in some positive action. They planned a grand operation against the British convoys in an area where they thought they would be least likely to meet any British warships. It was fortunate for us that the details of the operation were given to the Luftwaffe which was supposed to provide air cover for the Italian ships; it gave us the complete plan and we were able to pass it to Admiral Cunningham in good time. The operation disclosed by the Ultra signal was for two easterly sweeps by the Italian fleet, one to the north and the other to the south of the Island of Crete. It was to take place on March the twenty-seventh. The story of how Admiral Cunningham ordered his ships at Alexandria to get up steam and then himself went off with his golf clubs, only to return unseen to take his ships to sea at dusk, is well known; he was also careful to protect the Ultra source, and, despite the threat of Luftwaffe air power, he duly sent up a flying-boat which took care only to fly close enough for the Italians to spot it. As a result of being spotted, the nervous Italians cancelled their sweep to the north of Crete and all ships were ordered to rendezvous south of the island. This suited Admiral Cunningham better. The Luftwaffe was informed, but they never turned up. At the naval battle of Matapan the British fleet, informed of the whole plan by Ultra, caught up with the Italian battleships and cruisers and sent a crippled enemy squadron scuttling back to their home ports. The British victory of Matapan kept the Italian fleet off Mussolini's 'Mare Nostrum' for the rest of the war.

At the beginning of April came a signal from the German general in command of the invasion of Greece, Field-Marshal Wilhelm List, which informed Hitler that he was ready to move.

One of the crucial questions was whether the Yugoslavs would let the Germans through their country, a course which would so lengthen the line of defence of Greece as to make it impossible to resist the enemy. Prince Paul of Yugoslavia, who had become the Regent of his country when his brother, the King, had been assassinated, had so far resisted Hitler's pressure to throw in his lot with the Nazis.

Now, four years later, Ultra told us the crunch had come; Hitler wanted passage through his country. Paul refused but had to quit, and we learned from Ultra that part of General Maximilian von Weich's Second German Army had been ordered to advance through Yugoslavia at the same time as the attack on Greece by List's army from the north. There was little that Ultra or anyone else could do. To those of us who knew the vast German superiority in tanks and aircraft, the result had, from the beginning, been a foregone conclusion, but in Churchill's view a political necessity. What was saved of the Imperial Forces were evacuated from Greece to Crete. The strategic importance of this island was considerable. Its airfields on the north-east coast were ideally placed so that whoever held the island could threaten a large part of the eastern Mediterranean. Little wonder then that the Germans decided, after their short sharp conquest of Greece, to go on and take Crete as well. With the airfields of both Greece and Crete in their hands, they could dispose of any threat to the flank of the German invasion of Russia. I don't know who else besides Churchill thought that Crete could be held and, above all, supplied by the Navy in the face of a large German air force on the Greek airfields just to the north. The old sea dog had not yet learned the lesson that ships cannot function in such circumstances, and yet when Ultra informed us that Crete was to be taken by an airborne invasion and followed it up by also supplying all the detailed plans, there was some hope that we would inflict a defeat on the airborne forces, even if we had to evacuate afterwards.

At the end of April Ultra signals told us that units of the IX Fliegerkorps, which were to take part in the operations, were to proceed to Greece. At the same time they indicated that Goering had started to concentrate gliders and aircraft in Bulgaria. As a result, General Wavell went over to Crete and appointed General Sir Bernard Freyberg to command the island and warned him of what to expect. I had headlined the relevant signals to the Prime Minister pointing out that they indicated an imminent airborne invasion of the island and Churchill instructed me to make sure General Freyberg was kept fully informed. General Kurt Student, who commanded the paratroopers and airborne troops of the German XI Fliegerkorps, was fortunately meticulous about informing by signal every participating unit of every detail of the coming parachute and glider assault.

Freyberg was in possession of the most detailed plans of an enemy's proposed operation that were ever likely to be available to any commander. Churchill sent for me and I had to explain to him the whole operation on his big new map of Crete in the War Room. The assault opened right on time on May the twentieth, but thanks to our Ultra knowledge things did not go too well for the Germans; only at one aerodrome, Maleme, did the enemy get any hold. Alas, there was no counter-attack from Freyberg so General Student was able to consolidate his possession of the aerodrome, and fly in strong reinforcements. Freyberg had to retreat. The only consolation was that Cunningham's ships found one of the enemy convoys of seaborne troops. None of the little boats bringing German reinforcements ever reached Crete.

But the Royal Navy paid a heavy price for this small piece of consolation, for its losses during the Crete operation were out of all proportion to the loss of the island itself. It was at Crete that the hard lesson was learned that ships just cannot survive in waters dominated by large forces of shore-based hostile aircraft. One cannot help thinking that if only Freyberg had not been ordered to leave the Cretan aerodromes intact after all the RAF aircraft had been evacuated and if the aerodromes had been mined or obstructed, their immediate use would have been denied to the Germans, and the results of the airborne invasion might have been different.

The battle for Crete was frustrating from the Intelligence point of view. Despite the information provided by Ultra, the 'political' campaign in Greece and Crete had inevitably to end in disaster. But the potential of Ultra had made a profound impression on Churchill, the chiefs of staff and the commanders in the Middle East. Churchill had scanned every signal of the Cretan battle that we had been able to decypher and it had whetted his appetite for this 'miracle' source of information. Now he looked forward to the time when we could use it to its full effect, whilst the field commanders began to wonder how such accurate advance knowledge of enemy intentions was going to affect their orthodox conduct of war. It was General Alexander who told me much later in Tunisia that 'Ultra had altered the whole concept of modern warfare'.

Back in North Africa the port of Tobruk had been isolated by the German advance along the coast of Cyrenaica in April 1941. Tobruk was now like a fishbone in Rommel's throat. The gallantry of the Australian, Polish and British forces that held on to this fortress posed a constant threat to Rommel's supply lines. While Churchill was exhorting Tobruk to hold out, Rommel became obsessed with a determination to reduce it. This became evident in the Ultra signals which he sent back to Rome and Berlin. But Tobruk held. The OKW was obviously getting a little tired of Rommel's obsession because in an important Ultra signal about mid-May Rommel was ordered to leave the siege of Tobruk to the Italians and to press forward with all his own forces to Sollum and the Egyptian border.

Wavell, although warned of Rommel's orders to press on, was unable to stop the Afrika Korps, and a week later Rommel had recaptured the all-important Halfaya pass, the gateway to Cairo. Almost as if in retaliation against his order to leave Tobruk and in spite of the fact that Ultra showed he had received reinforcements of some units of a new panzer division, Rommel, now perpetually short of fuel, began sending Ultra signals to Kesselring complaining bitterly about the lack of every kind of supply, demanding new equipment and criticizing the Italians for failing to land supplies at Benghazi instead of Tripoli, five hundred miles farther west away from Rommel's forward troops but a much shorter route for their ships. The OKW, its hands obviously full with the imminent attack on Russia, refused to reinforce Rommel any further and, to make matters worse, now moved most of the Luftwaffe away from the Mediterranean theatre to the Russian front; Ultra became acrimonious. It should be remembered that at this time Churchill was virtually directing the war single-handed, and I think that it was perhaps the knowledge of all this Ultra information which persuaded him to take a more optimistic view than the British commanders on the spot and to order Wavell to relieve Tobruk. In the event, the operation failed and Wavell himself was relieved of his command.

General Auchinleck took over shortly after Hitler launched Operation Barbarossa. The attack on Russia had been delayed four vital weeks by the operations in

Yugoslavia and Greece. Before its launching a number of German army and air force movement orders were received on Ultra; names we knew from the Battle of France and were to know again later, ourselves: von Bock, von Kluge, Guderian of the Panzer Group, von Reichenau, von Kleist, von Rundstedt and many others were gradually assembling their own Army Groups, Armies and panzer divisions along the River Bug, such an unromantic place for Hitler's jump-off to change the world.

Churchill wondered how much information we ought to give the Russians. He consulted Menzies and then wrote a letter to Stalin saying that we had excellent information to the effect that there was a very big build-up of forces in Eastern Germany. Stalin did not reply.

Despite Wavell's 'failure', Churchill continued to take Rommel's complaints about his shortages a little too optimistically, although I had played them down in my headlines. We were getting to know Erwin Rommel. Now it was Auchinleck's turn to get Churchill's orders to mount an offensive against Rommel who, in an Ultra signal to Berlin, had now outlined his proposed attack on the British to open the road to Cairo.

Unfortunately Auchinleck's offensive in the spring of 1942, which was designed to hit Rommel before he could mount his operation, had to be postponed for a month due to our own shortages of equipment; and before he was ready, Rommel made his attack; a premature announcement by the OKW claiming Rommel's victory at Alamein in July must have angered him somewhat, for in a signal to Rome and Berlin he told them bluntly that Auchinleck was now holding him and that reinforcements were now reaching the enemy. Auchinleck had made good use of the Ultra signal in which Rommel had told us his plans.

Albert Kesselring, whom I had first met at one of Rosenberg's lunches in Berlin in 1934, and whom I had turned down for the job as German air attaché in London, had carved out a remarkable career for himself in the Luftwaffe during the rest of the 1930s. I had watched his rise with interest and was not surprised when he was given command of one of the great air fleets at the outbreak of the war.

During the Battle of France and the Battle of Britain in 1940 we were able to watch Kesselring at work and to learn both how ruthless and efficient he could be, but like Goering he had not known what he was up against in the RAF.

When all the preconceived ideas of victory by Luftwaffe were finally shattered, Kesselring must have seen little future for his career under a discredited Goering, and must have started to look about for some other field for his undoubted talents and qualities of military optimism and Nazi political fervour which Hitler so admired in him.

After the Battle of Britain we had lost contact with him on Ultra but now, at the beginning of 1941, he appeared in Rome, airman turned soldier.

From Rome, Kesselring was now to advise Rommel by signal that he and the Italian general who headed the Italian Supreme Command would visit him in mid-July. One could imagine that Rommel could have well done without them. To us it gave an indication that all was not well with the Axis forces in Africa, but it was not until Kesselring had returned to Rome that Rommel had to admit in a signal to Rome and Berlin that he had finally been brought to a standstill. With the aid of Ultra, which had told him where and in what strength Rommel was moving his forces, Auchinleck had outwitted him like a lightweight boxer with quick punches just where Rommel least expected them. Rommel's signal to his bosses in Berlin was, I remember, a very long one. He reported heavy German losses, putting much of the blame on the Italians. His German units were under half strength, his replacements were sub-standard, he was short of fuel and supplies, he hoped his own position would hold if attacked. It was the turn of the tide. I doubt if the OKW took as much notice of Rommel's signals as Winston Churchill did. They were too engrossed in their operations against Russia.

Kesselring did manage some reinforcement of the Afrika Korps by the parachute troops which had been used in Crete. This was important news because about this time we had had a number of reports from agents, of gliders arriving in Southern Italy and being assembled there, but in July 1941 we did not know if or when an airborne attack on Malta might take place. There had been no direct indications of such an attack on Ultra. The use of the parachute troops to reinforce Rommel was an important indication that any such attempt on Malta was now off.

The plight of Rommel's forces as disclosed by his signals to OKW led Churchill once more to believe that Rommel's army could now be eliminated, despite more warnings in my headlines and also from the chiefs of staff that Rommel was thought to be overplaying his hand. Auchinleck was told to go over to the offensive, although his army was very tired and he rightly believed that his adversary was by no means down and out, as he in fact proved when, despite his shortage of fuel and ammunition, he held Auchinleck's attack.

Churchill desperately needed a victory, both for political and morale reasons, and he felt that Auchinleck had failed him. On his way to see Stalin in Moscow in July 1942 he stopped off in Egypt for a conference with his chiefs of staff in the Middle East and, as a result, Auchinleck was relieved of his post, Alexander was put in his place as Commander-in-Chief, Middle East, and Montgomery was brought out from England to take command of the Eighth Army.

CHAPTER NINE

Alamein

Churchill, on his way back from Moscow in mid-August 1942, where he had had to suffer the taunts of Stalin that Britain was not pulling her weight, stopped off again in Egypt to meet his new generals, Alexander and Montgomery. The latter had put his own caravan at Churchill's disposal, parked close to the sea so that the Prime Minister could bathe in the warm Mediterranean. It was mid-August and the subject for discussion was the future of Rommel and his Afrika Korps.

In the caravan, the complete order of battle of Rommel's forces, their strength in men, tanks, guns and aircraft, and a close estimate of his supply position in fuel and ammunition had virtually all been supplied by Ultra.

While Churchill had been in Moscow it had been thought imprudent to forward any Ultra Intelligence to him. He had not yet got into the habit of taking an SLU with him and I did not wish to use any other cyphers than our own for security reasons. It must, therefore, have been a pretty dramatic moment when Alexander produced a long detailed signal from Rommel to Hitler, which had been sent during Churchill's absence, telling Hitler exactly what he was proposing to do in his final assault on the Eighth Army. In accordance with the best German textbook strategy Rommel proposed to make a strong surprise attack across the Qattara depression on the southern end of Montgomery's left flank and then, with a great northward sweep of the tanks of his panzer army, roll up the Eighth Army and drive them into the sea. Looking back to the Battle of France, it all sounded rather familiar, but now we also knew that this was to be Rommel's final attack to reach Cairo and Alexandria and the Suez Canal. He might as well have used the word desperate, knowing as he did that he simply could not go on with the shortage of supplies and his enormously long supply route. It was no doubt as a result of his complaints to Kesselring about the use of Tripoli that his supply ships were now trying to come to Benghazi, but this meant an easier target for the British Navy and there was still six hundred miles of desert to be covered.

Here then was the picture presented to Churchill as they sat in the caravan by the sea that August morning. All the Units in the attack carefully designated by Rommel; and finally the date. For us back in London this was the biggest 'plum' since the Battle of Britain; for the Eighth Army it was vital. I could imagine Churchill relishing the whole situation.

Over the years I was to get the impression that Montgomery did not like Ultra primarily because he knew that Churchill and the Chiefs of Staff would also be getting the same information. According to Menzies there had been a row when he first told Montgomery about Ultra in London. Montgomery had insisted that he alone should have the military information. This was of course impossible and Churchill told him so. As a result Montgomery never appeared to recognize the Ultra source as such; he realized that as with both Wavell and Auchinleck, Churchill could be breathing down his neck. Nevertheless on this occasion with Rommel's plan of attack before him he called a conference of his commanders and told them of his intuition that Rommel would try to attack round the British Southern Flank before our own attack at Alamein was mounted.

By contrast Alexander extracted every last ounce out of Ultra and, in addition, used to quiz me on any extra implications I might have found by reading between the lines and my personal knowledge of the Germans. His complete grasp of both the logistical and operational components of the enemy made him the totally efficient and quietly determined pillar behind Montgomery's successes.

It must be admitted that the whole situation in the caravan was bizarre, rather like playing a game of three handed bridge with one's opponents' hands, both Hitler's and Rommel's face up on the table, but whatever may have been Montgomery's ideas on the use of Ultra, Brigadier E. T. Williams, his G.2. Intelligence, devoured as much as he could possibly get, so that at least I knew it was reaching Montgomery in some form.

Apparently one of the reaons why Rommel had decided to make his final attack now at the end of August was because Kesselring had promised him some fuel by air. He had complained that the transport of the fuel by truck had used it all up by the time the trucks got to him. As far as I can make out from Rommel's signals, the air-lift never arrived, and to make matters worse the only ship bringing fuel by sea for the attack was sunk on the way over.

Thanks to Ultra, Montgomery had ample time to prepare for Rommel's final onslaught. Churchill came back to London more intrigued than ever with the output of his 'most secret source'. I had by this time established four Special Liaison Units in the Middle East. One in Cairo, which served both Alexander and the Air Officer Commanding in Chief Middle East, with a line to Alexandria to serve Admirals Ramsay and Cunningham. There was a second SLU with Montgomery near his Eighth Army headquarters and a third with Air Marshal Sir Arthur Coningham commanding the Western Desert Air Force. There was also a large SLU in Malta which looked after the needs of all three Services. Robert Gore-Brown was in charge of these SLUs and was responsible for the maintenance of good relations between the units and the commands they served. He had that facility of being able to get on with everybody and the wit to turn a scowl from a client into a laugh over a drink. In August 1942 he was for the most part with the SLU up at Eighth Army Headquarters.

Rommel's attack duly took place on the date that he had stipulated, the thirty-first of August, and followed exactly the plan that he had made. Montgomery had organized his defence in depth, centred on the high ridge at Alam Halfa itself which stuck out of the desert like a sore thumb. Despite the ample warning, it was a tough battle. Rommel's tanks weren't giving in easily, but when eventually his attack was brought to a halt, he had no alternative but to retire, leaving a number of tanks behind because of lack of fuel, apart from those which the Eighth Army had knocked out. With Montgomery's intuition so amply justified no one thought of what might have happened had Rommel's violent attack achieved the surprise he had bargained for. By September the second, Rommel had to admit failure and withdraw right back to his old position. His signal to Hitler giving the reasons for this showed us how bitterly disappointed he was with the way in which he had been starved of supplies. To those of us who were already watching the Russian campaign, it was not surprising. Obviously Hitler was fully occupied on the Eastern Front and the 'soft underbelly' in Africa didn't seem to merit his close attention.

According to his signals back to Berlin, now that Rommel's attack had been beaten back, he was ever more urgently faced with all his supply difficulties and apparent exhaustion of his troops. This time it really looked as if the Afrika Korps was in a bad state, and as a result Churchill urged Montgomery to open up his own attack against Rommel by the middle of September. The general said he was not ready. He told Churchill that he wasn't satisfied with the training of the troops or with the new tanks which needed a good deal of adaptation to desert warfare, so that eventually Montgomery's attack was put off until the end of October.

Meanwhile, Rommel was given six weeks' grace to prepare for the Eighth Army's attack, which he knew must now come. Montgomery was not going to take any chances, he had seen both Wavell and Auchinleck pushed into undertaking offensive operations before they were prepared to do so. Alamein was a battle which had to be won and it was here that the pattern of Montgomery's military thinking and determination to fight battles in his own way emerged. He was not prepared to tackle Rommel until he had absolute superiority in men and machines. There would be no surprise attack on the flanks, but a full-scale frontal assault, of which every detail would be thoroughly planned. Montgomery was ever cautious.

Nevertheless, it can be argued that the delay enabled Rommel to put down the great mine-fields and dig in his fuel-starved tanks, so that by the time the attack came he had a formidable defensive position. However his signal to Hitler summing up his chances was not very optimistic.

Montgomery didn't underestimate Rommel's ability and he knew that he would now have a slogging match until he had sufficiently softened up Rommel's defences to make a final breakthrough.

The second battle of Alamein started on October the twenty-third. Winston Churchill asked that the 'shadow OKW' at Bletchley should enable him to follow the battle from the German side. After eight days of vicious fighting, the writing was on the wall for Rommel. He repeated it to Hitler. On November the second Hitler sent his now famous signal to Rommel saying that 'there could be no other course but that of holding out to the last man and that for the German troops there was only the choice, victory or death'. Alamein was the first real German defeat of the war and also the first of this type of signal to come from Hitler. We were to get more of them in somewhat different forms over the next few years. Thanks to the oracle being in good form, this signal was immediately picked up by us and was in the hands of Montgomery and Churchill within minutes of its transmission by Hitler. Apparently Rommel had either got sand in his cypher machine or was deliberately stalling because, instead of acknowledging the signal, he sent a request for a repeat. It was probably the only time that a British commander has received a signal from the enemy's commander-in-chief before the enemy's commander in the field had got it, or at least admitted that he had. In either case it was a remarkable bit of team work by Bletchley. Meanwhile, earlier, on November the second, Rommel had himself sent off a signal to Hitler asking permission to start the retreat. In fact he had already started it without waiting for Hitler's reply. The story goes that it was only when Hitler's repeat signal had finally been decyphered and handed to Rommel the following day that he thought it was Hitler's negative reply to his request for permission to withdraw. Whether in fact he had seen the original signal and had asked for a repeat to cover up his orders to withdraw will never be known. However, in deference to his Fuehrer, on November the third he did order his troops to stop and fight again. But the Italians and many of the German troops were already out of touch on the way west and, as Rommel must have known, his order didn't amount to very much.

On the night of November the third and fourth, Montgomery's breakthrough attack was launched. Rommel's successes throughout his North African campaign had almost become a myth, and had sown the seeds of revolt against the British in many areas of the Middle East. The myth just had to be broken, and now that the Americans had joined with the British to launch an attack on North Africa at the other end of the Mediterranean, it was essential that there should be the first British victory to start opening the gullet of the Axis. The fighting by the armoured units was vicious, but by November the fourth we decyphered a signal from Rommel to Hitler admitting his defeat. The message arrived in London during the morning and I promptly telephoned it to Downing Street. It was in fact the first news that Winston Churchill had of the victory since the cautious Montgomery had obviously not been willing to claim it so soon. His own signal came later in the afternoon, by which time he too must have received Rommel's.

I do not think anybody expected Ultra information to be of any great importance during the actual battle, but it did in fact cause a vital change of plan just before the main breakthrough. Montgomery's plan had been to make the breakthrough thrust in the north, not far from the sea. His chiefs of staff had tried to persuade him to make it in the centre where the resistance would not be so great, a conclusion based on Ultra information which showed the movement of one of the German divisions to the north, combined with Rommel's instructions to infiltrate German units amongst the Italian units in the centre in order to try and stiffen them up. Finally, Ultra information revealed the sinking of a fuel ship on its way to Benghazi which made it unlikely that Rommel would be able to move his tanks southward, even if he wanted to. It was the presentation of all these factors which in the end induced Montgomery to change his mind and make the main thrust in the centre between the German and Italian armies.

It now seemed evident that it was about the time of Hitler's do or die signal that Rommel's disenchantment with the Fuehrer's mystique began. One cannot blame him; he was a brilliant young general who really looked after his men. He certainly had no intentions of standing and fighting to the last man if he could extricate the Afrika Korps and get them home. Now that the retreat had begun, it almost turned into a rout; but the cautious Montgomery did not follow through and somehow the German troops managed to get back. We learned from Ultra that Rommel's fuel was rapidly running out altogether and that Kesselring was unable to supply him with any more. Kesselring had his own troubles now in the form of an Allied invasion, launched on November the eighth, of Morocco, Algeria and Tunisia at the other end of North Africa, and to add to Rommel's despair, on November the seventh Hitler sent him a signal warning him to expect a landing of Allied troops between Tobruk and Benghazi. This was the result of a deception plan by the 'boys' in Alexandria where the story had been put about of an Allied landing to cut off the Afrika Korps. They had even gone so far as to start loading troops on ships together with their equipment. We knew that Hitler had a nest of informers in Egypt, and the deception plan had duly got back to him.

Just as Rommel had found his own lines of supply

getting longer and longer as he advanced eastwards, so Montgomery was now finding the same trouble as he went westwards and this was probably one of the reasons why he did not follow up his victory as some had expected. He did send the 2nd New Zealand Division across the southern part of the desert to try to cut off Rommel's retreat but unfortunately they were spotted by a patrol and unable to make a successful attack. Meantime, Rommel's retreat must have finally made some impression on Hitler, because Ultra signals now began to leave us in no doubt that Hitler himself had decided to take strategic command in North Africa, despite the fact that he was a long way away in East Prussia. Hitler's personal direction of the war not only provided us, through Ultra, with the topmost German decisions and directives, but was in itself a contributory factor to the Allied victory. This will become evident later. Hitler's signals made it quite clear that Rommel now had to do as he was told.

It was going to be a long walk home to Tunis anyway, and added to his worries we began a game of find and sink the convoys which were desperately trying to get supplies through to Rommel's tired army. The Special Liaison Unit in Malta was housed deep down in the rock next door to the naval and air force headquarters and it was to the naval and air forces on the island that the final forced withdrawal of Rommel's Afrika Korps into Tunisia belonged. Now, every time two or three ships were loaded in Naples or Taranto with food and fuel and spares and ammunition and were sent off in a convoy to try to reach Rommel either at the ports or on the North African beaches, Kesselring would send Rommel a signal telling him what supplies were loaded and at what time and date the ships would sail from their home ports, as well as the course they would take to their destination. No doubt all this information was necessary to allow Rommel to judge when and where the supplies would arrive; it was also part of that meticulous documentation which was so useful to us. It was of course a gift. Both Admiral Cunningham and Air Vice Marshal Sir Keith Park, the Air Officer Commanding Malta, were meticulous in sticking to the security rules for Ultra. They took great care to make absolutely sure that each convoy had duly seen the aircraft which was sent up and was supposed to have spotted it before the Navy turned up. Park would order an aircraft to fly just close enough to where he knew the convoy would be for it to be seen by the ships. Then a little while later the Navy would arrive and send all the ships to the bottom. After about the third of these desperation convoys had been sunk without trace a dense fog came down when the next one to go out had not long left Naples. Quite obviously an aeroplane couldn't be expected to see or to be seen by the convoy through a thick fog. Malta left the operation as late as possible in the hope that the fog would clear, but as the convoy was nearing the African coast, action had to be taken. It was unfortunate, from Ultra's point of view, that the RAF and the Navy turned up in a dense fog in exactly the right spot at the same moment and duly sank the ships, and not before one of them had reported this rather strange occurrence. This made Kesselring really cross and also a little suspicious. He sent a signal to the Abwehr, the German Military Security Service in Berlin, asking them to investigate these strange circumstances which pointed to some leakage about the sailings of his precious convoys. I sent a copy of Kesselring's signal to Admiral Cunningham in Malta. He told me later that he had expected a bit of trouble but there was little else he could do; it was a relief to see in their reply to Kesselring that the Abwehr could not account for the leakage. All the same I took the precaution of having a signal sent to a mythical agent in Naples in a cypher which the Germans would be able to read congratulating him on his excellent information and raising his pay. I can imagine the Naples waterfront was not a happy place for a while, but we could not afford to let up and the ships continued to fail to reach Rommel. Eventually the matter died down, no doubt because the Abwehr found they could not get any fruther with it. We did hear some time later that the Italian admiral in charge of the port of Naples had been relieved of his job on suspicion of himself giving the information away. It was reassuring to know that the idea we were reading their signals had not occurred to them.

By this time Rommel had made an orderly retreat west of the port of Benghazi and was now reaching the point where he could be supplied through Tunis itself. However, there was to be one final convoy which was ordered to sail as near as it could to a spot on the North African coast where Rommel's army was now concentrated, and there throw its barrels of fuel overboard so that they could be retrieved by the retreating Afrika Korps. The signal giving details of the sailing of this convoy and Rommel's reply, stressing the desperate necessity for it to get through, came into my office on a Saturday evening. I had as usual to wait until 2 a.m. on the Sunday until Churchill had finished watching his movie in order to telephone the signal through to him. I also read him Rommel's reply to it. There was, I think, silence for a full minute during which I almost knew what was going on in his mind. Then the characteristic simple instruction; I was to get in touch with the Chief of the Naval Staff and make sure that all action was taken to ensure the sinking of the convoy. This was the answer I had hoped for. I knew that he had been watching the situation closely and knew that since Montgomery had been following Rommel up somewhat cautiously, there was at least a chance that Rommel, without the supplies, might have to sacrifice much of his equipment before going back to Tunisia. I was also glad that by his action Churchill himself was willing to back up the sinking, even if it involved some security risk. He added that nothing was to be left to chance. I have reported this incident in full because I think it gives a good idea of Winston Churchill in action; his final sentence, which was one I was getting used to, was, 'Ring me back when you have done this'. The Chief of the Naval Staff was helpful as usual.

Once again there was patchy fog in the Mediterranean and this time the Malta aircraft couldn't find the convoy, which had evidently changed course in mid-channel as an extra precaution. The pilot of the RAF spotter plane, unable to find the ships through the fog patches, cruised around in those dangerous skies until suddenly, through a small break in the fog, he saw them on a different course to the one that had been given. It was virtual suicide for a single British aircraft to send a signal from the air if he was any great distance from the island since the Germans in Sicily would be able to get a fix on his position and enemy fighter aircraft would be sure to intercept him before he could get home, but the courageous pilot reported the convoy's position and paid for it with his life. The signal was heard, the Navy, which had been waiting not very far off, closed in and the final convoy was duly sunk just in time. Rommel's sense of humour rose above his anger and frustration and he sent a signal to Kesselring thanking him for two or three barrels which had floated ashore from the wrecks.

Personally, I look back on October 1942 as one of the most exciting times of the war. Very close association with Churchill taught me how to deal with other great men of World War II, and always to weigh fully in my own mind the responsibilities they were carrying. Although the Prime Minister got nearly as excited as I did over the chase of the Afrika Korps, we did our best to conceal it and yet, in some strange way, I began to sense what was going on in that great mind on the other end of the telephone.

CHAPTER TEN

Naval Affairs and Briefing the Americans

I did not mean to give the impression in my account that events in North Africa culminating in our victory at Alamein were all that occupied me or the attentions of Ultra for the 20 months between Rommel's arrival in Cyrenaica in February of 1941 and his precipitous retreat in October of 1942. While this theatre of operations claimed the bulk of our attention because we had so much at stake in the outcome, there were indeed other things going on. One of them concerned Naval operations in the Atlantic, and while I was not directly involved due to the Navy's insistence that all the Ultra signals dealing purely with naval matters be sent only to the Admiralty NID in the original German, I was aware of a number of interesting developments.

Many accounts of the Battle of the Atlantic have been written, but up until now none of them have been able to reveal the role of Ultra. One of the most dramatic examples occurred in the *Bismarck* affair. The sinking of HMS *Hood* on 24 May 1941 left a sense of shock with everyone. Then came the news that the great German battleship had made her escape on 25 May and we all knew that contact with her had been lost. Early on 25 May Admiral Lutyens, thinking that he was still being shadowed by a British warship, sent a long signal to his Naval Headquarters in Germany. It listed all his difficulties but mainly the loss of fuel from his earlier battle and he asked what he was to do now. It was this signal, picked up by us, which gave away once more his position. I remember the thrill that went through the office as the next signal came over the telephone from Hut 3 that *Bismarck* had been ordered to Brest where all available air and submarine protection was to be given to her. Later we were to know that the Admiralty had already made plans to cope with either her return northwards to Germany or southwards to France, but now her position was certain. On 26 May at 10.30 a.m. the *Bismarck* was again sighted. The rest of the story is well known.

Those in the know would agree that Ultra was the hub of the whole Atlantic battle. Nowhere was it more vital than in the battle between the German U boats and the convoys of merchant ships and their escort vessels whose supplies were vital to Britain's survival through the first years of the war, not to mention their role in supplying the troops and arms for the eventual Allied victory.

As the naval Ultra developed, we were able to read not only many of the instructions sent to the U boats at sea but also to gain accurate knowledge of their positions from the signals they sent back in order to keep their own naval operations people informed of their whereabouts. It doesn't take much imagination to realize the vital importance of such signals, not only to the Naval Intelligence Division, who were soon able to warn their shipping of where the U boats were operating, but also to Coastal Command, who were given the chance to spot and attack the U boats as they came within range of our aircraft on their way in and out of their home ports, from the Baltic to the Bay of Biscay.

That the battle against the U boats was highly successful, at least up to the middle of 1942, there is no doubt, but killings were obviously kept secret, and the main use of Ultra seemed to be the ability of Admiralty to route their convoys round or away from lurking U boats or U boat packs.

The Navy could not of course use the SLU system to all its ships. Instead, for all their instructions based on Ultra information, they used their own cyphers which worked much on the same principle as the tear-off, once-used pad, except that it was in book form and the pages of random figure groups were therefore used over and over again.

It was late in 1942 that the U boat killings started to fall off, and the German packs in the Atlantic began to play such havoc with our convoys—that in 1943 the Battle of the Atlantic became critical. Fortunately, an astute Commander Denning, who worked in NID on the Ultra material, 'smelt a rat' and with a change in the cypher book in 1943 the Navy once more got on top of the U boats. It was not until after the war that Admiral Karl Doenitz' diaries revealed the fact that our naval cyphers had been read during that critical period.

Just how important it is to have close liaison between makers and breakers of cyphers was illustrated by the fact that the Germans had been able over two years to fill in the random figure groups on their pages and columns of the Naval cypher book by the oldest crypto-graphic trick of concentrating on a recurring address. For instance, most signals would always begin with concise details of who it was for and at what address, such as: To the Commander-in-Chief Western Approaches, Naval Headquarters, Portsmouth; so that the code-book groups for these addresses were soon known to the Germans and they only had to subtract these groups from the cypher groups obviously representing the address on the hundreds of signals sent to that particular C-in-C and fill in the columns of their shadow cypher book with the groups that had resulted from their sums. Once they had got even a proportion of these groups, they could start decyphering the signals themselves.

Reading our signals, they must have been puzzled by our knowledge of their U-boat positions, but luckily they did not accept the fact that we had broken Enigma.

The tracking of the U boats in the Atlantic war was a superb exercise in co-operation of Intelligence and Operations Division at Admiralty War Room. There was, in addition, a highly efficient three-cornered liaison between Roger Wynn at Admiralty, who was briefed by Saunders in Hut 3, Max Horton in Liverpool and Coastal Command Headquarters. As a result, Winston Churchill was kept fully in the picture directly by Admiralty.

I think probably one of the most notable contributions that Ultra made to the submarine war occurred later, in 1943, when it was responsible for the location of the German submarine supply ships in the Atlantic. The most dangerous areas for U boats, as the submarines came and went to their bases, were the waters within range of the Coastal Command aircraft and naval destroyers. Therefore, in order to extend the time that the U boat could remain at sea, supply ships carrying fuel and other forms of supplies moved about the ocean and their changing positions were signalled to the U boats which would then rendezvous with the 'Milchcows', as they were known; in 1943 the changing locations of these Milchcows became available to us through Ultra. By this time too, there was very close liaison between Coastal Command and their American counterpart who were especially able to cover the southern Atlantic convoy routes. With typical enthusiasm the Americans were all for sinking the Milchcows at once; they were, however, persuaded by Jack Slessor, Commander-in-Chief Coastal Command, not to give Doenitz cause to suspect Ultra and the Milchcows were quietly sent to the bottom over a reasonable time; it must have been one of the greatest blows suffered by the U boats.

At last by mid-1943, the domination of the U boat in the Atlantic was checked and finally broken, due to the loss of the Milchcows, the use of new forms of radar used from aircraft to detect U boats (the older forms of radar had been susceptible to detection by the U boat allowing it to submerge before the Allied aircraft arrived), and finally, a relaxing of the strict security rules for Ultra which now allowed U boat positions to be radioed to Allied aircraft on U boat search operations. Bletchley got one bonus when the Navy captured a U boat with all its Engima and cypher keys intact. It saved a lot of work and acted as a very good cover against German suspicions that we might be reading their cyphers.

There were other naval occasions which were closely linked with Ultra. Some of these have been described in other parts of this narrative. But the inside story of the naval battles of World War II, both in the Atlantic and the Pacific, has yet to be told.

Another job that kept me very busy during 1941 and 1942 involved the establishment of SLUs with our units in the Pacific and the briefing of British and American generals and their Intelligence staffs on the significance of Ultra information and the importance of security in its use.

I don't know when Churchill first told Roosevelt about Ultra, but it was probably at their first meeting after Pearl Harbour. By this time the Americans were already picking up Japanese naval signals in one of the Enigma variations and sought our aid. The Germans had evidently been good enough salesmen to persuade the Japanese to buy some of their machines.

Thus it was that the American cryptographers were initiated into the mysteries of the Bronze Goddess, and Washington soon became operational with the Japanese counterpart of our Ultra. Admiral Nimitz and General MacArthur were the initial recipients. On the security side I found the Americans willing to adopt the measures we had so far worked out in Britain; in fact they were ready to draw the curbs even tighter and I was very happy to leave it all in their own hands.

In August 1942 General Eisenhower and his staff were installed in the old Norfolk House in St James's Square in London, and here he set up the headquarters of the Allied force for North Africa. With the arrival of the Americans, I started work on a whole new organization for the distribution and security of Ultra to cover all the Allied commands, whether in North Africa or, when required, in any other parts of the western theatre of war. It included an adquate briefing procedure for all those American and British commanders and selected members of their staffs who would now be put on the Ultra list.

It was at this point that Menzies told me he had decided to hand over my shadow OKW in Hut 3 to the General Administration at Bletchley.

One never quite knew where one stood with Menzies. He softened the pill by confirming me as his deputy, with full responsibility for ensuring the vital security of Ultra in the field, and also for the complete service of Ultra to the Prime Minister. He added that the job would take all my time and tact, now that we were going into offensive operations. It was a wrench to hand over Hut 3, but by now they knew the job well.

In early 1942 Colonel Palmer Dixon, a US Army Air Force officer, had been attached to the Intelligence Department at the Air Ministry, and at Charles Medhurst's request I had put Palmer in the Ultra picture with usual security briefing. Now with the prospect of large numbers of US Army Air Force units coming to Europe, Palmer asked me whether I could let him have Humphreys from Hut 3 to join the staff of the US Army Air Force Commander in order that he might have the best possible advice on the interpretation and use of Ultra Intelligence in operation. It was obviously going to be a highly responsible job and I was personally all in favour. It would, I felt, add tremendously to the full, yet secure, use of the Intelligence by the American air generals. Over the past two and a half years Humphreys had organized the output of the Shadow OKW so well that, in his opinion, it now only required a good administrator to keep it running. I therefore made arrangements for his transfer on loan to the American Air Force, where his first job would be to go to North Africa with Major-General Carl Spaatz, Commanding General Eighth Air Force.

The growing distribution and security problems meant the provision and training of a large number of new Special Liaison Units. Stewart Menzies had also stressed the point that in future I would have to travel to all the theatres of operations and make sure that Ultra, the greatest secret of the war, remained as such. He assured me that I could not only have this authority as his deputy, but that the Prime Minister himself would make it clear to all commanders-in-chief that I was acting with his authority also. This was a clear indication of the Prime Minister's view of the place this information occupied in the war effort. I felt that the time had come to codify security instructions and to get them fully agreed with Washington. The Americans had al-

ready agreed to the general outline of both the physical
and operational security precautions in the Pacific, but
I thought it better to have a US Joint Chiefs of staff instruction sent to Eisenhower to back up our SLUs
which would be attached to the commanders of the
American forces.

During 1940 and 1941 I had first been chiefly concerned with the physical security of Ultra, both on the
air and on paper, but I had now learned many of the
ways in which the secret could be jeopardized by too
hasty action in the field. I think one of the most difficult jobs in drawing up an amended set of security
directives was to strike a balance between what would
be practical in operation and acceptable to the recipients whilst allowing the SLU tactfully to insist on their
being kept. The sheet anchor was to be absolute ruthlessness in keeping to a minimum the number of people
who were allowed to receive and be aware of Ultra in
the commands at home and overseas. There was a per-
sistent attempt to get put on this list, either directly or
through the back door, by those who wanted to get in
on the act, often either out of pure curiosity or the
hope of some advancement. There were rumours
amongst the more ambitious that it was a good thing.
The list was restricted to four or five people at each
main headquarters, which themselves were restricted to
supreme headquarters, army groups, principal army
and air commands operating both in the European and
South-East Asian theatres of war, and the British and
United States air force commands operating from Britain.

I think it is worth while repeating the main security
provisions, which had been adopted after two years' experience, if only to give some idea of how the source
was in fact preserved. First, there was the strict limiting
of the number of people allowed to see Ultra, and no

names could be added to the list without my permission. The SLU officer was responsible for personally delivering the Ultra message to the commander or to a member of his staff designated to receive it. All messages were to be recovered by the SLU officer as soon as they were read and understood. They were then destroyed. No Ultra recipient was allowed to transmit or repeat an Ultra signal. Any action taken by a commander on the information given him by Ultra was to be by way of an operations order or command or instruction, which in no way referred to the Ultra signal or could lead the enemy to believe his signals were being read. Where action had to be taken which might seem suspicious (such as the continual sinking of the enemy convoys in the Mediterranean), some sort of cover, such as sending up a spotter aircraft, should be used. No recipient of Ultra could voluntarily place himself in a position where he could be captured by the enemy.

I was required to brief all the Allied commanders and their principal staff officers on Ultra when they took up their commands, either in the United Kingdom or elsewhere on the European front. I had imagined that all generals were much alike, with perhaps slightly different training on how to fight their wars. In the event, I found a vastly different variety of men, so that my approach to each one was different in order to get the best results. I had to tell them at one and the same time that they would be supplied with the actual signals of the enemy on the highest level, and that they must also conform to strict security regulations as to its use, the main one being that they must not take any immediate action on the information which might lead the enemy to suspect that we knew his plans. This often provoked a good deal of discussion as to what could or could not be done, and in the event we did have one or two near misses. Some commanders were a little incredulous, until I had shown them some of the actual signals from Hitler which had obviously proved correct already. A few were a bit unhappy about the restrictions put on its use, but by and large most were finally surprised and grateful, and the regulations were generally accepted.

The regulation about their personal security in avoiding capture irked one or two. They felt it restricted their own movements; one was Major-General George Patton, another Major-General Jimmy Doolittle. Patton always liked to be near the fighting and Doolittle certainly liked to go on bombing missions himself. Fortunately, the only really tricky case occurred when a senior Royal Air Force officer went on a particularly dangerous raid into France. He was shot down and Churchill had to be informed; there was a bit of an up and downer with the Air Staff. Fortunately, the escape people in France got the officer back uncaptured. One great advantage was that we, in turn, would know from Ultra if any German was in fact getting suspicious through the signals that he would send back to Berlin. On the whole, the help and co-operation I received from those now famous men made it comparatively easy. Both they and I knew that we were, after all, giving them the life blood of their Intelligence which no one wanted to see cut off.

The first American commanders that I had to brief were General Eisenhower's staff. One August afternoon, Menzies and I were ushered into the great room on the first floor of Norfolk House. Stewart Menzies had come with me to lend a bit of weight to the proceedings. Eisenhower came in with Lieutenant-General Mark Clark and his principal Intelligence officers. Eisenhower was shorter than I had expected but gave one the impression of inborn authority which is the essence of a successful leader of men. He introduced Clark and three members of his Intelligence staff and then he excused himself since, he said, he and his chief of staff, Major General Walter Bedell Smith, had already been told about it by the Prime Minister; Mark Clark was restless from the start. I explained not only what the source was, but in an endeavour to catch Mark Clark's interest gave some pertinent examples of what it could do. I had intended to follow this with an explanation of how the information would reach him, and the security regulations which accompanied its use. But Mark Clark didn't appear to believe the first part, and after a quarter of an hour he excused himself and his officers on the grounds that he had something else to do. It was a bad start and Menzies was considerably upset, but I felt that Clark's Intelligence officers were interested and I planned to have another talk with them later on. Meanwhile, I felt sure that Eisenhower would ensure the information was properly used by his deputy commander.

I talked over the incident with Palmer Dixon in case I was using the wrong approach. Palmer was already grateful that I had seconded Humphreys to his US Army Air Force and on the next briefing I found a very different welcome from General Spaatz, who was to command the US Army Air Forces in North Africa. I liked him straight away, and he was at once enthusiastic about the possibilities Ultra would throw open, as were also his Intelligence officers. When operations started in North Africa, they made maximum use of it.

Major-General Sir Kenneth Anderson, commanding the British First Army in North Africa, was a cautious Scot, but his astute questions showed that he had not missed a trick during the briefing. I already knew Air Marshal Sir William 'Sinbad' Welsh, who was in command of the British Air Forces Eastern Air Command, and he and his Intelligence staff were therefore easy to brief. It was, I thought, essential that all the principal staff officers of Operation Torch, the code name for Allied landings in North Africa, should be in the Ultra picture as soon as planning began, so that they could get to know the form, and the traffic going on between Rommel, Kesselring and the OKW in Berlin was an invaluable exercise for them to study. Meanwhile, I had to find and train a number of new Special Liaison Units composed of Royal Air Force cypher sergeants and officers with their own wireless unit, each man minutely screened for security. They had to learn to operate the one-time pad cyphers almost in their sleep, and the officers had to learn how to handle all the security arrangements and, more importantly, the commanders to whom they were allotted. However, I found that it was my own personal visit to the various headquarters, so my SLU officers told me, that kept security on the top line with the command staff. I would first find out from the commander himself whether he found everything satisfactory, but it was the Intelligence section who usually greeted me with 'Hello, what have we done wrong this time?' There were seldom any complaints on either count.

Just before Operation Torch, we were lucky to open up another avenue of Ultra which became of extreme importance to the Allied strategic bombing operations. This was the German weather reporting system. The weather over Central and Eastern Europe was vital later on in planning long-range missions and was therefore a top secret item with the Germans. We, of course, had the edge on the enemy when the weather was coming from the west, but at all other times this information was invaluable. When General Spaatz later took over command of the US Strategic Air Forces in Europe operating from the UK, he would invite me to attend the briefing of his formation leaders for bombing raids as far away as Austria. As we sat in what had been one of the old classrooms of the famous Wycombe Abbey Girls' School, and which was now the US headquarters, I would watch the care with which the meteorological officer would outline the weather all the way to the target and back. No one, I am glad to say, asked him how he knew it, but if someone queried the forecast, 'Tooey' Spaatz would look across at me with a twinkle in those shrewd eyes behind his gold-rimmed glasses and say quietly, 'I think you can rely on that'.

Despite the loss of my personal control of Hut 3 and the Shadow OKW, I still had direct access to it when required. I was never told by Menzies the real reason for the takeover, but gradually pieced together the facts that the Foreign Office and the directors of Intelligence of the armed services became alarmed at the power that Ultra had placed in Menzies' hands, so that the Foreign Office decided to place control of this vital source of information in the hands of the Joint Intelligence Committee, which was given a Foreign Office chairman (Cavendish-Bentinck). It had been considered advisable to put all the departments at Bletchley under one director, Commander Travis, who was put in to replace Commander Denniston, the real founder of Ultra, now posted back to London on other cryptographic duties.

CHAPTER ELEVEN

'Torch'

Before 8 November 1942 I flew down to Gibraltar to see that nobody got lost and to keep Eisenhower in touch before he went over to Algiers. It was an exciting moment. Eisenhower's SLU was installed in the operations block, hewn out of the rock. It was cool and moist. Quite suddenly all the planning had become a reality; now Ultra was to be put on trial in a great Allied amphibious offensive operation. Oddly enough Ultra's greatest value in those days, just before the landings in North Africa, was a negative one.

About a month before, there had been signals between Kesselring and Berlin in which each had kept the other informed of Intelligence reports concerning a coming Allied landing in the Western Mediterranean. Kesselring admitted he didn't know where the landing was to take place, but at the beginning of November he stated in an Ultra signal that he expected a landing either in North Africa, Sicily or Sardinia. This was particularly important information at this time, because had Kesselring had firm information of our intentions, he could probably have used the French in Algeria to resist us, which would have been disastrous. Nevertheless, he requested additional troops from Hitler to be concentrated in Sicily and Southern Italy as a precaution. Twice tersely refused by Hitler, Kesselring issued orders for the concentration of such troops as he had at his disposal in the South of Italy together with any transport aircraft that were available. After that, beyond signalling back to Berlin that convoys had been sighted near the Spanish coast, he was silent. Eisenhower was elated, it was our first lesson in non-Ultra, and it gave us every hope that we should, after all, achieve that highly valuable commodity, surprise.

Kesselring as we know was a Luftwaffe commander. We already know from Ultra that he was quietly consolidating his command position in the Mediterranean, and, since Rommel's defeat at Alamein, would waste no time once he knew where we were going.

Traditionally, German military thinking was 'Why go and land on the other side of the Mediterranean when your obvious objective was Europe?'. This had also been the American thinking when they wanted to go bald-headed into France before Churchill had finally persuaded them to try the North African operation first, and I believe it was why Kesselring did nothing except wait and see, as we too waited on The Rock. It was whilst we were still at Gibraltar that Rommel signalled Kesselring that he proposed to retreat right back to El Agheila on the Tripolitanian border in view of the possible Allied landings in North Africa. This was probably of more interest to Montgomery at that moment, but it posed the possibility that if Kesselring could hold Tunisia his forces would join up with the retreating Afrika Korps.

It hadn't taken Rommel long to learn about it, nor did it take Kesselring long to act when he too knew our objective. In an Ultra signal to the German Commission in Tunis, he ordered immediate agreement by the French for the Germans to take over the aerodromes and port facilities, both at Tunis and Bizerta. Shortly after Kesselring had sent this signal another one arrived from Hitler which gave Kesselring permission 'to seize these areas and prepare forces to despatch to Tunisia'. But as Hitler had recently refused to send him any reinforcements, Kesselring would have to act with what he had got available. We knew from Ultra what this force consisted of; what we did not know was how quickly they could be air-lifted over to North Africa. Unfortunately, but perhaps understandably, the political and military situation of the French in Algeria was, to say the least, confused. General Anderson commanding British First Army and the American forces arrived with his SLU in Algiers the day after the assault. That evening we read Hitler's signals to the German Army Command in Paris ordering the occupation of the rest of France. This signal set off a chain reaction in London about the security of the French fleet in Toulon. We naturally didn't want it to fall into the hands of the Germans. Approaches were made to the French in London to see if some arrangement could be made whereby it would sail out and join our own fleet in the Mediterranean. Eventually the situation was dealt with by the French themselves. They scuttled the fleet.

If before the landing Kesselring's reactions had been uncertain there was nothing dilatory about them now. There were urgent Ultra signals from him to the Luftwaffe and army formations ordering an immediate airlift of troops to Tunis and the transfer of fighter squadrons to Tunis and Bizerta aerodromes. He was able to report back to Berlin that Luftwaffe aircraft had landed at Tunis, together with an airlift of troops to guard them, the day after the Allied landings in Algiers. This was disturbing news for Anderson, and for the next two days Eisenhower was to watch the build-up of German troops airlifted from Italy at a speed which had not been anticipated when the American chiefs of staff had insisted on the more westerly landings at Casablanca,

Oran and Algiers instead of starting farther east, the course proposed by the British.

Eisenhower landed in Algeria on November the thirteenth; I had managed to get over there on the tenth on a submarine hunting aircraft. Half-way across we started to dive as the pilot pointed to a black object moving in the sea below, and an inoffensive porpoise nearly had a shock. The warmth of Algiers was very welcome after the cold of London; the purple bougainvilleas, the bright blue plumbago and the pink oleanders were still in full bloom. Oranges were plentiful. I never really settled the argument with the medical officer whether it was the oranges or the yellow fever injections which caused so much jaundice. The Saint George Hotel, the Allied HQ half-way up the hill above the town, gleamed white and clean, but alas when I got there I found that both 'Sinbad' Welsh, commanding the RAF component, and General Anderson, commanding the British First Army, had moved out. I tracked down Welsh to his new HQ near Maison Blanche aerodrome. He told me he had found the King George much too crowded to operate efficiently. Anderson was more difficult to find; he had taken his HQ to an isolated farmhouse amongst the bracken-covered hills some thirty miles east of Algiers. It looked much like Anderson's native Scotland. He explained with a wry smile that he had chosen a spot where he could keep his eye on the single railway line which had to carry the supplies up to the front. Due to the news on Ultra of Kesselring's rapid moves into Tunis, he was doing his best to get the armies on the move eastwards before the Germans could seize too much ground. He was grateful for the immediate Ultra signals, but somehow that evening at dinner in the old farmhouse the conversation got on to secondary education in Scotland in which he seemed passionately interested. However, later on that evening we received Kesselring's orders signalled to the air command at Tunis for a parachute battalion to seize the coastal aerodrome at Bone which lay in the path of the advancing Allies. It was essential that the Allies should have this aerodrome. Airfields were few and far between. Kesselring's orders were for the Germans to seize it on November the twelfth, the following day. It was a busy evening at HQ. A small battalion of British parachute troops who had had very little training, but at least were keen and available in Algiers, were ordered to seize the Bone aerodrome on the morning of the twelfth before the Germans got there and a number of American Dakota aeroplanes had to be got together in order to transport them. Despite the late hour, the operation was duly laid on. I shared a restless night on a camp bed with Anderson's RAF liaison officer in his room. We got up before dawn awaiting news of the race against the Germans. At least we had the edge on them since they did not know that we should be doing the same job as themselves. Fortunately they left Tunis later than we left Algiers, the American aircraft ferrying our parachute troops having left at dawn. It was an exciting race and the result was a win by a short head for the Allies. The German aircraft arrived just as the last British parachutist landed and the Germans had to turn back to base. It was a rather joyful, if late, orange juice, bacon-and-egg breakfast at the old farmhouse. The incident I think convinced both Anderson and his staff that Ultra could be of tactical as well as strategical use and that this was a classic case where Kesselring could not, in fairness, suspect we had read the signals.

Back in Algiers I saw Admiral Cunningham who was, in addition to his purely naval Ultra, being given the general situation reports by the SLU at the Saint George Hotel, which looked after Eisenhower and also Welsh.

I did not discuss the naval Ultra with the admiral but I had learned from the Air Officer Commanding at Gibraltar, who incidentally had been my first flight commander in France in 1917, that Ultra had got the German submarine position in the Mediterranean well buttoned up.

The U-boats certainly gave us no trouble either at Algiers or at those other amphibious operations in the area later on.

I had to hitch-hike in one of those remarkable warhorses, the Douglas Dakotas, back to Gibraltar, then on a flying-boat back to Plymouth. I had arranged to return to Algiers in six weeks' time. Meanwhile, I should have to watch the operation from the German point of view in London with Kesselring's help.

I found that the arrangements I had made for headlining the signals going over to the Prime Minister had worked smoothly during my absence, but I also found that the urgency which had characterized his demands for Ultra had eased a little. Now that Eisenhower was accepted as Supreme Commander of Torch, Churchill was able to sit back and relax his direction of the war in North Africa, which hitherto had been his main preoccupation.

We learned now from Ultra that the OKW had promised Kesselring massive reinforcements, a promise that was treated with some scepticism after the experiences of Rommel. Nevertheless by the end of November Kesselring was able to report back to Berlin that he had landed some fifteen thousand troops with a hundred tanks at Tunis and there were approximately eight thousand Italian troops which had been drafted into the area. The indications were that the Germans would now be able to hold the Allies by making the best use of the rugged terrain.

From the end of November onwards the picture given by Ultra included not only the German forces in Tunisia commanded by Walter Nehring, but also Rommel's Afrika Korps retreating from Cyrenaica in the East. Hitler, according to Ultra, had taken remote control of the Afrika Korps and ordered Rommel to make a stand at El Agheila. This signal from Hitler prompted Montgomery to send the 2nd New Zealand Division to try and cut off Rommel's retreat. Rommel eventually had to abandon his stand. He duly signalled Rome and Berlin and announced his intention of withdrawing to the Homs Line in Tunisia, but we learned from Ultra that Hitler had ordered Rommel to make a stand and defend it as far to the East as possible, which was why Rommel then decided, probably against his own better judgment, to dig in at Buerat. He signalled Hitler to this effect. Once again it was on this information that Montgomery decided to send the 7th Armoured Division through the desert to attack the position from the Western flank.

Rommel had given us his strength returns after the El Agheila stand, and despite his tremendous difficulties with fuel and supplies he still had a fair tank force available.

By Christmas I was already getting requests for more SLUs for the forward areas in Tunisia so I decided to see the position for myself before extending Ultra distribution. It would mean a greater security risk which would have to be justified. I found some changes at headquarters; Tedder had come from Cairo and taken over command of all the Allied Air Forces, and was generally helping Eisenhower to get a bit of co-operation from everybody. This was good news for me. He was an old friend with whom I had worked during the

1930s, and I felt I now had a good ally right at the top who would watch the security of Ultra. These two men were of much the same quiet temperament; they understood each other and it was no surprise when, after the Casablanca conference, Tedder was chosen by Eisenhower to be his Deputy-Chief for the great events of 1944. Tedder wanted to see me as soon as I arrived. He had Spaatz with him in his office, and now came a request from Spaatz for Ultra to go to his forward operational headquarters. Humphries who was now Spaatz's adviser had given the project his support and Tedder wanted it done. We organized a SLU from the spare staff I had sent out for emergencies. Spaatz was delighted. He was using Ultra to the utmost advantage, bombing endless targets such as newly arrived German aircraft on the outlying airfields, and any other targets which Ultra identified.

Tedder also told me that Major-General Patton was now in Algiers and would like to be briefed. He had sailed direct from the United States with his landing force to Casablanca, so I had had no opportunity to brief him before. Hearing so many stories of his gold-plated tin hat and his personal armament, I was a little nervous as I knocked on his office door. I needn't have worried; he greeted me with a broad smile and a cheery welcome and a 'Now, young sir, what's it all about?' He was delighted at the idea of reading the enemy's signals, but when I got on to the security angle he stopped me after a few minutes. 'You know, young man, I think you had better tell all this to my Intelligence staff, I don't go much on this sort of thing myself. You see I just like fighting.' He had summed himself up pretty accurately. One point he didn't like was the one which referred to personal safety. I was to meet him often in the next few years; he had always smiled but never would submit to any restraint. I just had to rely on Tedder to keep an eye on him, and on his very excellent Intelligence staff to keep him 'wised'.

An old colleague, George Lawson, who was liaison officer at General Anderson's headquarters with the RAF, up in Tunisia, asked if I could go up and see him and another old friend, Lieutenant-General Allfrey, commanding British 5 Corps. They too wanted their Ultra direct from Bletchley, since they were so far from Algiers; I found Lawson convinced that there were many more fighters and dive bombers operating from the Tunis area than Ultra made out. However, I convinced him that because they could operate from several fully equipped aerodromes the fighters had been able to carry out three, or even four, sorties a day whilst Lawson himself was almost desperate for even temporary aerodromes in that mountainous country. The Luftwaffe squadrons had a considerable advantage at this time, and the clashes over possession of existing airfields outside the Tunis perimeter were fierce. This was an area of operations where Ultra information was vitally important in helping Spaatz's fighter-bombers to deny their use to the enemy. Allfrey was pretty well up to date with the position and strength of the German army units which now held the difficult passes in the mountains. It was an exercise in adapting the Ultra services and SLUs to meet requirements; but I did not repeat it in future operations: too risky.

When I got back to Algiers I was overjoyed to find that my old friend Georges Ronin from the Deuxième Bureau in Paris had managed to get out of France, when the Germans took over the south, in a small civil aeroplane and had flown, along with his late chief, across to Algiers. When Stewart Menzies had heard the news in London he flew out so that he could meet his old opposite number and between us perhaps start up a new French Intelligence service based on Algiers. Colo-

nel Rivet and Georges Ronin gave Stewart Menzies
and me a splendid lunch on the sun-drenched roof of a
a little house in Algiers. With the coffee came the news
that Darlan had been shot in his house a few hundred
yards away. They could not have cared less.

In January 1943 Churchill went to the Casablanca
Conference, which meant sending across a SLU from
Algiers to keep the Prime Minister informed. While he
was there Rommel's signal to the OKW again report-
ed that he had been forced to abandon the Buerat Line
and was retreating to Homs. This time the Eighth
Army didn't give him time to dig in and almost immediately another signal from Rommel told Hitler that he
was withdrawing to the Mareth Line in Tunisian terri-
tory. General Alexander came over from Egypt and in
February was given overall command of the British
First Army and the American Forces, together with the
Eighty Army on the other side of Tunisia, to form
Eighteenth Army Group. By February too the Americans began to threaten the Afrika Korps both from the
flank and the rear as the Allied armies came closer together. By early February the two German armies, the
Afrika Korps and the army commanded by General
Juergen von Arnim, had joined together with the First
Italian Army under General Giovanni Messe to form
Army Group Africa commanded by Rommel. Ultra
confirmed their appointment. We noticed that the Ultra
signals between Kesselring and Rommel had begun to
be far from friendly. Kesselring had been trying to hold
the ring between Rommel and the Italians, who were
accusing Rommel of abandoning Tripoli, and Hitler,
who kept ordering Rommel to make a stand. Von Arnim, who obviously didn't relish the Rommel take over,
was also at odds with Rommel himself. In fact Kesselring was playing it all very skilfully, quietly gathering
the real decisions into his own hands.

It was unfortunate that Ultra failed to give any warning of Rommel's attack on the advancing American forces at Kasserine on 20 February. As a result, American troops got a vicious punch on the nose. When briefing the Commanders I had always warned them of the possible fallibility of Ultra and that adequate air reconnaisance should never be dispensed with. On this occasion the absence of Ultra and the quiet secrecy with which Rommel himself set up and directed the operation seemed to us at the time to indicate some serious discord between the Axis Commanders in Tunisia. The first reference to the action on Ultra came in a rather prosaic signal from Rommel to the OKW stating that owing to the pressure of the French Division to the south-west he was now withdrawing all his forces back into the Mareth Line.

Almost at the same time came a signal from Kesselring to Rommel, repeating orders from Hitler, to the effect that the Mareth Line was to be held; there was to be no withdrawal. The Mareth Line was, in fact, a well fortified and strong position, originally built by the French. Perhaps one of the most detailed reports ever sent by Rommel now followed. Maybe he wanted to keep Hitler quiet for a bit; in effect it gave the complete layout of the Mareth Line with the positions of every unit in its defence. Montgomery now knew exactly what he was up against; whatever the reasons for the Eighth Army's inability to trap the Afrika Korps in the open, the result was that Montgomery was now confronted by a well-defended fortress position. Kesselring's signal ordering Rommel to hold the line at all costs was followed by an order from Hitler that a delaying attack should be mounted against the Eighth Army. Kesselring was now having to pass on the orders he received from Hitler, despite his own views on the situation. This order drew a bitter reply to Kesselring from an obviously disillusioned Rommel who knew his opponents well enough by this time to realize the futility of such an operation. He signalled back to Kesselring that an attack on the Eighth Army could only have a slight delaying effect and that as an Allied attack on the Mareth Line was expected anyway, he suggested a further withdrawal from Mareth to unite the Army Group on a shorter perimeter. A signal came straight back from Kesselring that Rommel's proposals were over-ruled. One couldn't help feeling a little sorry for the man at this time. He had shown himself a brilliant fighter in the desert; three times he had escaped Montgomery's efforts to surround his panzer army; he had been consistently starved of supplies and equipment. He must now have seen the beginning of the end of the whole North African operation and it seemed obvious that Hitler was so fully engaged with the worsening situation in Russia that he was completely out of touch with the situation in Tunisia. It is true that by this time, as we learned from Ultra, more supplies were at last beginning to come over to Tunis, but by the beginning of March it began to look as if the Axis forces had shot their bolt. Churchill was scenting the kill in North Africa and, once again, came the polite request for more signals.

I suppose Rommel felt that somehow he had to carry out the orders from Hitler, and in the operation he now mounted Ultra was to play a leading role, for the signals warned Montgomery of the precise Axis forces to be used for the holding attack on the Eighth Army at Medenine, 15 miles south-west of the Mareth Line. Rommel had managed to get together three panzer divisions as well as two Italian divisions for the operation. What was even more important, he had also given us very adequate details of where the Axis armoured thrusts would come from. Rommel's 20th February attack failed. Montgomery had been too well briefed and the Eighth Army beat back the panzers with concentrated anti-tank fire. For Rommel it was obviously the end in Africa. He had already conducted a heated exchange of signals with Kesselring before the attack; now he pleaded sick leave and left for Germany. We didn't get the actual Ultra signal of his leaving. I don't suppose he had wanted to send an ordinary Ultra signal to Hitler on this personal subject and it probably went by despatch by aircraft, so the first time we knew that Rommel had left was when von Arnim was appointed in his place. It was a sad end to the story of Rommel in Africa as we read it in London.

Once Montgomery had disposed of Rommel's attack on Medenine he duly went ahead with his main attack on the Mareth Line itself now well aware of its weakest points.

Once again the Afrika Korps slipped away from Mareth. It was Easter and von Arnim signalled Kesselring that he doubted he could hold out much longer, and boldly stated that he proposed to put in a counterattack against the armies now closing in from the west. It may have sounded all right to Hitler, but in fact there was only one composite panzer division available for the final German armoured assault of the Tunisian campaign.

At the beginning of May I was able once again to get out to Algiers. The fall of Tunis was now imminent and I wanted to sort out what SLUs would be available for the next step to Sicily. I went up to Constantine to see the large SLU which was now operating there. Since my visit in December of 1942, we had been able to switch a large part of the traffic on to the Typex cypher machine. The Algerian SLU served principally the

North-West African Air Forces, the US XII Air Support Command, which later became the Northwest African Tactical Air Force, and the Mediterranean tactical air force, as well as the Eighteenth Army Group. I found a busy, and now victorious team. I also learned a good deal about the ingenuity and ability to improvise that the SLUs had to employ. Supplies were always a problem; Sergeant Reynolds told me that they had to adapt their Typex machines, first of all to work off the French 120-volts and then the American power plants of 110-volts and finally they had to use some old German equipment. There was an interesting incident, too, of how little things can prove dangerous to security. The SLU had at one time got prior information of an enemy air raid on Constantine and quite naturally they took their tin hats with them when they went on duty. When the air raid arrived other people at headquarters got suspicious, so after that it was no tin hats even if there was a warning on Ultra.

Kesselring, on Ultra, was now preparing the OKW for the surrender of Tunisia. He was getting both dirty ends of the stick, from Berlin and Tunis, but already he was asking the OKW for help and instructions as to what he should do against the next Allied move, whatever it would be. The end came quickly after the final Allied assault on May the sixth. Ultra was able to give all the North African Air Forces the movement orders for the fleet of German JU 52 transport aircraft and their ME 323 gliders which were to be used in the evacuation of German troops from Tunisia. The SLU told me they had a job to restrain the Allied Air Forces from taking too quick action; however, in the event, most of them were shot down. The same fate was suffered by the Hermes, the last German destroyer in the Mediterranean, and also the Belino evacuation convoy, although some senior German officers managed to escape in a hospital ship. Ultra became silent until Kesselring, on May the thirteenth, repeated to Berlin, quite shortly, the total loss of Tunisia and of the Army Group Afrika.

CHAPTER TWELVE

'Husky'

In May 1943 I toured Algiers, Cairo, Alexandria and Malta checking that all was in order at my various SLUs so that they were ready to give maximum help and information for Operation Husky, code-name for the planned invasion of Sicily.

In Algiers Tedder had given me the command set-up for Husky. He himself was taking over command of all the air forces in the Mediterranean and suggested that I wait until the principal commanders for Husky had assembled at La Marsa near Carthage in about two weeks' time, when it would be easier for me to contact anyone I wanted to see.

During my tour, I found that at all the main SLU stations a great deal of high-level traffic was being sent over the SLU channels by the chiefs of staff in London to Eisenhower and Alexander, and also between the various commanders-in-chief in the Mediterranean area.

This was primarily because so much of the planning for Sicily and Italy was based on Ultra information and any discussion or change of plan based on this intelligence had rightly to be sent over our own channel; added to which the top brass as well as Winston Churchill found our channel quicker than the normal signals organization, and its maximum secrecy was useful when personalities had to be discussed. The SLUs were, in consequence, working flat out.

During my visit to Malta, Lord Gort, the Governor, told me of the value of Ultra during the 1940 campaign in France. Over lunch at Government House we talked about Ultra and the effect Brauchitsch's famous signal had had in convincing London that we had to get out of France as quickly as possible, a conclusion that he had already come to. 'I think', he said, 'there are many who would bless your code-breakers if they knew what they had done'.

I left SLU 5 and a fair reserve of personnel with Tedder at La Marsa and arranged that, as one of the most experienced units, part of SLU 5 should go with Alexander when he moved to Sicily. The SLU which had been with the Eighth Army for such a long time stayed to look after Montgomery while the SLU that had been with Anderson went to strengthen Patton's SLU. It was later to be transferred to Mark Clark's Fifth Army. An amalgamation of the others was allotted to the various British and American tactical and strategical air forces or kept as reserves. Admiral Ramsay had his direct link at Alexandria whilst Admiral Cunningham had a full service from the large SLU at Malta as well as at La Marsa. All the SLUs were now old hands at the game. They had worked out methods of keeping on the air even in times of rapid movement, since they told me that the commanders didn't like being without their Ultra even for minutes.

The SLU at La Marsa was handling two hundred signals in the twenty-four hours, many of them very long ones, and it kept all three watches fully occupied. Even after operations began we found that once again the SLU channel was being used for inter-communications on planning the Italian landings when Ultra was closely involved. This added to the pressure on the

SLUs. I couldn't complain because the plans right from Husky onward were in fact based so completely on Ultra information.

When I visited General Alexander's small camp near Carthage he suggested that we should take a walk amongst the sand-dunes where we could talk. He was fascinated with the Ultra story and I gave it to him in detail. Hitherto he had not been able to understand how we managed to get it to him so accurately and quickly. He wanted to know the prospects for its continuance for the Italian campaign, and I told him that unless there was a serious boob by anyone, I couldn't see the Germans changing Ultra now and, barring accidents, there was every hope for good results seeing that Hitler and the OKW were a long way from Rome, and all signals would go on the air. He seemed very satisfied with the whole outfit. He was fascinated, too, by the tough character of his opponent, which I was able to draw from my personal knowledge of Kesselring. He also wanted to know just who in his new command was in the Ultra picture. He told me that he had known from his first meeting with Churchill in Egypt before Alamein that the Prime Minister was well informed from Ultra but he had no idea, until I had just told him, that he received direct signals annotated by me. Alexander was a little thoughtful on this subject. He must have realized that Churchill would be following the campaign almost as closely as he would be doing himself. I did, however, take pains to assure Alexander that I only annotated them from the German point of view since I was unaware of any orders or actions on the part of the Allies.

There had been one interesting incident in June; Ultra had disclosed that Kesselring's forward headquarters in Sicily were in the San Dominico Hotel, which stands high on the cliffs at Taormina, overlooking the sea. The RAF had been precise and dropped a bomb right in the centre of this once ancient monastery. Kesselring himself was evidently in Rome, but the bomb struck the officers' mess and there had been considerable loss of life.

Before I left Tunis, Kesselring thought it wise to inform the OKW by Ultra of the complete set up of the Italian and German forces in Sicily. This, of course, was an absolute gift. Ultra gave no indication of German reactions to the 'man who never was', the body with the false plans for Torch which had been 'washed ashore' on May the ninth on the Spanish coast. However, later signals told us that with the exception of the Herman Goering Panzer Division no major reinforcement of Sicily had taken place, so that it looked as if Hitler was still uncertain. It looked too as if Kesselring, whatever his own ideas about where the invasion would come, had gone along with his Fuehrer. Kesselring was obviously desperately anxious not to make a mistake, and from the signal that he sent, giving the distribution of his forces, it was evident that he had taken some precautions in Sicily. But from Ultra it appeared that Kesselring feared a landing at Palermo on the north coast because he had stationed part of the German 15th Panzer Division with two Italian field divisions in that area. However, his uncertainty was helpfully obvious since he then split the remainder of the 15th Panzer Division, together with the Herman Goering Panzer Division, into three groups in the centre of the island, ready to move in any direction.

The defence of Sicily was officially in the hands of the Italian General Guzzoni and his Sixth Italian Army, which consisted of four field divisions and two coastal divisions. Kesselring, in his signal, had given the precise positions of these Italian divisions, and it was evident too from his signals that, although the German units were officially under Guzzoni's command, they were in fact ordered to operate on their own initiative and that Kesselring was in direct contact with them through the German liaison officer at Guzzoni's head-quarters. From the disposition of all the Axis troops on the island, it was evident that the landing areas were only lightly guarded by Italian coast brigades and that, in view of the mountainous country, if the few roads to the coast could be denied to the German panzers, the landing operations should meet with little resistance. It was evident too that both Kesselring and Guzzoni were unsure as to when and where the attack would come. Thus Ultra not only gave the full strength and disposi-tions of the enemy, it also showed that the Allied could achieve tactical surprise and, in the event, allowed Al-lied parachute troops to block a number of the German panzers in their race towards the beaches. This was Ul-tra at its best.

By now we had learned that the last few days before a seaborne invasion were the most tense; once again every available Ultra signal had to be scanned with care to see if there was a clue about any awareness by Kesselring as to exactly where the blow would fall. It was only when the armada of ships coming up from Al-exandria had been spotted by the Germans on July the ninth that Ultra informed us that the troops on Sicily and elsewhere were put on the alert. The Axis uncer-tainty as to the precise objectives continued, however, and the Allies did attain a strategical advantage when they landed in Sicily on the tenth. Kesselring advised the OKW as soon as the landings began and for the time being there was no 'Victory or die' order from Hitler. Kesselring did not use Ultra direct to his panzer units, which were now operating on their own initiative, so there was little on Ultra to tell us the details of how well it was progressing until Kesselring's situation reports and his claim to have checked the British south of Catania on July the fifteenth. The Luftwaffe was of little use to the Germans. In fact, shortly after the landing Goering had probably had a rocket from Hitler on the subject, for he had sent a signal tearing a strip off his Luftflotte pilots and he had thoughtfully sent it through Kesselring. On July the twelfth Kesselring received an Ultra signal from the OKW advising him that parachute troops reinforcements would be flown to Sicily on the following day, and that there would be more reinforcements of parachute troops and a Panzer Grenadier of the XIVth Panzer Corps had been ordered to cross to the Island from the mainland. In addition, part of the 29th Panzer Grenadier Division started to arrive on July the nineteenth. Kesselring had again wasted no time once the objectives were clear, but it was all to no avail. Patton, taking full advantage of the move of the panzers to hold Montgomery, and knowing from Ultra that there was nothing to stop him, was already making his famous high-speed left hook towards Palermo and Messina and by August the eighth, Kesselring reported to the OKW his withdrawal from Catania, followed shortly after by his decision to withdraw all units to the Italian mainland. He had evidently secured OKW agreement. The conquest of Sicily ended on August the seventeenth. Ultra had played a vital part and Alexander's previous comment to me that Ultra had brought an entirely new dimension into the conduct of warfare summed up the situation accurately.

CHAPTER THIRTEEN

'Avalanche'

Churchill had always been convinced that if the Allies invaded Italy the Italians would throw in the towel. Latterly, Roosevelt had been brought round to the same view. Mussolini, who in 1942 had suffered the effects of his fruitless visit to Cyrenaica, was now facing the collapse of his whole regime after the success of the Sicilian Operation Husky. He was an extremely worried man and Hitler had no illusions about the difficulties he might have in keeping his Axis partner in the war. Mussolini's ebullience at their meeting on July the seventeenth had not deceived him, but he probably didn't bargain for the rapid chain of events which followed. Only one week later Mussolini's Fascist Grand Council told him to quit; the next day he was arrested by the King.

Marshal Badoglio took over the Government and assured Kesselring that Italy would stay in the war. Kesselring repeated this assurance in a signal back to Hitler, who rightly didn't believe a word of it; within a week the Italians started secret negotiations for an armistice with the Allies. Hitler had seen it coming and was already making preparations to send German troops into Northern Italy if and when the Italians should defect. The first definite news we had of this, however, was in a signal from Hitler to Kesselring in Rome telling him to expect German divisions in North-

ern Italy and to tell the Italians that the troops were to
form a strategic reserve for the whole Balkan area, in
order not to upset them too much. This corresponded
with Hitler's views which he had expressed in an appreciation sent earlier to Kesselring that the Allies might
well try an invasion into the Balkans after they had
cleared up the North African position. The unpleasant
fact for Kesselring must have been that this northern
force was to be under the command of Field-Marshal
Rommel and designated as Army Group B, which
meant Kesselring would have no authority over it at all.

The Italian situation worsened. Earlier in August,
Hitler ordered Kesselring, in the event of an Italian ca-
pitulation, to move all German troops northward and
to join up with Rommel's Army Group and hold the
line along the northern Apennines and the River Po; he
added that Rommel would assume command. The sting
was certainly in the tail, and was a bitter pill for Kesselring to swallow. He didn't swallow it; he had worked
hard for the position of commander-in-chief in the
Mediterranean theatre and, knowing Kesselring, it was
no surprise to see the way he resolutely set out to cir-
cumvent Hitler's orders and fight the whole Italian
campaign so as to keep his command. During August
we received a signal which duly reported Rommel's divisions as moving into North Italy and at the same time
Kesselring reported the position of his own divisions in
Southern Italy. There were more detailed signals giving
the route of the reinforcements and the times that they
would be passing through Grenoble; in consequence,
the 15th US Air Force had a field day and apparently
did a great amount of damage. Kesselring's signal
showed us that in the toe of Italy were the 26th Panzer
Division and the 24th Motorized Division, whilst
spread around Italy's heel was part of a parachute division. Further north, covering the Salerno area, was the

16th Panzer Division, whilst north of Naples was the 15th Herman Goering Motorized Division; close around Rome was stationed a motorized division and part of a parachute division. In an Ultra signal, Hitler had given orders to Kesselring that all the units, except those around Rome, were to be formed into an Army which would be commanded by General Vietinghoff, in order, as Hitler put it, to relieve Kesselring of the details of tactical control.

The Allies now knew exactly where the opposition was on the Italian mainland, and also that at the end of August Kesselring had sent a signal to the OKW in which he stated that he had ordered the Tenth Army to start the northward withdrawal of the units in the extreme south. This, so far, fitted in with Hitler's orders and, although it was now getting near the time for the invasion of Italy, code-named Operation Avalanche, at the beginning of September, it was still evident from the signals passing to Berlin that Kesselring had absolutely no idea where the main landing would take place. He favoured, in a signal to Hitler, the probability that the Allies would land north of Naples in order to have the shortest possible distance to march on Rome; in the same signal he reported that the withdrawal northward of the panzer divisions from the extreme south was now in progress. Montgomery's Eighth Army was, in consequence, able to cross from Messina on to the mainland of Italy without any serious opposition. Kesselring signalled Berlin that he did not consider it was the main effort, which he still expected nearer Rome, and that he would continue to withdraw north in accordance with Hitler's instructions.

It was fortunate for us that Ultra at Bletchley was in full operation during the first half of September 1943.

If one analyses the amount of knowledge about the enemy's strength, disposition and intentions available to the Allied command at that time, one cannot help feeling that had the Allied plans been more flexible and had we been able to keep the Italians on the hook a little longer, Kesselring might have been given time to withdraw northward and the misfortunes of Cassino and Anzio might have been avoided. But as things turned out, on the day the Allied invasion fleet was spotted off the Gulf of Salerno, General Vietinghoff had not yet started to withdraw his troops from this area. Nevertheless, General Mark Clark's Fifth Army obtained complete strategical surprise for the actual landing. As soon as Vietinghoff had news of the landing, he at once signalled Kesselring and tried to get a ruling as to whether he was to oppose it or retire northwards to Rome in accordance with his previous orders. This was now a vital decision for us, and as we waited there was, alas, no reply by signal. Twice the Prime Minister's secretary rang me to ask if we had got the answer. One can only imagine that Kesselring was pretty busy with the confrontation by the Italian units round Rome which he later reported in a signal back to Berlin. Meanwhile, Vietinghoff took matters into his own hands and decided to stand and fight, he moved his panzer corps quickly to the landing area. Kesselring's signal came at mid-day approving his action; it was probably the most important decision Kesselring had to make in the face of his Fuehrer's orders. As a result, despite the US Fifth Army's almost unopposed landing at Salerno, Vietinghoff's reactions were quick and fierce, and after four days of bitter fighting there was deep gloom in London when a signal from Vietinghoff to Kesselring stated that enemy resistance was collapsing and that the Tenth Army was driving the Allies back on a wide front.

I did not know at that time that Alexander had evidently ordered Montgomery to come to the rescue without delay, because it was after receiving Vieting-hoff's signal that Churchill rang up to ask if there was any evidence to show any opposition to Montgomery's advance. As far as one could see, there was none. However, although the Eighth Army did not physically come to the aid of the Fifth Army, the latter just managed to hold on and no doubt the threat of the Eighth Army's advance was partly responsible for a more than welcome signal from Vietinghoff on the sixteenth, asking Kessel-ring's permission to withdraw due to the intense naval and air bombardment. Kesselring gave permission, but ordered Vietinghoff to delay the enemy as best he could and to deploy his retiring army right across Italy. Kessel-ring stated in his signal that he would do his best to pre-pare a defensive position on the Volterno and Bifurno riv-ers. Hitler himself had obviously been impressed by Kesselring's ability and his strategy, for he was now persuaded to change his mind and his own original or-ders to move to the North, and he sent a signal to Kes-selring ordering him to hold the line running eastward, north of Naples, for as long a period of time as possi-ble.

Somehow, despite his loyalty to Hitler, I didn't think that Kesselring would willingly agree to the idea of withdrawing all the German forces away to the north of Italy and then calmly handing over the command to Rommel. These two had not parted on the best of terms when Rommel left Tunisia, and although Rom-mel was Hitler's pet general, Kesselring had proved himself a quick-thinking operator both in Tunisia and now in Italy. He knew the Italian terrain and its possi-bilities for defensive action, he had virtually held com-mand of the Mediterranean theatre for some time, and I don't suppose he relished the idea of either playing second fiddle to Rommel or perhaps relegation to the command of some depleted Luftflotte on the Russian front.

Kesselring's signal to Vietinghoff had given Alexander the overall picture and the welcome news that the Allies would have the port of Naples. Admittedly, the port had been badly knocked about, but it could soon be put in working order, and in any case it seemed unlikely that Kesselring would now mount any serious counter-attack southwards.

The Eighth Army was making good progress up the east coast. On October the fifth they had captured Termoli harbour with a brilliant seaborne attack. Kesselring, evidently considering that this breakthrough opened up the danger of a drive to Rome from this easterly direction, signalled to Vietinghoff to send the 15th Panzer Division from the Volturno area right across the peninsula to the other side to try and stop Montgomery's army. The cautious Montgomery had meantime, however, halted his forces in order to reorganize his supply position. Vietinghoff later reported to Kesselring that the Eighth Army did not appear to be ready to exploit the position. After Major-General Lucian Truscott Jr. and the United States 3rd Division had made a brilliant crossing of the Volturno river, Vietinghoff had evidently gone on leave, for a new name, General Lemelsen, appeared on our signals as Commander of the Tenth Army. As I had predicted to Alexander when I had seen him at La Marsa, Ultra had so far provided a clear picture of Hitler's and Kesselring's moves and intentions.

Churchill had gone to Teheran at the end of November, stopping off at Cairo, where he and Roosevelt had an important conference and selected the men for the jobs for Operation Overlord, the code-name for the invasion of France. This time Churchill wanted Ultra Intelligence to go with him and a short note came over from Downing Street in the usual courteous language: 'Pray make the necessary arrangements.' During the whole of the Teheran Conference Churchill used the SLU channel whenever he wanted a quick reply. There were to be a few special occasions when the SLU was used both by Churchill, Eisenhower and finally by Harry Truman when they wanted to put through an Ultra secret person-to-person immediate signal which they did not wish even their own signals organizations to see.

The New Year saw Eisenhower and Montgomery back in London and the beginning of the planning for the great adventure across the Channel, but for the moment we will stay with Alexander, who had now moved his headquarters to Caserta, and with General Sir Oliver Leese, who had taken over the Eighth Army from Montgomery.

What can one say of the agony of the Anzio beach? Back in London, before it all started, we felt that this at last would force Kesselring to abandon his Gustav line and put an end to the bloody battles round Cassino, so once again we scanned every available signal to see if there was an indication that Kesselring had even a suspicion of what was going to happen. From his signals back to the OKW, it was apparent that he felt he could hold the Allies on the Cassino line, at least for some time. There was no sign of any troop concentration in the direction of Anzio. Kesselring did show concern at the growing strength of the French colonial divisions, and some more troops were brought south to Rome, but not far enough to indicate a threat to Anzio. At the end of the third week in January, in fact right up to the moment of landing, Mark Clark was assured of complete strategic surprise and the probability that no new opposition could be brought to bear before forty-eight hours. Alas, the story of Anzio is now too well known, the successful seizure of the beachhead and then indecision by the US commander until it was too late to make the drive inland to cut the Tenth Army supply lines, too late to do anything but dig in and await the inevitable counter attack. It was not too late, however, to read Kesselring's signals to Berlin that the landing area was now contained. In February he made a near successful attempt to liquidate the beachhead, but it just managed to hold on; after that he was content to seal it off with a new Army, the Fourteenth, which Hitler had ordered him to form for the purpose. He now had twenty-two divisions between Rome and the Cassino line; for four months the narrow beachhead held on, and we now noted from Ultra the arrival of the tough mountain troops who had fought in Crete.

In due course, an important signal from Kesselring advised the OKW that he expected an all out attempt by the Allies to break the Cassino line as soon as the flooded rivers and the countryside permitted. So far, this airman turned soldier had done a remarkable job stopping the Allied drive to Rome and overcoming the defection of his Italian Allies. Nor had he been idle during the winter months, for, in signals to Berlin, he had told us about the defensive lines he had been building behind his present position, the Adolf Hitler line across the Liri valley, and a final line, the Caesar line, on which both the Tenth and the Fourteenth Armies would combine to protect Rome. Hitler seemed satisfied with these arrangements, but right up to May the tenth Kesselring reported that he was uncertain when and where the expected Allied offensive would come. It was, in fact, the signal to Vietinghoff, commander of the Tenth Army, addressed to him at Hitler's headquarters and telling him to return immediately, which advised us not only that he was absent in Germany but also that the timing of the offensive was a surprise to Kesselring.

At midnight on 12 May 1944, Alexander's offensive at Cassino began. Kesselring then reported that the main attack on Monte Cassino had been repulsed, but that some ground had been lost south of Cassino town. In a signal on May the thirteenth he told the OKW that all available German reserves had now been committed. It was about mid-day on Sunday, May the thirteenth, that I had a telephone call from the Prime Minister at Chequers. He asked that I meet him at his flat at Storey's Gate that evening at 9 p.m. and would I bring round all signals dealing with the Cassino front. I wondered what it was all about. His private secretary rang a few minutes later and put me wise. Apparently Winston had returned to Chequers on Saturday night from a secret visit to Alexander's headquarters in Italy; I knew the Prime Minister had been getting more than worried at the inability of the Allies to make progress in Italy. He desperately wanted Rome before he started on Overlord across the channel. The Anzio fiasco, though no fault of Alexander's, had been a morale booster for the Germans, and now, before we landed in France, we needed to shake it up a bit. It was obvious that Churchill had been briefed by Alexander, but I had only two or three signals reporting small advances by the Eighth Army around Cassino, and Kesselring's claim to have beaten off the attack on Monte Cassino. They were not a specially joyful selection to present to Churchill. It was a cold evening for May and the Prime Minister was sitting in his boiler suit deep in his green leather chair in front of a good fire. He looked tired. As he asked me to sit down and tell him my news, he was puffing gently at a large cigar. I had the distressing

feeling that he took my normal quiet, but factual, opening of the conversation as my own way of telling him
something exciting. I had given him the various small
details of the fighting which had come in during the afternoon. When he said 'Is that all?' I had to say that I
was afraid that was so. We went across to the map
room where the few alterations I had brought over
were flagged up, but Churchill was obviously puzzled
and disappointed. In his usual courteous manner he
thanked me for coming over and then, with a broad
smile, he said, 'See that I get anything more first thing
in the morning. I think you will find there will be something of interest.' It was now late but I phoned the
watch at Bletchley and warned them to keep their eyes
skinned. It came through about 3 a.m. with Mrs
Owen's knock on my office door and a welcome cup of
coffee. The French Moroccan troops had scaled the
mountains south of Cassino. Kesselring was calm, but
obviously dismayed at the feat; he reported to Hitler
that 'the whole Cassino line was now in danger'. I sent
the signal over to Storey's Gate before seven-thirty in
the morning and gave a ring to General Ismay to let
him know what was afoot. I hadn't seen him the night
before. How he ever got any sleep, I never knew, he
was usually up with Churchill until 2 a.m., then up
again at 7 a.m. That day signals reported to Berlin that
now both the British and the Americans were gaining
some ground, and Kesselring again stressed that all reserves had been thrown in. Kesselring was a worried
man and he was also not being properly kept in the picture by Vietinghoff, for, early on the fourteenth he sent
a 'snorter' to Vietinghoff telling him to report to him
by mid-day exactly what was happening. (I was happy
to put a note on this for Churchill saying that it probably explained why Kesselring had not reported the

French success on Sunday. I didn't want him to think Hut 3 had fallen down on the job.) On the fifteenth Kesselring sent a signal to Hitler reporting a breakthrough by another strong French force over the massive Monti Aurunci which dominated the whole Liri valley and the supply routes to the Cassino line. On the sixteenth came reports from Kesselring of the successes of the British and Polish forces around Cassino, and then on the seventeenth came the one we had been waiting for: Kesselring ordered the evacuation of the entire Cassino front, since, as he said, the French had penetrated twenty-five miles behind the German lines. His signal was repeated to the OKW. Bletchley was in good form and Churchill, Alexander, and the US chiefs of staff in Washington had it within a few minutes of its despatch by Kesselring.

The attack by the Moroccan troops across the mountains was, according to Kesselring's report to Berlin, entirely unexpected. By the nineteenth it was hard, even from the Ultra signals, to sort out just what was happening. The German Tenth Army signalled desperately for reinforcement, having lost most of two divisions; that communications were extremely bad was evident from a further signal by Kesselring demanding to be told what was going on. Vietinghoff seemed to be out of touch with his divisions. He didn't reply. Kesselring ordered withdrawal from the Liri valley on the twenty-second, and the Allies started their break-out attack from Anzio the next day. Kesselring signalled to Berlin that his Tenth and Fifteenth Armies had been divided by the Allies, and he asked Hitler's permission to abandon the Adolf Hitler line, some ten miles behind the now abandoned Cassino line, and withdraw to the Caesar line, which was some twenty miles south of Rome. In another signal he ordered his last reserve divisions from Northern Italy into the battle. Hitler signalled his permission to withdraw to the Caesar line on the twenty-fourth of May.

Stewart Menzies told me that on his visit to Italy, Winston Churchill had agreed with Alexander's plan to try to trap and destroy the German armies south of Rome rather than try to drive them northwards. The plan, if successful, would obviously dent the morale of the whole German army at this critical moment before Overlord.

General Mark Clark had been fully briefed on Alexander's plan and had received his instructions to use the forces now ready to break out from Anzio to move rapidly eastwards to trap the retreating Tenth and Fifteenth Armies from the rear. (Ultra had given him the weak point.) Instead, he chose to ignore them, and whilst sending a small token force to the east, decided himself to try and make a dash up the west coast to Rome. The result was that neither objective was attained. Clark neither unlocked the door to Rome—nor trapped the Germans. By this time Hitler had sent one of his death-or-glory signals to the troops in Italy which Kesselring duly passed on to Vietinghoff. No signal from Vietinghoff acknowledged it, which was not surprising in the circumstances, but by May the thirteenth Kesselring signalled to the OKW that the Caesar line, to which both the armies had now retreated, was holding, despite heavy losses. Nevertheless, his report was shortlived; the next day he reported that the Caesar line itself had now been breached. There was no doubt from his signals that he had managed to restore some sort of cohesion and had got the Tenth and Fifteenth Armies together.

It was on June the second that Kesselring asked Hitler for permission to evacuate Rome without fighting.

Hitler agreed on June the third, by which time Kessel-ring's forces were already slipping away to the north, and now General Clark finally took some notice of Ul-tra. He knew from Kesselring's signals that Rome was undefended. He organized two flying columns and made a triumphal personal entry into the Eternal City, ahead of anyone else.

It is, I think, greatly to Kesselring's credit that he did not defend Rome; perhaps he didn't want his name linked with Nero, but I believe that under the rough, tough, thrusting exterior, there must have been some sensitivity to history and the arts which induced him to save Rome and, later on, Florence.

Churchill had got his Rome just two days before Overlord broke the quiet of the English Channel.

I suppose, looking back on it, the Italian campaign had given us almost as complete a picture of the Ger-man side as could have been found in Kesselring's files in his office in Rome. It had obviously been necessary to put all signals between Kesselring and the OKW and Hitler on the air, a point I had previously made with Alexander.

In my London office, where only the main strategic plans for Avalanche and Anzio were known to me, it was as if I were sitting at Kesselring's right hand watch-ing the campaign entirely from his point of view.

I have given a fairly detailed account of the cam-paign of the road to Rome from the Ultra Intelligence point of view in order to show how, with this 'new di-mension of war', not only the commanders in the field, but also Churchill, Roosevelt, and the Allied chiefs of staff had all the cards in the pack spread out on the ta-ble face upwards.

Some people may draw the conclusion that the army commanders did not understand how to play them, but that they did provide the opportunities for them to carry out Alexander's plans cannot be doubted.

In the event I think that the picture I have given is one which entitles Kesselring's fighting withdrawal from Sicily to Rome to rank amongst those other masterly retreats in history.

CHAPTER FOURTEEN

Preparation for 'Overlord'

Lieutenant-General Freddie Morgan had been chosen by the Allied statesmen and chiefs of staff, after the Casablanca Conference, to act as COSSAC, or Chief of Staff to the Supreme Allied Commander, for the purpose of setting up a planning organization for invasion of France by the Allies. As early as March 1943 he took up his post in the now empty Norfolk House where Eisenhower had previously set up his headquarters before Operation Torch in North Africa.

I had discussed with him the provision of Ultra for his planning operations, and agreed that he could find all the information he required already digested and co-ordinated at the War Office and Air Ministry. However, I told him I would bring round any item of urgent or special interest, should it arise.

The story of the V1 flying-bomb has been told by a number of well qualified people, but so far the part played by Ultra in the Intelligence investigation into the nature of Hitler's secret weapon, together with the location of the experimental station where it was being developed, and the actual launching and performance data, has not hitherto been disclosed.

The investigation was primarily carried out by R. V. Jones, who had been working on secret scientific Intelligence in our SIS office. The way in which he unravelled the problem gives some idea of the co-ordination which was possible between reports from secret agents, Ultra, and spy plane photography.

The first time the V1 turned up on Ultra was on a signal in which special anti-aircraft protection was being ordered for the 'FZG76' site on the Baltic Sea. This was the first time we had heard its correct official name.

Early in 1943, before the Ultra signal, we had heard something about a secret flying-bomb from our agents. These two reports had together established that some sort of missile was under construction.

Then Jones took a long shot. He was aware that the Germans, having had trouble in establishing the trajectory of the long-range gun with which they bombarded Paris in World War I, might try to use radar to plot whichever new missiles they were developing. If so, he rightly judged that they might call on the most experienced radar plotters that they had. He believed that they were in the 14th and 15th Companies of the Luft Nachrichten Versuchs Regiment. He therefore briefed his contact in Hut 3 at Bletchley to look out for anything concerning these two companies and to inform him immediately if one or other of them moved up the Baltic coast. A month or two later an Ultra signal was spotted which showed that the 14th Company had in fact moved up, and had started to plot the flights of flying-bombs. Luckily the plots were broadcast in a simple letter-for-figure code that we could break ourselves. From the plots, Jones was able to work out the disposition of all the plotting stations and obtain detailed performance figures on most of the flying-bomb trials. When he had worked out the co-ordinates of the launching point at Pennemunde, by backtracking from the radar plots, he asked for a spy-plane sortie over that pinpoint and also over the other launching point, which he had similarly identified a few miles along the coast at Zempin. The photographs showed the two launching sites, and it happened that at Pennemunde we got a V1 on the ramp. Pennemunde was duly bombed in August 1943 and the damage was so great that production of the V1 was put back by six months. Both the radar plots and the Ultra ceased for a while. However, Ultra came into its own again when the launching site was transferred to Poland and signals had again to be put on the air.

It had all been a brilliant bit of deduction on R. V.'s part and, as the time for Overlord approached, in 1944, we began to get a great many reports from agents of the construction of launching sites on the French coast. These sites were photographed and bombed as soon as they appeared, so that the Germans were forced to make prefabricated mobile ramps in order to avoid their destruction.

It was in April 1944 that Ultra finally came up with the orders from Hitler himself to establish a special headquarters near Amiens in France to control the V1 operation, and everything clicked into place. The new headquarters was to be commanded by Colonel Wachtel and was called the 155th Flak Regiment. Since the signal was also addressed to General Heinemann, commanding the LXVI Corps, it was evident that the new regiment would come under his administrative command.

At the end of May 1944 an Ultra signal from Watchtel to Heinemann reported that fifty sites were ready for launching. This finally determined Churchill to press for the start of Overlord in June at all costs. Time was obviously going to be very precious. It was on D-Day, June the sixth, that Wachtel received a signal ordering him to prepare for an immediate all-out offensive to start on June the twelfth. As it turned out, it was not until the thirteenth that the first V1 landed.

But to go back to 1943. In November there was a piece of important information for Morgan; it was a signal from the OKW to all units in the West, notifying them of the arrival of Rommel to undertake a general inspection of the coast defences of France and Belgium —Hitler's Atlantic Wall.

Since 1942, when Rundstedt had left the Russian front and re-appeared on the scene as Commander-in-Chief in the West, there had been a fair stability of the Ultra output for this area. The usual strength returns of the sixty-odd divisions in the Western Command changed very little. We learned from his signals that it was part of Rundstedt's job to rest and re-equip the tired and depleted divisions from the Eastern Front. We were given a rough picture of the manpower, equipment and other shortages as well as the difficulties experienced over the policy of introducing prisoners-of-war contingents into the German units. We learned, too, that the actual strength of the new divisions did not amount to more than fifty per cent of the establishment total. On the few occasions that Rundstedt himself went on the air to the OKW, it was usually to complain about the state of inadequacy, both as regards manpower and the general condition of the defences in the West. All this was vital knowledge for the planners.

One subject, however, which came over with great clarity, and was of extreme importance to Morgan in late 1943, was Rundstedt's own appreciation of where he considered the Allied invasion would take place. True to orthodox German military thinking, he gave it as his opinion that the Allies would surely take the shortest sea route and attack in the Pas de Calais area. I think it is true to say that it was this signal that sowed the seed of the elaborate deception plan to install a phantom army in Kent, opposite the Pas de Calais, in order to bolster up Rundstedt's views.

General Morgan had presented his initial plan for Overlord to the Quebec Conference in August 1943, but it was not until November that Roosevelt and Churchill finally agreed on the command structure, when they were both in Cairo on the way to the Teheran Conference.

Tedder had told me back in July, in Tunisia, that he hoped to get a top job with Eisenhower, and now I learned that he was to be Deputy Supreme Commander under 'Ike'. This was very good news.

In February 1944 Eisenhower set up his headquarters of SHAEF—Supreme Headquarters Allied Expeditionary Force. I now started to make my own plans for the provision of a new network of SLUs, and made it my business to get to know all the commanders and their staffs personally. This was a very special sort of Intelligence and required a special relationship if the best was to be got out of Ultra. I was not a subscriber to the view which seemed to be held by Montgomery that all Intelligence must be entirely impersonal and under no circumstances must there be any contact, or acknowledgment, of the source by the commander. With Ultra, the broad coverage provided those who continually handled it with a large amount of background information, in addition to that culled from reading so many of the signals of the German High Command; I found it was this that the majority of commanders were always interested to know about.

When the principal commanders had settled in I therefore 'made my number' with each one. There were long green wooden huts making up a little American township in Bushey Park. Here the Stars and Stripes flew at the masthead and received the full ceremonial to which it was entitled. Around the tidy square were the huts of the Supreme Commander and principal staff officers, and it was to Tedder's hut that I usually gravitated, to find out if there were any particular aspects which SHAEF wanted watched.

General Bradley had been aware of Ultra in Tunisia, but now I was able to give him a full briefing, together with those members of his staff that he had asked me to put on the Ultra list.

With Bradley's G2 Intelligence officer—Colonel Monk Dickson—I became great friends as the war progressed. I would meet him in his working caravan, situated in some corner of a field or wood, and find him always the same quietly efficient soldier. Lieutenant-General William Simpson, who was to command the American Ninth Army when it became operational, moved his headquarters into Clifton College at Bristol. He was a tall, courteous and friendly person who never wasted a word, or asked the same question twice, and he seemed to fit quite naturally into the headmaster's chair in the book-lined study which was now his office. When, later, I went to see him in France or Germany, I found he usually managed to set up his headquarters in a school-house. I found, too, that the instant catering arrangements were superb. I think they took it as a compliment that I always managed to turn up in time for lunch, or for a night's lodging.

General George Patton was, by now, an old customer, although he preferred—as he told me at our first meeting—to leave the Intelligence to his highly proficient Intelligence staff. A compulsive fighter, he never failed to use every opportunity that Ultra gave him to 'bust open' the enemy.

I met General Sir Miles Dempsey—Commanding the British Second Army—for the first time when he asked me round to his flat in London one evening to tell him all about Ultra. He was a newcomer to the source and I spent a long time with him, giving him every facet of what he might expect. As we drank our Scotch and sodas he would occasionally laugh outright at the thought of reading Hitler's signals. When I eventually left at midnight, I felt sure he would use Ultra to the full and be meticulously careful of this precious source.

Major-General Lewis H. Brereton's staff had, I think, been warned of my mission by Tedder and I had a big welcome from them. They hadn't been long in England, nor had they come across many members of the Royal Air Force at the time; they had set up a blackboard for me, evidently expecting a lecture, but instead they just kept me talking for an hour or more. Once again, the full story paid off. The US Air Forces were some of the most practical users of Ultra, even if a little impulsive at times.

Lieutenant-General Henry Crerar, Commanding the Canadian Army, was also a newcomer to Ultra. He had set up his headquarters at Lord Beaverbrook's house near Leatherhead. It was a peaceful spot. General Simmonds, one of his corps commanders, was also put in the picture at Crerar's request and was to prove, not only a brilliant commander, but an enthusiastic Ultra customer.

General Spaatz had come back to England from Tunisia to command the Strategic Bomber Force. By now I knew this American commander well, and I found him at General Doolittle's new headquarters in Wycombe Abbey girls' school at High Wycombe. He was not directly responsible to Overlord, but his force was, when necessary, to be at Eisenhower's disposal. He was therefore very much involved. I had looked after him well in Tunisia, and he was always an enthusiastic user of Ultra, especially grateful for the German secret weather reports for Europe. His headquarters were not very far from Bomber Command so I arranged that they both had a direct line from Hut 3. When Spaatz later moved on to SHAEF in France he was served directly by their SLU.

With all the customers we already had, and those which no doubt would request SLUs as more operational units got under way in Overlord, there was a fairly large programme for the training of SLUs to be started. I needed some sixty RAF Cypher sergeants and a dozen officers; they all had to be very thoroughly screened—a process in itself which took some time— and only when we were satisfied on security grounds did I myself interview each one to make sure we had the right type of man for the highly responsible and exacting job. In an evacuated school in North London, day after day they learnt their cyphers and security. They were quite an exceptional and highly intelligent selection of men and became absolutely dedicated to the job.

The SLUs were ready by the beginning of May to be attached to their commands, where they began taking Ultra direct from Hut 3.

There was no noticeable increase in the signals of importance to Overlord during March, but by April we learned from an OKW signal that Rommel had been given command of Army Group B, which was responsible for the defence of the coast from Holland right round Normandy and Brittany, as far south as Nantes. Army Group G area, which comprised most of the southern half of France, looked after the West Coast from Nantes to the Spanish border. As soon as Rommel got his command he started to throw his weight about. Evidently the results of his inspection of the coast defences were unsatisfactory, for in April he started sending impassioned requests for materials and labour to make a proper job of Hitler's much-vaunted Atlantic Wall. It was evidently considered by Rommel

as being largely inadequate, but signal as he might, and
did, for cement, steel, timber and guns, nothing much
appeared to happen. Eventually, Rommel warned the
OKW that what was being done was being accomplished by the troops themselves, which meant that
their state of readiness was badly impaired. The signals
outlining Rommel's constant demands were now being
backed up by aerial photography and the two together
gave us a fairly good time-table of the construction of
the beach and coastal defences we should meet later. It
became obvious from the aerial photographs that despite his incessant bullying of Berlin for more of everything, he had made a pretty good job with what he had
got.

During the spring of 1944 the Germans made what
was to be probably the most important decision of all
those affecting the Allies and the Overlord plans. The
decision arose from a clash of views between Hitler,
Rundstedt, Rommel, Guderian and Schweppenburg,
who commanded a group of four panzer divisions
which made up the panzer reserve stationed near Paris.
In view of the importance of this whole affair, I think
it would be of interest to give the full facts of what
went on, as we learned them from documents captured
after the war, and then to show how much we learned
from Ultra at the time.

The discussions between those top level commanders
were mostly conducted personally with Hitler in Berlin,
but fortunately there were times when he was away at
his eastern headquarters at Rastenburg, and it was the
exchange of just one or two signals on these occasions
which gave us the vital clues we needed.

I have already referred to an appreciation by Rundstedt, in which he considered the Allied invasion would
take place across the Pas de Calais; but documents
show that both Hitler and Rommel—who, incidentally,

had a personal telephone line direct to his Fuehrer, which avoided the necessity of going through Rundstedt—firmly believed the invasion would come on the Normandy beaches.

Whether Hitler had, in fact, been more impressed than he admitted at the time with the supposed Overlord plans stolen by a German spy in January from the British Ambassador in Ankara (he had told his generals that they were obviously an Allied trick) or whether both he and Rommel were now being more realistically briefed by German Intelligence sources one cannot tell. But the result was that Rommel, who had obviously studied the techniques employed by the Allies in their amphibious landings in the Mediterranean, was convinced that the only way to repel an invasion was on the beaches themselves. Quite early in the year Rommel had made plans to deploy the powerful reserve panzer divisions, which were normally situated not far from Paris, to positions he chose behind the Normandy defences, where he could quickly get them to the landing areas. He knew only too well that, with a totally inadequate air defence over Normandy, it would be impossible to move these divisions along the roads by day and that time would be the vital factor if he was to be able to take his tanks, as he said, 'to the water's edge'.

Hitler, who knew Rommel pretty well by this time, trusted the man on the spot and backed up his appreciation of the situation, rather than the views of the older, more orthodox, Rundstedt.

General Heinz Guderian, who in 1943 had been made Inspector-General of Armour, now entered the ring. He, like Rommel, had personal contact with Hitler, and he argued that to commit his precious panzers to the beaches was far too dangerous; he said that, in the event of a landing elsewhere, they could not be withdrawn to meet any new threat which might come across the channel.

Hitler, however, apparently stood firm in his support of Rommel, but he must have wavered a little because he went on to suggest to Guderian that he should go back and talk the matter out with Rommel himself; a course which seemed to suggest the first doubts in Hitler's mind as to whether Rommel was, in fact, right. It seems probable that the little man must have been in a rather testy mood and probably beginning to have doubts about the whole future of his thousand-year Reich as well, because, according to Guderian, Hitler had flown completely off the handle when he, Guderian, had suggested strengthening the very inadequate Atlantic wall coast defences.

When Guderian went to Rommel he took with him General Geyr von Schweppenburg, who was now commanding the panzer group in France, to back him up. Rommel evidently refused to budge an inch from the dispositions he proposed to make and it was at this point that he sent a signal to Hitler at Rastenburg, reinforcing his previous views that the panzer divisions should be deployed behind the Normandy beaches and repudiated Guderian's idea of keeping the armoured reserve near Paris. He stressed the point that the vast air superiority of the enemy would make the rapid movement of the armour impossible.

This was the vital clue we wanted. We knew, of course, from the usual 'inventory' returns over the previous months, what the panzer reserve consisted of and where it was located; now for the first time we learned that there was a possibility it would be moved towards the Overlord assault areas, that is if Rommel had his way. The vital requirement of the Allies, apart from the smooth operation of Overlord across the channel, was to attain as much surprise as possible as to the time and the precise place of assault and somehow keep the German infantry divisions stationed opposite the Pas de Calais and the panzer divisions near Paris. Unfortunately, we did not get the signal giving Hitler's reply to Rommel—he was evidently back in Berlin—but we now knew what to look out for and every signal dealing with these infantry and panzer divisions was scanned for any sign of them moving, or making any preparations to move westward.

Just how far the creation and carrying out of the brilliant deception plan of Patton's phantom army in Kent, opposite the Pas de Calais, was responsible for reinforcing Rundstedt's views and adding to Hitler's doubts, is still hard to tell. German Intelligence must have picked up and analysed the vast amount of bogus wireless traffic that went on in the phantom army area. General Patton himself was constantly in evidence, along with his white bull-terrier, in and around the area of the hutted encampment, which was manned by a skeleton staff of US soldiers. And the whole deception plan was well backed up by the German double agents, which we were now operating from Britain. Anyway, in the face of the two schools of thought, Hitler wavered.

Finally, in May, Schweppenburg himself personally appealed to Hitler to allow him to retain the bulk of his panzer reserves near Paris.

The result was a compromise, and in May we at last picked up a signal to Rundstedt from Hitler which confirmed that the four panzer divisions, which constituted the reserve, would be held where they were, as an assault force, under the direct control of the OKW. This, of course, was the plum we had been waiting for; had the final decision gone the other way it would have seriously jeopardized the chances of success of operation Overlord as it then stood. There continued to be no signs of a move by any of the infantry divisions of the Fifteenth Army from the Pas de Calais area.

After this bit of information it was not surprising that I found Tedder puffing his pipe contentedly as he looked out of his office window and watched the United States buglers sounding the Retreat as 'Old Glory' was carefully lowered and folded. Maybe the Swastika was also being lowered at La Roche Guyon, where a finally disillusioned Rommel waited and wondered about the fallibility of Fuehrers.

Rommel had lost control of the main armoured force, and he never had control of the coast batteries which belonged to the German Navy along with a few odd destroyers and motor boats which seldom put to sea; his air force—Luftflotte 3—we knew was down to about fifty operational aircraft. Both General Sperrle, commanding the Luftflotte, and the Fliegerkorps commander whose two fighter squadrons, in fact, made up the whole air fleet, eventually gave up asking for more aeroplanes; none ever arrived in reply to Sperrle's signals. In desperate uncertainty, Hitler had fallen back on the orthodox views of the older general.

On the Eastern front the situation reports by the German commanders showed the relentless Russian pressure now pushing the German armies back. Kesselring, in Italy, after a masterly defence over the winter, was falling back northward from Cassino. As one watched the signals going into the OKW, one wondered how much the faithful Generals Keitel and Jodl were, in fact, telling their Fuehrer. Nevertheless, Hitler was now, too late, taking more interest in the defence of Normandy and, for the first time, we found the word fear appearing in his signals to Rommel. From OKW came Hitler's fear that 'the Allies might not be able to be held on the beaches'. Little comfort for the man who had been stripped of his tanks. There was, too, a subtle change from the positive decisions by Hitler of earlier times. Perhaps he was already entering that state of fantasy which must have become his defence mechanism against his journey to Valhalla. His signal to Rundstedt confirmed his 'fear that after all the landing might come at the Pas de Calais' and justified his decision to keep the armoured reserve near Paris.

One simply could not help feeling sorry for Erwin Rommel during those weeks before Overlord. It was just like old times in the western desert, but instead of the signals demanding fuel and spare parts, they now demanded men, concrete, steel, trucks and the authority to plan his defence of Normandy his own way. At one point he asked to be allowed to employ the Luftwaffe as troops, who presumably had little else to do, but Goering, already discredited by the Army, and his Air Force in shreds, had retired to his lush living at Karinhall, and flatly refused to let his idle Luftwaffe ground troops lend a hand, or to relinquish any control over the anti-aircraft batteries. We were beginning to get a picture of Rommel, frustrated and disillusioned and without hope of being able to repulse the Allies' attack, but those who had had some experience of him in North Africa were very well aware of his ability to produce a tough nut out of an, apparently, empty hat. Montgomery knew quite well that with the troops Rommel had at his disposal he would not be as soft a touch as he was making out to the German Army General Staff.

The lack of support for Rommel from Berlin did, however, engender some speculation as to the German Army's politics. There were those who argued that some of the generals would much prefer a rapid advance by the Allies to Berlin and any sort of peace, rather than have Germany over-run by the Russians, but Hitler still lived and I, for one, was quite sure he meant what he said when he talked about 'no surrender'.

The end of May once again emphasized the negative role of Ultra, in so far as Overlord was concerned. Every signal was scanned for clues of any change in the strength and location of the German units and formations, or any indication that the enemy knew the timing and exact location of our landing beaches. There was nothing. Fortunately, the RAF screen was so tight that no Luftwaffe planes dared to cross the channel and the German spy network in Britain was working for us, the story which has now been given in Sir John Masterman's book, *Double Cross System of the War of 1939–45*. Nevertheless, those first few days of June 1944 were about the tensest I have ever known.

German signal traffic was normal; there did not appear to be any real jitters amongst the high command. The Italian campaign was now progressing rapidly, but Winston Churchill's mind was on Overlord and, from such neat red-ink comments as came back on the Ultra signals from No. 10, I gathered he was well satisfied with the negative news.

Eisenhower moved his headquarters to the south coast, not far from Admiral Ramsay's naval headquarters at Portsmouth. The tall gates in the high wall, which opened on to the park surrounding an old country house, gave no indication that this was the vital supreme headquarters of the whole affair.

Montgomery was here, too, with his staff, and Bill Williams, his Chief Intelligence Officer, remarked to me that it was rather like old times with Rommel just across the water, instead of just across the desert. I found both the SHAEF and Montgomery's SLU in good order and they were fully operational. Compared with Whitehall, here a terrific atmosphere of coming adventure had replaced the tensions of the past three months of endless planning and logistical build-up. Tedder was relaxed as usual as we discussed, once again, the possibilities of the OKW continuing to believe in the Pas de Calais assault for long enough. I expressed the view that Hitler seemed to be losing a bit of his grip and as long as he continued to believe he was God's gift to the Army, all would be well. The roads between London and Portsmouth were well-nigh impassable, with mile after mile of tanks, transport, stockpiles of shells and stores, big guns and little guns. It was the same all over the south of England, as I paid a last-minute visit to the SLUs with the other commands. Where one could see any country, through the vast camouflaged parks of equipment, the summer lay lazily on our green and pleasant land. Then in the first days of June came the tempest.

CHAPTER FIFTEEN

The Battle of Normandy

We had tackled the 'soft' underbelly of the Axis; now we were about to crack the hard shell.

My direct contact with Tedder in no way cut across the work of Brigadier Strong and his American colleagues who formed the SHAEF Intelligence unit. They had a large staff dealing with every type of intelligence, of which Ultra admittedly was the king-pin, but Tedder was more anxious to get my overall impressions. Just as in the days when I had been in close contact with the top Nazis, the Chief of the Air Staff had been much more interested in my general impressions than in the items which went to make them.

I suppose that living with the German high command signals as I was now doing, coupled with my personal knowledge of Hitler, who obviously dictated most of them, helped me to sense what they were up to.

The appalling weather on those first days of June put everybodys' nerves on edge; we knew that the ships and the men were already on the move, and the risk of leakage and detection must increase with every hour's delay. I had a call from Tedder on the fifth asking me to go down to Portsmouth to see him, and before leaving I scanned every available signal for the slightest clue as to whether there was any alert the other side of the Channel. I could find nothing. We now know that Rommel and his army commanders firmly believed the

assault on Normandy was imminent; but they thought
no one would attempt the invasion with the high seas
and winds which prevailed on the fourth of June. Rommel had, in fact, gone back to Germany. I got down to
Portsmouth early in the afternoon and I found that the
conference which was to decide 'Yes' or 'No' had been
held early that morning in Eisenhower's room on the
ground floor of the old manor house. I was told that
Tedder was in with the Supreme Commander but
would probably be out soon. So I waited in the big hall
at the foot of the main staircase. He came out; he was
in a hurry. I only had time to get his nod and a quick
'Tomorrow', and for my part I shook my head and
gave him the brief message—'Absolutely nothing'. He
smiled and took the stairs two at a time. As I left the
Portsmouth area and came up the Winchester by-pass,
the lines of tanks were getting on the move towards the
coast. The wind was still blowing; it would be a rough
ride tomorrow.

I gave instructions to be called at midnight.

It was somewhere around 2 a.m., on D-Day, June
the sixth, that the first signal came through from the
German naval headquarters in Paris. It was addressed
to both the C-in-C West and to Hitler at his headquarters at Rastenburg in East Prussia. It stated simply that
the invasion had commenced. It was not until after the
war that we heard how both Rundstedt and the OKW
had refused to believe the story. Rundstedt is reputed
to have told the Navy that they had seen a flock of
sea-gulls on their radar. Nevertheless, still believing in
the short sea route invasion, he alerted the Fifteenth
Army in the Pas de Calais. His signal was an absolute
godsend to us all at that moment, especially as he evidently did not think it worth while alerting the Seventh
Army in Normandy. He seemed determined to believe
that the parachute troops, now being reported back to

him by the Seventh Army, were, in fact, a bluff. It was dawn before Rundstedt's chief of staff, General Guenther Blumentritt, sent a signal direct to the OKW advising them of the urgency of the situation and at the same time asking Hitler's permission to employ the OKW panzer reserve. There was no signal so far from Rommel, which puzzled us, and it was not until later in the morning that we picked up a signal from Rommel to his chief of staff, General Speidel, ordering him to use the 21st Panzer Division against the Allied landings west of Caen. The signal came from Germany and showed that Rommel was not on the spot in Normandy. It also explained why Blumentritt had sent the signals to the OKW, because there is little doubt that had Rommel been in Normandy he would have himself appealed direct to Hitler for the release of the panzer reserve. We guessed that Speidel had managed to contact Rommel by telephone. Hence the latter's signal.

It was essential at this critical time to watch every move by Rundstedt, Rommel and Hitler and to analyse their thinking behind the orders they were sending out. These then were the signals which I sent over to the Prime Minister on D-Day morning. There was, as yet, nothing from Hitler.

One cause was, as we know, that Hitler was asleep and Keitel and Jodl had not dared to wake him up until well into the afternoon. Under the circumstances it was not surprising that it wasn't until the evening of the sixth that we picked up a signal from Hitler releasing to Rundstedt the 12th Panzer Division from the OKW reserve. But it was already too late. Rommel's plan to defeat the landings had been to meet them with tanks at the water's edge. By evening the Allies were well ashore and, in any case, the 12th Panzer Division did not dare move until dusk, with the sky full of Allied aircraft. Nevertheless, this was the first sign that Hitler was taking the matter seriously. Late that night Rommel signalled his situation report to the OKW that 'the British advance on Caen had been halted and that the 21st and 12th SS Panzer Divisions were in position west of the town from the north round to a point some seven miles to the south-west'. The 12th SS Division had made remarkable speed as soon as dusk fell.

Churchill was obviously getting Montgomery's reports on the progress of the operation. He was a little puzzled at the lack of reaction from Hitler, and his secretary phoned me midday to ask if there was anything new. I didn't, of course, know at that time that Hitler was asleep, so there was little I could do until the signal giving Hitler's orders to Rundstedt came in late in the afternoon.

After the tremendous effort of the actual landings, the tough resistance put up by the enemy in defence of the town of Caen made it eveident on June the seventh that the British were held to the west of this important objective. This was confirmed in a signal from Rommel in which he also advised the OKW that he had ordered the withdrawal, from Brittany, of a motorized and an infantry division together with the XI Parachute Corps to try and hold the Americans on the Cotentin peninsula.

Rundstedt must have stretched Hitler's orders releasing the 12th SS Panzer division because we picked up a signal from him ordering another of the reserve panzer divisions—the Panzer Lehr—to move to the Caen area in addition to the 12th SS Division.

With this strong reinforcement, Rundstedt evidently considered that Rommel had now got enough armour to mount an operation against the Allies, because on June the ninth he signalled to Rommel to counter-attack. But the armoured reserve which had been subject to so much argument must have been caught napping, because in a signal back to Rundstedt and the OKW, on the ninth, Rommel summed up the situation as follows: 'The 12th SS Panzer Division has arrived short of fuel and the Panzer Lehr Division is quite unready for action. Under the circumstances no immediate dislodgement of the enemy is possible and a return to the defensive on the Vire-Orne front is necessary until preparations for a counter attack are complete'.

This was an important signal which gave Miles Dempsey of the British Second Army a short and welcome breather.

'Monty' went over to Normandy on the tenth and soon realized the unlikely chances of the British and Canadians being able to take Caen in face of the mounting German panzer forces revealed by Ultra, and it was at this point that he changed the original plan and, instead of trying to complete the capture of Caen, decided to pin down as many of the main enemy armoured forces as possible, in order to give Bradley's First Army a chance to try and break out to the south against less heavily armed resistance. A British thrust by the 7th Armoured Division towards Caen on the tenth drew the German armour into the open and the Panzer Lehr Division was reported by Rommel on the night of the thirteenth as having 'lost 100 tanks and as now being unable to thrust towards the sea'. So Montgomery's strategy was working. The losses were serious for the Germans as their tanks could not be replaced, at least for some time, whereas the 7th Armoured Division's loss of only twenty-five tanks could be made good immediately.

Meantime, on the thirteenth, Bradley's forces had secured the important little town of Casteau at the eastern base of the Cherbourg peninsula, with its main road and railway connections. Rommel signalled the loss to the OKW on the fourteenth, but at the same time he reported: 'I am satisfied at the moment that the American landing at the East of Vierville [Omaha beach] is only making slow progress and the Caen front is now held.' We were to learn after the war that three days later, on the seventeenth, Hitler himself came to Soissons in France for a personal conference with Rundstedt and Rommel. At the time we knew nothing about it but we got the result next day when Hitler signalled his orders to Rundstedt to attack Bayeux and also signalled the garrison commander at Cherbourg that 'the port must be held at all costs'. But the American VIII Corps pushed right across the peninsula to the western coast, cutting off Cherbourg and the northern half of the Cotentin. Rommel had to signal the news to the OKW on the eighteenth and to admit the almost total loss of his 91st and 77th Divisions.

Now Ultra had shown us that Hitler himself was directing main strategy, and as the Americans started closing in on Cherbourg, Hitler sent a personal signal to General Schlieben, commanding the garrison, saying: 'Even if the worst comes to the worst, it is your duty to defend the last bunker and leave the enemy not a harbour but a heap of ruins. German people and the whole world are watching your fight; on it depends the conduct and result of operations to smash the Allied beachhead and the honour of the German Army and of your own name'.

All that poor Schlieben could do was to signal to Hitler; 'In view of the great superiority of the enemy in aircraft, tanks, and artillery and now finally the naval bombardment, I must state in the line of duty that further sacrifices can alter nothing.' The poor man must have been desperate.

Rommel's reply was short: 'You will continue to fight to the last cartridge in accordance with the orders

of the Fuehrer.' One felt that if Rommel hadn't had the
Fuehrer breathing down his neck, he would have given
Schlieben some leeway, but in the light of later events
Rommel must have been taking every care to avoid any
suspicion of disloyalty to Hitler. Despite all that was
happening, the Fuehrer was still omnipotent.

Around Caen, Ultra told us that the three German
armoured divisions were now in full working order,
even if a bit short of tanks, and that two further armoured divisions, the 9th and 10th, were on their way
from the Russian front to the Caen area.

The fact that Hitler was bringing armour from the
hard-pressed Eastern Front to Normandy meant he was
now determined to stop us from a break-out in the
West. It was bad news, but it was soon to be followed
by a further signal from OKW to Rundstedt and
Rommel, stating that the 1st SS Panzer Division was
coming across from Belgium, and the 2nd SS Panzer
Division was coming up from Toulouse to the St Lo
area on the American sector.

This might seriously affect Bradley's chances of a
break-out, and Montgomery decided to do something.
Dempsey attacked; the Scottish 15th Division made
such progress that General Paul Hausser, who commanded the German Seventh Army, relayed a signal to
Rommel from General Sepp Dietrich, who commanded
the I Panzer SS Corps, saying that unless reinforcements were sent to him that night there would be an
Allied breakthrough. We had obviously frightened
them more than we had thought. Rommel, who was all
this time trying to get together a force to carry out Hitler's orders for an attack on Bayeux, with some reluct-
ance signalled Seventh Army to use the 9th and 10th
and the 1st SS Panzer Division to help Dietrich. More
importantly, he was to 'bring back part of the 2nd SS

Panzer Division' which was at the time facing Bradley
at St Lo. Ultra had worked again, showing Dempsey
precisely the weak spot to go for.

By June the twenty-seventh, the British Second
Army's thrust had made further gains, but evidently
both Rundstedt and Rommel were away in Berchtesgaden, because the commander of Seventh Army sent
his situation report to them there that night. In his signal he expressed his intention of mounting a counter-
attack at 7 a.m. on the twenty-ninth on the salient created by the British thrust. So well was the Oracle working that this signal reached all commanders in good
time for the 2nd Tactical Air Force to be alerted, and
just before 7 a.m. they found their targets to such good
effect that Hausser later reported to Rommel that 'as
soon as the tanks had assembled they were attacked by
fighter-bombers, and were so disrupted that the attack
had to be put off for some seven hours'. Here was Ultra at its best in actual battle. The Navy also had a go
with their big guns and, as a result, both sides eventually withdrew when the operation was finally halted. But
once again the British thrust had done its job of holding
the panzers.

After the war we learned that around the last week
in June Rundstedt, Rommel, Hausser, and Geyr von
Schweppenburg had got together and agreed that they
would ask Hitler's permission for a phased withdrawal
from Caen in order to put their divisions out of range
of our naval guns. They had also decided to ask for
reinforcements to be sent from the Fifteenth Army,
which was still sitting around in the Pas de Calais area,
awaiting Patton's phantom attack. As a result of this
meeting, Rundstedt and Rommel had gone to see Hitler
at Berchtesgaden to put their case. They no doubt
stressed the fact that both Hausser and Schweppenburg
were in full agreement with them. Safety in numbers

when suggesting withdrawal would not have escaped them, and it was interesting to see the careful Rommel, who would normally have been expected to ask Hitler direct, taking shelter with the other three principals of the Normandy scene. Even so, it was no go. Hitler, evidently still afraid of another landing in the Pas de Calais, flatly refused and told them that 'mobile warfare must not be allowed to develop'. None of this was known to us at the time, but the day after Rundstedt got back from Berchtesgaden with Rommel, Hitler—as was his custom—sent a signal to Rundstedt confirming his decision and stating: 'Present positions are to be held.' It was Ultra's first indication that Rundstedt and Rommel had seen the red light and wanted to withdraw.

It was not until after the war that we also learned the story of how Rundstedt had eventually phoned Keitel and told him that it would be impossible to carry out Hitler's orders to attack Bayeux. The conversation is now well known. Keitel is reported to have said: 'What shall we do?' 'What shall we do?' Rundstedt replied. 'Make peace you fools; what else can you do!' The next day Rundstedt was relieved of his command. The first indication we had over Ultra that Rundstedt had gone was a signal by Field Marshal Kluge as C-in-C West. His first signal had promptly repeated Hitler's 'Present positions to be held' order to all commands.

It was just as all this upheaval in the German command was going on that I decided to go over and see if all was well with the SLU system and security. Bradley was making little progress and, for the moment, the Allies seemed to be stuck. Montgomery was coming under some strong criticism from SHAEF and although he never admitted the existence of Ultra, I didn't want any come-back against Ultra from either of them. In this respect, Churchill was an excellent barrier against any excuse of poor Intelligence by a commander in the field.

It was just over three weeks since D-Day; Omaha beach itself was tidy once more, and just inland the airstrip was alive with the ubiquitous Dakotas. Robert Gore-Brown had somewhere acquired a jeep and he met me. We made for Bradley's HQ, a few miles westward along the coastal road, and drew up by the side of the road opposite a hole in the hedge. From here onwards it was on foot only.

We scrambled up a muddy bank, through the hedge, along a muddy path at the side of a small meadow, through another hedge and there, ranged in a semi-circle around the seaward edge of a small wood, was the caravanserai of the United States First Army Commander. It looked for all the world like a village green. The SLU had made themselves comfortable in tents under some apple trees; it might have been a camping holiday in a peaceful corner of Devon except for an occasional boom of gunfire some way to the south, where Bradley's army was inching its way through the difficult Bocage country.

Monk Dickson, Bradley's G2, had warned me that his chief was depressed over the inability of the First Army to make headway. Nevertheless, as I went up the steps of his outsize caravan into his workmanlike office, the general greeted me with his customary courtesy. He paid tribute to Ultra which was good to hear. 'Never,' he said, 'did I expect to get such concise information about my opponents, the only trouble is that there seems to be too many of them.'

He was lucky in one way, he said, in that most of the panzers were up around the British sector, but his boys were finding the Paratroop Corps tough fighters, and they were contending every hedgerow—and there were plenty. Was there any indication that any panzers were coming this way? I told him that Ultra was still showing them concentrated around Caen, and I knew Montgomery was doing his best to hold them there. We talked of Rundstedt's replacement by von Kluge. I could not tell him much about the new German commander but I did point out to him that Rundstedt's removal, coupled with Hitler's order to hold the present position, and von Kluge's repetition of the order to his armies, must surely mean that Rundstedt had seen the red light and wanted to withdraw; it seemed to cheer him up.

As I left he said: 'Just see that no more of those panzer boys get around here.' Monk Dickson and I left to get down to the job of analysing the latest signals.

The grass was still a bit soggy from the recent rain as we walked across in the sunshine to Monk's own smaller caravan, which was next to the one provided for visitors. I had expected a ground sheet in one of the SLU tents, but now I had been given a comfortable berth in the VIP Department. We talked the whole afternoon and I explained to him how to read between the lines of Rommel's and Hitler's signals and how to insist on SHAEF keeping him up to date with the full details of strength of men and equipment of the enemy divisions; details were purposely not sent to him direct, partly because we did not want to overload both the SLU and the G2, but also because once the Ultra information was incorporated in the order of battle its particular identity was camouflaged and, although still classified as top secret, did not have the same restricted circulation as Ultra.

This procedure also gave access to the order of battle to all the planners who were not necessarily in the Ultra picture.

I helped Monk to annotate the more important signals for Bradley in the same way as I did to Churchill, and we did a few exercises in paraphrasing the signals in the form of orders for onward transmission to corps and divisions. In fact I learned as much from him about the difficulties of a G2 trying to get the best out of Ultra as I think I taught him.

It was a much more cheerful Monk who invited me to take the ample meal in the officers' mess tent.

I spent the evening with the SLU under the apple trees. They were on top of their form enjoying every minute of their job.

I woke up the next morning to find a considerable stir in the caravanserai. I had left the top half of my caravan door open and now, as I leapt out of bed and looked out, I saw half-dressed officers moving rapidly about the village green, even Bradley himself was hurrying back from the far corner of the wood. I called to Monk Dickson in the caravan next door. He was himself trying to do a quick shave. I asked if the enemy had broken through and whether we were about to evacuate. His half-shaven face appeared over his caravan door with the news that Montgomery was coming over at eight o'clock to see Bradley. I don't know whether Montgomery was trying to impress on Bradley, as he had done on Winston Churchill, the importance of his keep fit campaign. Perhaps Bradley hadn't realized that this early bird business was just part of it. However, it was not going to be a scramble to get some breakfast before the familiar figure of the C-in-C arrived. I don't know whether it was the first time that they had met in conference since Montgomery had set up his headquarters in France, but it was certainly causing a bit of a kerfuffle.

Later, I found Monk Dickson thoughtful, as also was Bradley, but now there was a glint in his eye, and as if to stress the necessity for action, we received through the SLU—while I was there—confirmation of the arrival of the two panzer divisions from Russia into the Caen area. This was evidence enough of the tough job that Montgomery had taken on, as was also the earlier signal telling us of the transfer of part of the 2nd SS Panzer Division away from St Lo to Caen.

It was around midday that I saw Patton on 'the village green', complete with his white bull-terrier. There was a cheery greeting and he explained with a broad grin that he just couldn't bear sitting around any longer, so he had just flown in. Patton, of course, was still supposed to be commanding his phantom army in Kent, ready to make the phantom dash across the channel to Calais. The whole essence of this deception plan was that Patton should constantly be seen at his phantom HQ as long as possible. Just one photograph of him in France published in the Press might blow the gaff. Monk Dickson acted with some speed. He summoned all the members of the American Press to attend a press conference immediately and asked me to go along. All the press men came hurrying in, thinking, I imagine, that they were going to get some news of Montgomery's visit. It was, however, the shortest, sharpest press conference I have ever attended. 'Gentlemen,' said Monk, 'I don't know whether any of you have seen what you took to be General Patton around here with his dog. You were mistaken. Good morning.' After that all was well. Patton and Bradley emerged from the caravan and strolled off through another gap in the hedge to the general's private mess tent.

That afternoon I went in search of Major-General Quesada, commanding the Ninth US Tactical Air Force. I had put an American officer in charge of the SLU here, with the usual complement of RAF cypher sergeants and W/T personnel. Quesada himself was tickled to death with Ultra, especially the movement orders which gave him ready-made targets without having

to search for them, and woe betide any German tank or
transport that put its nose out from under a hedge or
wood in daylight. Quesada had devised a brilliant system of communication between his aircraft and the US
tanks which worked in practice much the same way as
the dive-bombers had done for the German tanks in the
Battle of France in 1940. I found the US Air Force
lads boisterous with good spirits. They knew that the
hedgerow battle must soon come to an end and then
their chance would come in open country. Quesada
suggested I stop the night. There was a bunk-bed in a
wooden hut. There had been air sorties right up to
dusk, and at first light next morning the fighter-bombers were off again. I was back in another part of
France in 1917, lying in my own bunk in another
wooden hut listening to B flight take off on a dawn patrol over the other side of Arras.

I don't know whether it was the smell of hot oil, of
the noise of the aircarft revving up, or just the whole
atmosphere of the Normandy front, but somehow it
gave a new flavour to the paper work I had to do in my
London office, just as my visits to Biggin Hill had done
in the Battle of Britain. I understood why Churchill
wanted, from time to time, to get nearer the fighting.

Back along the muddy tracks between the battered
hedgerows to the main road and I had left the TAC behind.

Some of the farmers and their families were coming
to life again and drifting back to their homes, such as
they were. There was little livestock about that had escaped the shells and bullets of the past three weeks. On
the sides of the roads near the little villages were piles
of decaying grey-green camembert cheeses. They were
hard and useless.

The ancient town of Bayeux was almost back to normal. Goodness knows what would have happened to it

if the offensive that Hitler had ordered Rundstedt to carry out had come off. I found time to look at the famous tapestries before going to Montgomery's headquarters, a vast tent covered all over by an even vaster camouflage net. It was pitched on the gentle western slope of a small hill. Some two hundred yards away, right on the top of the rise, was a neat row of brown bell tents for visitors and a small mess tent of the same colour. The overcooked cold beef and salad did little for me when I thought of the corn beef hash at the American units. Nevertheless, whoever ran the catering had bought some Normandy butter. Montgomery himself was not available. I'd already got used to the formula, but as I only wanted to check up with Bill Williams that he was fully satisfied and that the SLU had no complaints on security matters, it was just as well. The latter, poor chaps, on instructions from the C-in-C himself, had been banished to a solitary spot in a little quarry some half a mile away. It meant a long walk at night. I complained to Major-General Graham—the G3—but apparently the C-in-C was adamant. His excuse was that he feared that the enemy might get a bearing on the W/T. As we used very short-wave transmissions and the acknowledgement signals from the SLU were equally short and at different times each day, and since no enemy, either in North Africa or Italy, for the past two years had shown any interest in the whereabouts of our SLUs, I was forced to the conclusion that it was the presence of RAF personnel concerned with Intelligence which for some reason the general did not like. However, Williams was as enthusiastic as ever. We had, after all, given him very full information about the opposition and also the main enemy intentions ever since D-Day, and now the numbers and strengths of the panzer units, even if unpleasant reading, were pretty accurate accounting. The SLU had to grin and bear it. I asked Graham to try and look after them a little better when the HQ moved. Both he and Major-General Freddie De Guingand, the chief of staff, knew full well the value of what we were giving them, but maybe it was Montgomery's knowledge that both Churchill and Eisenhower, who were breathing down his neck at the time, were getting it too that irked him.

It was Graham who thoughtfully came out to my tent next afternoon and told me that if I cared to look skywards in a few minutes I would see the strategic bombing of the Caen defences by RAF Bomber Command. As I stood outside my tent on the top of that little hill in Normandy, I watched four hundred and fifty Lancasters, black against the evening sky, their deep drone rising to a roaring crescendo as they swept overhead. Then came the thunderous roar of their bombs on the dug-in tanks of the defences of Caen. The earth trembled, even though we were some miles away. I had warned the SLU, who came over to watch with me. I thought a posse of RAF in the visitors' lines, where all the headquarters staff had also come to watch at that moment, might do them all a bit of good.

Dempsey's tent at his Second Army Headquarters was a much smaller affair than Montgomery's, nor had it got a camouflage net. It was pitched in a warm, sheltered, grassed-over quarry. Here the SLU was only some fifty yards away and they were well looked after on Dempsey's own orders. He gave me a warm welcome and told me he was completely sold on Ultra and had no idea, when the show started, that he would be kept so completely in the picture about the German intentions. He asked how Bradley was bearing up, and was evidently aware of the frustrating sort of war he was having to fight; so totally different, as he put it, from the rough, tough, fighting on the plain around Caen that his men were engaged in. He, too, wanted to know if I knew anything about von Kluge, but alas I had never met him before the war. His record both in France in 1940 and later in Russia had been good. I also told Dempsey what I had told Bradley. Miles Dempsey would obviously make the best use of what we sent him, as he had already done.

Near Bayeux, I found a little shop which was selling large, round and nicely ripe Port Salut cheese, so I collected a couple on the way to the air-strip and put them under the seat in the aircraft, together with some Normandy butter. The smell caused some consternation amongst some of my fellow passengers.

Von Kluge turned out to be a methodical general. When he took over from Rundstedt he had a good look at the various formations under his command; he listed them carefully and sent the inventory back to the OKW and the Army HQ in Berlin. His signal, which we were able to pick up, was particularly valuable since it not only put us right up to date as regards the actual strength of the various units, but also gave us a pretty good idea of the German losses. He had probably been warned by Rommel that Hitler had a habit of ordering attacks by non-existent or non-operational units, so it was as well to start off on the right foot. This valuable check-up of Kluge's command, as C-in-C West at the beginning of July, showed that it now included the Army Group in Southern France as well as Rommel's Army Group B in Normandy, and that in Rommel's command, the Fifth Panzer Army had no less than nine panzer divisions around Caen. The Seventh Army facing the Americans was made up of II Parachute Corps at St Lo, and LXXXIV Corps in the south of the

Cherbourg peninsula. But the real value of Kluge's signal was that it showed the Fifth Panzer Army had even fewer serviceable tanks than we had estimated.

It was against II Parachute Corps, that Bradley's efforts to reach St Lo had been brought to a temporary standstill. Now it was vital to take the town, and its cross-roads, as a jump off for the coming break-out operation Cobra, before any panzer division came west again. Bradley renewed the attack on the tenth and the capture of the town was finally accomplished on July the seventeenth. Only then did II Parachute Corps request to be allowed to retire. We picked up the signal as it was being sent by Seventh Army Commander to Rommel at Army Group B, and we were puzzled when there was no reply. We had been expecting the usual uncompromising no withdrawal order from Rommel. The Parachute Corps however, did withdraw, but it was only very much later that the full story came out as to what had happened after receipt of Hausser's signal. Instead of the request going right back to Hitler for approval as it should have done, Army Group B chief of staff telephoned back to Seventh Army at once and told Hausser to take whatever measures he thought best, which must have surprised the general somewhat. It turned out there was considerable confusion at Army Group B and little wonder. The first indication that we got on Ultra that something had happened to Rommel was when we got Kluge's signal to all units that he had assumed command of Army Group B. The story of how Rommel's car had been shot up by an Allied aircraft and Rommel thrown out came through to us a few days later from the French Resistance, though at first they reported him dead. It was like suddenly losing a pen pal. We had lived with this irrepressible young general ever since the first clash with his tanks in May 1940 in France, when I think for the first and last time he had panicked. We had got to know all his little quirks during the western desert campaign; we had watched his bumptious audacity turn to acid disillusionment as he retreated back to Tunisia after Alamein, and finally went back to Berlin in a huff after his tiff with Kesselring. We met him again in November 1943 and we watched him through his battle with the OKW for the right to fight the invasion in his own way—a way that might well have been disastrous to our Overlord Operation—and now the poor chap was out of it all. He would never know how useful he had been to us with his direct access to Hitler. We should miss those signals badly. The story of his secret implication in the bomb plot of July the twentieth and his subsquent forced suicide are now well known. I should like to have met him just to see if my picture of him was quite correct. Runstedt, who had also vanished from the scene, had been thankfully and utterly predictable; a soldier, typical of those generals of that close-knit German institution—the Officer Corps, he had learned his business strictly according to the textbook.

It is, I think, difficult for those who have not been involved in a world war to understand how every facet of the enemy's behaviour becomes a matter of vital interest. For those of us who were watching the enemy through Ultra, the removal of a general, the discomfiture of his army commanders, his difficulties in replacing his losses, the no withdrawal and 'fight to the last cartridge' orders of the Fuehrer, all were to us of the greatest importance in assessing the enemy's potential and morale, and the difference between World War II and other wars was that now we knew. But we had yet to learn about von Kluge.

As Bradley was at last moving into St Lo, Montgomery was again set the task of bringing pressure on Caen to keep the Panzers away from the Americans, for now the planned break-out by the United States First Army was possible. The attacks by the British and Canadians were so successful that by July the eighteenth the whole of Caen was cleared of the enemy. And to confirm how successful Montgomery's whole strategy had been, signals came in showing that the two SS Panzer Divisions the 11th and the 12th, which had come from Poland and had evidently been allotted to the Seventh Army facing Bradley, were now ordered to be kept at Caen. This meant that there were still nine armoured divisions facing the British and Canadians. Admittedly they were not up to strength, but it was a formidable force of armour.

Perhaps at this critical phase of the war I should remind the reader that, unless I have stated otherwise, all the enemy signals referred to in this book were read by us, more often within minutes of their origin and duly distributed to the Commands.

CHAPTER SIXTEEN

Hitler's Miracles

The attempt on Hitler's life at Rastenburg was announced over the ordinary wireless on that fateful twentieth of July. It was not surprising that the majority of German generals wanted Hitler dead. Barring one or two, they had seen the end of the Third Reich for some time. The Rastenburg bomb was only the logical conclusion of the deep-seated mistrust and antagonism between the Nazis and the generals.

I had seen the massive concrete base for Hitler's headquarters rising out of the sandy woodland soil of Rastenburg in 1938. In July 1944, it nearly became his tomb. His escape was heralded as a miracle. Maybe it helped him to regain his powers of decision which, as we have seen, were wavering a bit, for he was now ready to perform his own miracles of strategy, for which his hard-pressed armies in Normandy had been waiting.

Bradley's break-out Operation Cobra struck on July the twenty-fifth and that evening we picked up Kluge's signals to the OKW which told them that 'as from this moment the front has burst'. I phoned the signal over to the Prime Minister, who I knew would be waiting anxiously for news. He took the call himself and I heard a quiet grunt of satisfaction. On July the twenty-seventh, German resistance in the lower part of the Cherbourg peninsula was declining rapidly, and that evening Bradley was able to report to Eisenhower, 'that we are riding high tonight is putting it mildly'. Cobra was turning into a rout. It must have been a wonderful moment for Bradley. He had gone through an anxious time, as Monk said 'bogged down in the bloody bocage for seven weeks'. Now the village green must have been a hive of activity. As the Americans advanced, a large pocket of German troops on the left of the German line had been cut off and surrounded and General Hausser, commanding the German Seventh Army, ordered them to break out to the south-east. His signal which we did not get was evidently picked up by von Kluge and, fearing for his already disintegrating left flank, he promptly signalled orders countermanding Hausser's order for the break-out of the surrounded troops. It was this signal that showed us that not only was Kluge completely out of touch with the situation, but that at last we had got the German command off balance. On the strength of this Ultra signal, General Quesada's fighter-bombers had a field day, and only a few of the enemy who escaped the pocket were to get back to their comrades, with all their transport and equipment destroyed.

As the rout gathered momentum, it became quite evident that Kluge was unable to find out what was going on. His signals to Hausser's Seventh Army, demanding information, remained unanswered, but Hausser couldn't help much himself, and it was not until July the thirty-first that Kluge was finally able to signal to Hitler at OKW that the Americans had already occupied Avranches. They had, in fact, arrived the day before. Kluge's signal went on to admit that, apart from Avranches, the situation was completely unclear, that the Allied air activities were unprecedented, and that the Americans had ripped open the whole Western

Front. His signal must have ripped open the OKW front as well.

This was the sort of stuff we had waited so long to hear. There was no need now to headline the copies to Churchill. The German line had come completely unstuck, Brittany was at the mercy of the Americans, and the road to Paris looked wide open. At last George Patton's frustrating weeks of deluding Hitler from his empty camp in Kent were over and his Third Army became operational.

If one has been to Avranches, it is not difficult to grasp the importance of this old mediaeval town perched on the top of its tall circular hill dominating the vast area of country to north, south, east and west and now, as Patton's men and tanks streamed up and through that ancient fortress town with its well-laid-out little park, its cafés and shops around the broad square on the summit of the hill, some turned west into Brittany but most turned east towards the Seine.

George Patton's Army had originally been earmarked to clear up Brittany, but as he now turned east, he was scenting the open country and speed. At this moment Hitler, the infallible military genius, signalled Kluge that he had taken over command of the whole western theatre. From our experiences in North Africa and Italy, this signal was almost the best bit of news so far. His next signal was to the Todt organization (named after Dr Todt the Minister for War Production, who had been killed in an aircraft accident in 1942), the great concreters, who were building V1 and V2 launching fortresses in the Pas de Calais area, telling them to stop work and transfer their activities to defensive positions further inland. He then signalled orders to all the units in the west that 'if withdrawal was ordered, all railways, locomotives, bridges and work-

shops were to be destroyed and that the commanders of
the fortress ports were to fight to the last man to deny
the ports to the Allies'. To those of us who were unused
of late to this sort of decisive action by Hitler, the signals were a bit of a surprise. It looked as though he had
snapped out of his dreams and delusions and was getting down to real business.

Then on August the second, in a long signal, which I
remember covered two whole sheets of my Ultra paper,
Hitler told Kluge 'not to pay any attention to the
American break-out, which would be dealt with later'
followed by instructions in considerable detail, to col-
lect together four of the armoured divisions from the
Caen front with sufficient supporting infantry divisions
and make a decisive counter-attack to retake Avranches and thus to divide the American forces at the base of
the Cherbourg peninsula. He was then to roll the
American forces to the north of the armoured thrust
back to the sea. It was to be a repetition of his successful strategy in the 1940 Battle of France. Here then
was the master-plan straight from the Fuehrer, who
was now personally directing what was obviously going
to be the decisive battle of the war in the west. This
highly important signal arrived just as I was preparing
to go back to my club for some food. It had been an
exciting day after the anxiety of the past weeks. I knew
Churchill would want to see Hitler's signal right away
and I sent it over to him with a note to say I would
send over any follow-up material as it came in. Eisenhower, I knew, had established a close link with
Churchill through his own chief of staff, General Bedell Smith. It was, therefore, important that Churchill
should be ready to talk to Bedell Smith on the same
wavelength when any important strategical decisions
had to be made.

For Bradley everything was going well, and it was

just at this time that he got his command of the Twelfth
Army Group, and with it a new chief Intelligence
officer, General Sibert. I was very sorry he had lost
Monk Dickson at this critical moment. SHAEF was
still down at Portsmouth so Tedder took the rather unprecedented step of ringing me up and, as he put it, 'in
view of the extreme importance of Hitler's signal', asking if I would be quite certain that it was not a bluff.
Again he said that the substance was of such importance that Eisenhower didn't want to take any chances.
I phoned Hut 3 to make quite sure that the original
German version was in Hitler's own distinctive style
and language. They told me we had no reason to doubt
it on any score, and the signal had without doubt come
from Fuehrer headquarters. Tedder was satisfied.

The question which we were now all asking was how
long had we got to prepare for this blitzkrieg attack and
just where and when would it arrive? If we could have
two or three days it would give Patton time to get eastwards around the southern flank of the Germans and it
would also give Bradley time to prepare a defensive
stand near Avranches, because no one doubted the
thrust would be vicious. The German divisions had
been waiting for their Fuehrer's miracle and if, as they
thought, they could achieve surprise, the Fuehrer must
be right again. Surprise was the last thing he was going
to achieve.

Hitler may have snapped out of his indecision, but
Kluge must at once have seen the grave danger of this
miracle cure, for on the following day, luckily, the Oracle spoke again, and we saw he had the temerity to reply to Hitler in an equally long signal setting out all the
possible consequences of such a move. His action was a
surprise. 'Apart,' he said, 'from withdrawing the essential defensive armoured divisions from Caen, such an
attack, if not immediately successful, would lay open

the whole attacking force to be cut off in the west.' Now this, of course, was just what Eisenhower was thinking, and he had already warned Bradley to be ready to push Patton's Third Army swiftly eastwards so as to be able to move north behind the attacking force; only one corps was to be left behind to clear up in Brittany.

Now the vital question was who was going to win the argument, Hitler or Kluge? My money was on Hitler. This was once again his chance to show his doubting armies that he still remained a genius and to rekindle the Hitler myth. I felt sure he would insist; so did SHAEF. Bradley was told to make the necessary preparations to meet the attack with defence in depth in the Avranches area, whilst a warning was sent to Patton to make provision for turning a corps northwards from Le Mans. Would there be time? Excitement was mounting, not only in London, but in Washington too, everybody was waiting for the Oracle. Hitler didn't keep us waiting long. Next day another long signal came from him in which he had the courtesy to acknowledge Kluge's arguments, but now he said 'the situation demands bold action. The attack to split the American forces must be carried out'. Kluge must take the risk of temporarily withdrawing the panzer divisions from Caen. Thanks to Kluge's spirited arguments, we had already been given three days warning and Eisenhower, seeing this as a Hitler-sent opportunity, now prepared to change the whole plan of the broad frontal advance eastward across France, and seize the chance to encircle and destroy the bulk of the German armies in the west. It was a bizarre situation with Eisenhower and Ultra deciding the fate of the German armies with the help of Hitler.

Menzies told me that despite the signals from Hitler,

Montgomery was still in favour of an advance on a broad front to the Seine, but that Eisenhower's directive to him was to be ready to surround the German forces from the north with the Twenty-First Army Group, whilst the US Twelfth Army Group was to close in from the west and come up from the south. Montgomery was still officially Commander-in-Chief of Land Forces until Eisenhower could move SHAEF to France and take command of both Army Groups himself. Only then would Bradley and Montgomery be on equal terms, but the orders for the encircling movement now had to be issued by Montgomery's headquarters. However, the opportunity that had been offered to us was such that the decision to alter the entire strategy became one for Eisenhower himself, and I understand it had also to be approved by the joint Allied chiefs of staff.

Churchill was quite evidently elated and on one occasion, when I had to enlarge on a point in one of the signals on the telephone, his voice the other end sounded almost gay; he was getting Hitler's signals in London within an hour of Hitler despatching them. Hut 3 at Bletchley had risen to the occasion and, with a supreme effort, had provided the answers for several days running at record speed. There was little need for me to comment on them; Eisenhower himself went over to France, ostensibly on a visit to Bradley. We all waited. Meanwhile, the German forces east of Avranches were hanging on grimly, no doubt under orders to do so and to await reinforcements. But the stubborn Kluge wasn't finished yet, and on August the fifth he had one more try to dissuade Hitler. Churchill had gone to Chequers on August the fourth, so this was going to be a pretty busy weekend on the telephone for me. Everybody, from the Shadow OKW to the Prime Minister, was deeply involved in the Hitler-Kluge drama and I certainly wouldn't leave the office while it was being played out.

Kluge staked his whole career on trying to stop this attack. In his last signal he pulled no punches and boldly stated that it could only end in disaster. It was not hard to imagine the feelings of this courageous man; one could get a glimmer of his utter hopelessness from his signals. He must have known it was the end for him anyway. Back now, without even a comment, came the order from the Fuehrer to proceed. Kluge had now no alternative; Eisenhower, too, knew what to do.

When I was reading these last signals over the telephone to Churchill, I sensed his controlled excitement at the other end. I think we all felt that this might well be the beginning of the end of the war.

On August the sixth Montgomery duly issued the order swinging three Allied Armies, the British Second, the Canadian II Corps and the US First Army, into the flanks of the German forces, and for the US Third Army to pass them on the southern flank. On that same day, Kluge faithfully carried out the Fuehrer's orders. His tenacity in arguing the case with Hitler and our ability to read all the signals which passed between them had given us a vital four days. Lieutenant-General Guy Simonds, the Canadian Corps Commander, was already prepared for a jump-off to the south to capture Falaise, Dempsey moved south on Simonds' right, the First US Army (now commanded by General Hodges) began to move its northern corps south-east while at the same time preparing to meet Kluge's attack at Mortain just north of Avranches, and Patton started his famous right hook around the southern flank of the German armies.

For me, this was a testing time for Ultra's security. When I saw what was going to happen, I sent a signal

to all the SLUs concerned warning them to watch
'points' very carefully. I knew it was going to be a difficult job for the commanders to get the right orders to
their subordinate units without giving away the fact that
we knew just what the enemy were up to. This was especially the case in the setting up of the defensive position at Mortain, but I need not have worried. Bradley
had given careful instructions for defence in depth so
that the Germans in fact had a small initial success to
allay their suspicions, as it turned out their attack was
so vicious that it penetrated a bit further than expected.
Patton had been bound to inform General Haislip of
the source of the information, as it was his XV Corps
that was to turn north to meet the Canadians behind
the German armies. On the whole, security was quite
marvellous, considering the moves which had to be
made in a hurry.

I was awake at 5 a.m. on August the seventh, waiting for the first news of the assault. However here, for
the sake of continuity, I will try to put together in one
picture both the Allied and the German accounts of the
battle; the former I got from Monk Dickson some days
later. It was at first light that the 4th Panzer Division
roared through the forward American road blocks and
into the little town of Mortain. Their tremendous momentum took them forward seven miles beyond the
town and then the Allied aircraft started on them. Quesada's fighter bombers and the British Typhoons firing
their rockets must have played havoc with the unsuspecting panzers. They then ran into Bradley's massed
artillery. The German tanks were halted, their commanders bewildered; their tank losses were mounting so
rapidly that the panzers began to dig in feverishly
around mid-day. The terrific American artillery fire
must have aroused some suspicion that their attack was
no surprise, but this aspect never came out in any of

their signals. Most of the enemy went to ground and covered their tanks with camouflage nets, and only a few units actually penetrated the main American lines.

By the evening of the seventh, seven American divisions were ready and waiting to throw back the attackers. In the afternoon Kluge, who had obviously been in close contact with the battle, had to send his situation report signal back to OKW. It read, 'The attack has been brought to a standstill with the loss of over half the tanks.' He went on to say that he proposed to disengage his remaining forces at Mortain to cover the British strike towards Falaise. Hitler must have been more than a little cross.

As for poor Kluge, his only hope now was that he could again establish some sort of line east of Falaise preparatory to a general withdrawal, a course which he had already recommended to Hitler in his signals of the last two days. But no; the next signal we got straight back from Hitler read: 'I command the attack to be prosecuted daringly and recklessly to the sea, regardless of the risk.' He went on to instruct Kluge that far from reinforcing General Eberbach's remaining panzer group at Falaise he was to 'remove forces from Eberbach and commit them to the Avranches attack in order' as he put it, 'to bring about the collapse of the enemy's Normandy front by a thrust into the deep flank and rear of the enemy facing the Seventh Army'. The Fuehrer, of course, totally unaware that we knew all about his attack long enough beforehand to allow Bradley to make the necessary arrangements for its failure, went on with his rather hysterical rhetoric. 'The greatest daring, determination and imagination must give wings to all echelons of command. Each and every man must believe in victory. Cleaning up in rear areas and in Brittany can wait until later.' End of signal.

Now, if Kluge complied with this latest signal, we might get the lot in the bag.

I didn't hear anything from No. 10; I just sent signals over as they came in. I think Winston Churchill must have enjoyed the last one. Now it was Hitler's turn to rally his nation and he was giving a rather poor imitation of Churchill's inimitable style. Stewart Menzies was getting reports from the War Office and kept me abreast of our side of the battle.

Kluge sent a signal to Eberbach early that evening telling him to send three of his precious panzer divisions, with which he was desperately defending Falaise, to Mortain to comply with the Fuehrer's orders. He went on to tell Eberbach that the continuation of these attacks on Avranches, if they were a failure, could lead to the collapse of the entire Normandy front, but 'the order from Hitler was so unequivocal, it must be obeyed'.

Kluge's signal reached all our commands later the same evening, and just as the panzer divisions were getting ready to start out for their dash to Mortain, General Simonds began the famous Canadian onslaught to try and cut through the German armour guarding the way to Falaise. Nearly a thousand Allied aircraft laid a barrage of bombs on either side of the corridor down which the Canadians tried in vain to reach the town. It was a gallant effort, but, alas, the panzers finally stopped the Allied attack eight miles short of their objective.

Montgomery might have done better to let Eberbach's panzers go west before the Canadian attack, but the participation of the bombers no doubt made postponement impossible. When the attack started one of Eberbach's panzer divisions had just set out for Mortain, and von Kluge promptly cancelled the movement westward of the two others. In the middle of the night he sent a signal to Hitler informing him that the attack could not now take place, but still the German troops around Mortain fought on and fought hard, waiting for the panzer divisions which now would never come. It was obvious from all the Ultra Signals by OKW, Kluge, Eberbach and Hausser, that the whole situation was out of control.

SHAEF was not due to move from Portsmouth to Granville, on the west coast of the Cherbourg peninsula, until August the ninth, but as a result of the Ultra signals, Eisenhower was already at Bradley's headquarters and set in motion the operation to surround the three German Armies.

Hitler was hundreds of miles away and all that Kluge had feared was now happening, but still Hitler wouldn't take 'no' for an answer. He was so completely out of touch with reality that in reply to Kluge's signal he sent another: 'The front attack has been launched too early and was too weak, a new attack must be launched on August the eleventh.' (He was now specifying the actual date.) 'A massive attack by several corps to be commanded by Eberbach himself.' Eberbach himself replied that there could be no attack before August the twentieth, and on August the tenth Kluge signalled OKW that the Americans were moving north to Argentan, and for the first time he warned the OKW that he was threatened with envelopment. I think this was one of the signals that brought home to me the tremendous difference that Ultra was making to our operations. We had all known what was happening for the past four days, but von Kluge had only just learned that his worst fears were becoming a reality.

Little wonder that, after the war, Eisenhower had written to Stewart Menzies to the effect that Ultra had been 'decisive'.

As the signals flashed to and fro and flashed also to the Allied commanders, not to mention the shuttle service of red boxes to Downing Street, those in the Ultra picture in the office came flooding around my teleprinter room, until Mrs Owen sternly ordered them out. As far as I could make out there was no work being done anywhere in Whitehall. All my WAAF had come on watch, their blue shirtsleeves rolled up to their elbows. The Oracle of Bletchley was working as never before, no doubt the very high volume of high-level signals had stimulated her digestion.

Early that evening of August the tenth, Kluge sent another signal to OKW recommending to Hitler that the Seventh Army should be withdrawn from Mortain and switched against the American thrust from the south. Only a short while later the OKW replied that whilst admitting the American thrust required quick action, Hitler still wanted another attack on Avranches. We noted he didn't reply himself. He had obviously got himself out on a limb and didn't know how to get back and now, despite the OKW signal, Hausser began to withdraw his Seventh Army from Mortain. The Hitler myth wasn't working any more. By August the eleventh, Hausser signalled to Kluge that he had lost a hundred tanks, and from Eberbach, who had had orders from Kluge to drive off the threat from the US XV Corps from the south, came a signal to say that 'my ammunition and fuel supplies are already short. Due to Allied aircraft, I cannot move in the daytime and some of my divisions exist in name only.' Eberbach in fact carried out no attack, but instead built up a line of defence which the Americans eventually came up against when they reached the outskirts of Argentan on the thirteenth. Now there was a gap of only thirty miles between the Canadians and the Americans, and 'in the bag' to the west, which was slowly shrinking under the pressure of the First US and the Second British Armies, were all the forces of the Seventh Army, and the Fifth Panzer Army. They had warned Kluge by signal that if the front was not withdrawn immediately, the Army Group would have to write off both Armies. This signal, which was repeated to the OKW, must have given Jodl a tricky few minutes with Hitler. How could the Fuehrer's inspired strategy have gone wrong. We knew that what was left of Eberbach's armour was virtually immobile; he was short of ammunition and fuel. It looked as if the American corps could close the gap. It was at this moment of high tension on the thirteenth that, unable to get any news from our side of the operation, I asked Stewart Menzies what was up. He was smilingly evasive. The Air Ministry didn't appear to know anything either. I rang Hut 3 at Bletchley, who couldn't make out what was happening at all. Everyone there had been waiting for Eberbach's report on the battle for Argentan by the Americans. Nothing came. It was to be a long time later before I heard the story, as told me by the Americans. Apparently, just as General Haislip was preparing his XV Corps to attack northward to capture Argentan, he had a signal from Bradley telling him to stop offensive operations and assume blocking positions and to wait further orders. Haislip must have had every reason to be puzzled. Even if Montgomery couldn't make headway from the north to close the gap, what had happened to stop Bradley doing it from the south? It transpired that in the plans for Overlord a line dividing the operational zones of the British and American forces had been drawn and it passed through Argentan, which meant that in normal circumstances Montgomery would have to give Bradley permission to cross this line from the south. As Eisenhower was with Bradley, no doubt he had had to advise Bradley to stick to the agreement not to cross the line until Montgomery should suggest it, but I don't suppose that either of them thought that Montgomery would fail to do so. For twenty-four vital hours Bradley waited.

On the fourteenth the Canadians made another attack on Falaise. This time they got within three miles of the town, but there were still fifteen miles separating the Allied armies. To us, in the office in London, the situation seemed about as unrealistic as the signal which now arrived from Hitler to the effect that 'the present situation in the rear of the Army Group is the result of the failure of the attack at Avranches. A further attack was to be launched'. I can only assume that Keitel and Jodl had been much too frightened to tell Hitler the truth, both as regards as the perilous position of Kluge's Army Group and the state of their armament. Perhaps too much had happened lately to make them risk changing their velvet collars for a rope. To us, who always watched Hitler's signals with a close scrutiny for any signs of a psychological breakdown, despite a return to his earlier self-assurance after the Rastenburg bomb in July, the latter stages of the battle of Falaise again reinforced our impression of his lack of decision and failure, or perhaps unwillingness, to face up to reality.

After his fruitless twenty-four hour wait, Bradley told Patton to leave half the XV Corps at Argentan and to send the rest rapidly eastwards to the Seine with a view to trapping the German Armies there, if they should now break out of the Falaise bag. Meanwhile, the US XII and XX Corps of Patton's Third Army were already streaking eastward. We now know that on the next day, August the fifteenth, Kluge went into the pocket to talk to Hausser and Eberbach and he got lost. We only guessed that something had happened when signals from the Seventh Army were unanswered, and when a little later Kluge's own headquarters were asking the Seventh Army where he was. Already the British Second and the US First Armies were squeezing the bag to death, as the trapped German armies came to a standstill on the roads crowded and littered with wrecked vehicles and dying men.

A signal was sent to Hitler telling him of Kluge's disappearance, and in the evening Hitler signalled back appointing Hausser temporary commander in the west, and ordering him to destroy the American forces near Argentan which threatened all three armies with encirclement. So the penny had dropped at last. One wondered whether Hausser had time to read this signal. It couldn't have mattered less. On the sixteenth Kluge had evidently turned up, for he soon came on the air again. Later we learned he had spent the day in a ditch with a broken radio; now he signalled OKW, recommending an immediate withdrawal of all forces through the Argentan/Falaise gap. He added that 'hesitation in accepting this recommendation would result in unforeseeable developments'. Because of the rigid code of having to get Hitler's permission for every withdrawal, added to the fanatical unreality of Hitler's orders, Army Group B lost a vital day which might have saved a few of them for a little longer, for, on the sixteenth, the Canadians finally took Falaise, now only a pile of rubble; only then did Montgomery propose to Bradley that they should now close the pocket, meeting half way between Falaise and Argentan.

The night of the sixteenth, Eberbach made a desperate attempt to dislodge the Americans from Argentan so as to keep open a corridor wide enough to allow the escape of the seven trapped German corps. The gap was still fifteen miles wide and after dark the escape from the pocket started.

As the Fuehrer cannot be wrong, he laid the blame

on Kluge, and a signal sent to Kluge that day informed him that General Model would take over the armies in the west. Kluge must have known this was the inevitable end of Hitler's mad strategy. I imagine, too, that he was tired, disillusioned certainly. For us there was little doubt that Ultra had been primarily responsible for the massive victory.

On August the fifteenth the Allied Operation Anvil, the invasion of the South of France by the US and Fighting French forces, had begun and on August the seventeenth a signal from Hitler to the Army Group G, which covered the southern half of France, ordered them to give up southern France and retire northward to the Seine. On the eighteenth, too, the Canadians captured Trun, the village proposed by Montgomery for the meeting place with the Americans, who themselves were now nearing the village of Chambois just a few miles away, and yet on the night of August the nineteenth in a drizzly rain and early morning fog thousands of trapped German soldiers made their way stealthily through the narrow gap, and when the fog lifted on the morning of the twentieth the gap was still packed with the escaping enemy. Only by midnight on August the twentieth was the exit from the bag finally sealed.

It was some time later that Patton's bitter remarks to Bradley about Montgomery were allowed to be known, but even at the time there were some questions being asked in London as to why Patton could not try and close the gap from the south?

But it had been an epic story. The Ultra signals between Hitler and von Kluge which led up to the Battle of Falaise and the destruction of a large part of the German Army in the west were probably Ultra's greatest triumph. The back-room boys at Bletchley were superb.

It was the beginning of the end of the war in the west for Hitler, despite the fact that it was estimated that between twenty and thirty thousand men had escaped east, many of them veteran panzer troops. For von Kluge it was the end. He wrote a letter to Hitler which we found after the war. In it he told Hitler the true facts and declared that the grand and daring operational concept ordered by him was impractical to exercise, a moderation of expression worthy of his officer corps background. On the night of August the eighteenth the Field-Marshal who had dared to question the Fuehrer's orders set off for Germany. He never arrived; he committed suicide on the way.

CHAPTER SEVENTEEN

The Beginning of the End

The Overlord operation had rather overshadowed the fall of Rome on June the fourth, but although the Prime Minister's attention was for the moment firmly focused on Overlord, the flow of signals to commanders in Italy continued. Kesselring, pulling back from Rome, had got his two armies into a dangerous position with a wide gap separating them. His signals told us that the withdrawal was not going smoothly and both he and his army commanders, were a bit panicked as to whether the Allies would wade into their open flanks.

Kesselring signalled an appreciation to Hitler in which he stated he was endeavouring to conduct a co-ordinated withdrawal to the Albert Line and eventually to the Gothic Line which was now being fortified. The Albert Line was obviously a temporary position and it was half-way from Rome to the Gothic Line in the north. His Fourteenth Army had suffered the virtual loss of three infantry divisions, whilst the others were only at half strength. Material losses had been high and withdrawal along the coastal road was proving difficult.

Despite all this information of the German troubles, Mark Clark, who was now in Rome, did not move his Fifth Army after the reteating enemy and, according to a signal from a very nervous Vietinghoff to Kesselring, Clark missed the opportunity of not only over-running the Fourteenth Army but also of encircling the Tenth

Army. This, of course, was only an appreciation by a retreating enemy, but once again Kesselring had been let off the hook. Kesselring, too, admitted in a signal to the OKW that had the American Fifth Army concentrated their offensive against the junction of the two armies, it would have torn the German front for good.

The Gothic Line to which he was now retreating was a fairly formidable obstacle, and was principally based on the Apennine Mountains which ran most of the way from west to east across Northern Italy. We knew from Ultra of the massive fortifications which the OKW had ordered to be constructed here, but we also knew that since Italian labour had been forced to do the job, the final result might not be too formidable.

There were but few passes through the mountains and at the eastern end marshes and lakes made attack difficult.

Fortunately Kesselring's Ultra signals had pinpointed the junction of the two armies and it was this point that Clark wisely chose for his main attack.

On September the eighth had come the usual Hitler signal that the Futa Pass, one of the few through the Apennines, was 'to be held to the last man and the last bullet'. On the strength of this Ultra signal Clark attacked through another pass, just east of the Futa Pass, on September the tenth, and after bitter fighting the American Fifth Army penetrated to the northern slopes of the mountains overlooking the great Lombardy plains and the River Po.

The Italian campaign was virtually over. Ultra had pinpointed the weak spots in the Apennine defence and Mark Clark had at last reacted to it.

In France the race to Germany was on.

Once Model had got the remnants of his retreating armies over the River Seine he signalled to the OKW that his armies, such as they were, were falling back in three columns. He made an impassioned plea for thirty new infantry and twelve new tank divisions, and also asked for new army and corps headquarters staff to replace his losses. How many new units he really expected is hard to guess.

But Model's signals had some result because the OKW ordered some hundred fortress battalions, composed largely of the unfit, the old and the maimed to be sent to the front. This signal brought home to me a vivid memory of my prison camp in Silesia, when in October 1918 the old chaps and the wounded who had been our guards were turned out for active service once more. It was a pitiful sight. There was one old man who had always been helpful to the prisoners and I gave him a cake of soap to take with him. He nearly wept as he tore off his Iron Cross and pressed it into my hand.

The OKW also signalled to Kesselring, ordering him to send two divisions up from Italy. Next they ordered the combing out of all existing non-combatants in order to form twenty-five new divisions. Now at last the reluctant Goering had to disgorge his Luftwaffe men. It was a pleasure to hear from him again.

Despite all the measures that the OKW were now taking, Hitler himself was obviously quite out of touch with the real situation. He sent elaborately worded signals all round the commands ordering them to build and hold a defensive line behind the Somme and Marne rivers.

I had flown over to France because Robert Gore-Brown was getting worried at the inclusion by some of the American Army Intelligence units of too much Ultra in their Intelligence summaries which had a wide distribution. It was obviously a great temptation to show how much they knew, and Robert suggested a visit by me to the various HQs might tighten up the security. We didn't want our secret blown at this stage even if the end of the war in the west was in sight. There was still the Pacific war and Ultra was being particularly useful there.

I decided to go straight to Bradley and tell him and his G2 that I proposed to go to his Army HQs and, at the same time, ask Brigadier-General Sibert to keep a keen eye on the whole question of including Ultra in normal Top Secret summaries.

It was good to see Bradley a much more confident and less worried man than I had seen near Omaha beach. He thanked me for the remarkable effort by which Ultra helped to close the Falaise gap. Sibert gave me a map reference where he hoped I might find Patton.

Patton was obviously in his element. We had chased after him all day and passed a lot of American tanks, stuck on the road out of fuel. Their crews lay on the roadside getting a few hours rest; goodness knows they needed it. A few days before they had been lucky enough to capture part of a German fuel train that had been left behind, but it couldn't supply them all for very long. Late that afternoon, after a good many enquiries from cheerful GIs, we at last found a track leading off the road and up to a wood which fitted the map reference that Sibert had given us. Here we learned Patton would rest the night, so said the bulldozer crews, who had the job of carving out the tracks into the wood in order to let the caravans come in for cover.

The bulldozer crews were right, but Patton's men had also captured a trainload of champagne, in the local station. As a result the bulldozed avenues in the wood were works of art but no caravan would be able to get round the curves. The SLU had just arrived and pitched their tents. We were hailed with cries of delight by everyone.

They deserved every drop. They had been going flat out ever since they left Avranches in Normandy. Someone had had the idea of trying to get some petrol out of the local inhabitants. Like good Frenchmen they had not failed over the years to 'win' and store quite a bit of the precious fuel. Now they were prepared to exchange it litre for litre for Veuve Cliquot. The tanks would roll again at daybreak, at least for a few more miles.

Patton himself was in holiday mood. He said: 'Now, young man, tell me anything better than this.' 'This' was obviously his kind of war. He asked where the Germans were. I told him it looked as if they were now on their way back to the Siegfried Line just as fast as they could go. He agreed with me and said, 'I got to try and get there first. If only I can get some gas.' He took off his tunic and leant back in his chair in a characteristic attitude with his hands clasped behind his head. He was happy and relaxed as he looked out of the windows of his caravan resting on the edge of the little wood into which it had been unable to go. I, too, looked out across the small green fields of France to a village nearby where once again the farmers were going about their work and the church bell was giving out its evening message. How quickly freedom and peace had come to this countryside again. I said as much to Patton. 'Sure, sure,' he said 'but we gotta get after them.'

A few days after I got back to London we received Hitler's decree to his armies of the west that they 'should hold out as long as possible in front of the Siegfried Line and then occupy the line itself.' Jodl had evidently put the right pins in his map at last. Then came a signal with Hitler's battle cry number one: 'All German forces in the channel ports and the Scheldt fortress are to fight to the last man.' He went on to state that there was to be a new headquarters set up in Holland to rally all the troops of whatever category, that the Fifth Panzer Army was to be reconstituted with two divisions from Italy, that a decisive counter-attack was to be made against the American Third Army. Despite all the nonsense which we had received from Hitler of late this was to be an important signal both to Montgomery and Bradley. It warned Montgomery that there would be a number of German troops in Holland, and it warned Bradley and Patton to look out for a German attack.

It was at this point that Hitler reinstated Rundstedt as Commander-in-Chief in the west. Rundstedt's appointment told us how badly Hitler needed to restore confidence in the army and in the nation as a whole. Once again he had fallen back on the orthodox old soldier.

CHAPTER EIGHTEEN

Arnhem

By the beginning of September a British armoured division was in Antwerp and Montgomery was urging Eisenhower to allow him to push forward across Holland in order to try and get over the Rhine whilst the Germans were still off-balance. But Eisenhower was, quite understandably, looking at the supply position of the whole Allied front and he considered it far too critical for an advance in strength. We were still denied the convenience of the channel ports still in the hands of the Germans, and all the fuel and supplies still had to come hundreds of miles from Normandy. In any case the enemy was getting himself together rather more quickly than anyone suspected.

Nevertheless, Eisenhower finally agreed to Montgomery's plan for an armoured and airborne thrust across Holland to seize the Rhine bridges and outflank the German defences. It was a bold idea, but many people felt there was some underestimation of the stubborn resistance now beginning to manifest itself from the reformed German units which were being filled up with all the available man- and boy-power that wasn't already in the fighting line. General Bradley was critical of the plan, and what was described by Montgomery as a springboard for a 'powerful full-blooded thrust to the heart of Germany' drew the comment from

Bradley that it would be a 'sixty-mile salient drive up a side alley of the Reich'.

Montgomery had won part of the concession he wanted. There was also strong pressure being brought to use the boundless energy and high state of training of both the United States and the British parachute forces, who were understandably getting a bit restless and feared they might be relegated to the role of infantry, as had happened to the German Parachute Corps.

Experience with Overlord had shown that, however highly trained are the parachute troops themselves, the difficulties of making accurate and concentrated drops at night were too great, and it was also found that there would not be enough aircraft available for a simultaneous drop of all parachute troops together. This meant that the British drop would have to be done in three lifts, and to overcome the inaccuracy of night drops, daylight ones were finally accepted. When the crews of Bomber Command were consulted on this aspect they pointed out that the anti-aircraft fire-power in that particular area would be intense, as it was in line with our bombing raids on Germany. Nevertheless, the plans went ahead with haste despite the protests of that other quiet, efficient general of the British Second Army, Dempsey, who rightly doubted its feasibility.

This then was the background against which we had to try and provide some Intelligence as to what the airborne attack was likely to meet in the way of resistance and whether the essential factor of surprise might be lacking. There was little to go on from Ultra except that we knew that Holland was to be a rallying point for Model's armies. Otherwise there were few signals coming out of Holland at all. But there were other sources of information. First, we had one or two good agents in Holland who were able from time to time to report troop movements to us.

Unfortunately the Dutch Resistance as a whole was, we knew, seriously penetrated by the Nazis, and the SIS had been forced to warn the SOE (the Special Operations Executive, which was set up to help the Resistance movements on the continent) that many of the arms they were dropping in Holland were going straight to the Nazis. Despite this, SOE decided to drop an extra large consignment of arms to assist the resistance in the coming operation. In the SIS's view this was more likely to alert the Nazis that something was in the wind. The same contacts in Holland who had supplied us with troop movements had advised us for some time past that Holland was used as the rest and re-equipment area for formations coming back from the Eastern Front, just as Rundstedt's signal had told us the same thing about divisions in France before Operation Overlord; finally Supreme Allied Headquarters' Intelligence had received information that troops of the 9th and 10th Panzer Divisions, who had escaped from the Falaise bag in Normandy, were in the area waiting for new equipment and arms. This was confirmed by our Dutch friends who reported that parts of the 9th SS Panzer Division had been seen around Arnhem on September the fifteenth. It seemed that the area was not so devoid of German troops, and tough ones at that, as Twenty-First Army Group optimistically forecast.

To complicate the Intelligence picture still further a member of the Dutch SIS, part of the Dutch wartime government mission in England, defected to Holland just before Arnhem. He was, in fact, a secret Dutch Nazi and there is no doubt he knew of the coming operation in Holland. It was a delicate and dangerous situation which must have been known by Twenty-First Army Group.

Once the operation had been decided upon the US

parachute divisions and the Polish parachute brigade also wanted to join in, and so it was that on September the seventeenth Operation Market Garden was launched. Some fifteen hundred aircraft and nearly five hundred gliders took off from airfields in Britain.

The plan was for the airborne troops to capture the bridges across the various canals and rivers in Holland, finally securing the bridge across the Rhine at Arnhem, the key to any possible breakthrough to the Ruhr. British armoured forces were to follow up the parachute attack and consolidate the captured bridges.

The battle for the key bridges is now an epic story, and the reported presence of so many German troops in the area proved only too true. German resistance was vicious and immediate and proved too much for the Allied parachute units; at Arnhem alone, where the bridge remained untaken, twelve hundred paratroops lay dead and three thousand were taken prisoner, and on September the twenty-fifth, after eight days of gallant but fruitless fighting, what remained of the paratroops were evacuated.

We know now that Model was caught napping in his hotel when the Allied aircraft came over. On the other hand, General Willi Bittrich, commanding II SS Panzer Corps, who was reorganizing and refitting the men of the two panzer divisions that had got out of the Falaise trap, uncannily had some eight thousand of these battle-hardened, even fanatical fighting men in the Arnhem area, and a subsequent signal from Bittrich to Hitler stating that 'almost before the British had touched the ground we were ready to defeat them' looked as if he had somehow been expecting them.

In fact the whole area seemed to be crawling with German troops. General Student was there collecting and reorganizing his parachute army, and it seemed probable that this was part of the area which Hitler had

designated in his earlier signal for the headquarters of
the reformation of his panzer army. Ironically, from
Montgomery's point of view, the limited success of his
plan was mainly due to the men of the crack SS panzer
divisions who had been allowed to escape from the Falaise pocket.

Churchill had meantime gone to Quebec, for which I
was grateful, for he would certainly have expected Ultra material about the Arnhem operation and it was not
forthcoming. Despite the tragedy of Arnhem the operation was not judged a complete failure, since some
bridges over the many rivers which flow across Holland
to the sea had been secured, and the idea that the enemy was beaten and in confusion had been dispelled.

Throughout September the British and Canadians
were busy mopping up the channel ports. Hitler had repeated the usual signal to these ports to consider themselves fortresses to be defended to the last man. Fortunately he had sent the one to Dieppe a day too late
and the Canadians found no opposition, but the others
put up fierce resistance.

CHAPTER NINETEEN

The Japanese War

When he returned from Quebec Winston Churchill was obviously turning his mind to peace, as was Roosevelt. The Prime Minister was taking less interest in Ultra in the west but I had to furnish him with an outline of the Ultra position in the South-East Asia Command.

There were a number of questions that needed to be settled with regard to the distribution of Ultra in the Eastern Hemisphere and now, in October, it looked as if I should be able to get away for a while. In any case Churchill was due to go to Moscow during the first half of the month. Back in 1943 I had sent Squadron-Leader John Stripe out to India to organize the provision of Japanese Ultra to the Commander-in-Chief, India, in Delhi, and the C-in-C Fourteenth Army. Now he wanted me to go out and approve the SLU set-up for Lord Mountbatten and his South-East Asia Command, which had moved to Kandy in Ceylon.

Not being a cryptographer I was never closely connected with Japanese cyphers but I believe I am correct in saying that as far back as 1930 the Japanese purchased the early uncomplicated version of the Enigma machine and adapted it to their own use, primarily for diplomatic traffic. This cypher was broken by the Americans in 1940 and shared with the British. Just when the Japanese navy, army and air force began to use the more highly sophisticated Enigma as developed by the Germans I do not know, but I assume that the Bletchley system was brought in and shared with the USA in order to give complete coverage in the Pacific, since shortly after Pearl Harbour I was asked to supply Washington with my tried security regulations. As the Japanese war spread south, a further centre was set up at Brisbane, Australia, for interception and distribution of Japanese Ultra and I then supplied SLUs to look after the Australian forces operating with the Allied Command.

The establishment of the SLUs in India and later the arrival of an American officer whose job it was to look after the needs of the American Armies and Air Forces in China, raised the question as to who should have Ultra, where it was to come from, and to whom it was to go; Ultra information on Japanese army, air and naval matters was now being received from Washington, London and Brisbane, and was available to the whole of the South-East Asia Command forces, as well as United States forces in China.

I had been able to send a complete SLU out to Brisbane, SLU9, and they had proved so welcome that I now had a request for more, but I will deal with the Australian side when we come to it. With Ultra world-wide, there were new problems of great distances in the Pacific and problems too of security of signals and operational use in isolated areas. I thought the best way to sort all this out was to go out and do it myself.

The maintenance of the absolute security both as regards distribution and use of Ultra around the world was, in the event, a pretty remarkable achievement.

There was not a great deal for me to do in Delhi beyond ensuring that C-in-C India was getting such Ultra as concerned him. My real business was obviously with the Fourteenth Army at Comilla in Assam and with South-East Asia Command. I had also been asked by

Menzies to visit and check with our SIS posts in India, Ceylon and Australia to see if there was anything lacking.

We flew down to Calcutta, where Dum-Dum aerodrome, once the parade ground and barracks of the famous regiments of the Raj and the home of Kipling's ballads, was teeming with aircraft supplying the Burma front; thence north-east across the Ganges delta, over the tea gardens and forests of Assam, to Comilla, gratefully cooler than Calcutta.

General Slim's HQ was in a large old Indian house, its spacious grounds covered with scented shrubs and shady trees and a small tented camp in a sunken garden; beneath the house lived father, mother and three baby mongoose who kept the snakes away both from the house and our tents, which was a comforting thought. I found both General Slim and Air Vice-Marshal Alec Coryton were well satisfied with the information which was being received and were conforming to all the security rules. The type of Ultra information received from the Japanese was much the same as that received from the German Army in Europe, operational and movement orders, strength returns and locations of Japanese formations which not only formed useful targets for the air but gave General Slim a complete order of battle of the Japanese forces. Some of the most interesting signals had been those showing the shortages of rations and equipment. There were, too, some strategical signals giving a wider overall picture of Japanese operations in the whole of the South-East Asia area.

General Slim told me that the intelligence from Ultra about the Japanese forces had been invaluable throughout the campaign, but the real triumph had been the information which led up to the final attack by the Japanese at Imphal and Kohima. It had become very evident from Ultra that the Japanese supply position was desperate and that their attack was being planned in order to capture the Fourteenth Army supply depots, so as to keep the Japanese army 'in business'.

Ultra had also shown that the Japanese air force in the area had dwindled so as to be practically useless. It was these two factors which determined the plan to allow the Japanese attack to spend itself while the Fourteenth Army formed a defensive box around their bases at Imphal and Kohima whilst General Stratemeyer, commanding the Eastern Air Command, was able to supply the Fourteenth Army from the air with men and materials, without the menace of Japanese fighter aircraft.

It was a strategy which paid off, and which denied to the Japanese the stores and equipment they had relied on capturing. Ultra then showed their supply position to be impossible and SEAC's ability to fly in a whole division without enemy interruption was a deciding factor at Imphal. This time the Japanese retreat was for good. The Supreme Commander himself has paid a fitting tribute to this phase of the Burma campaign, even though he could not mention Ultra when he stated that 'we could not have held Imphal or Kohima without the uninterrupted air-lift'. 'Uninterrupted' is the operative word.

By the time I got to Comilla, Imphal and Kohima were past victories and preparations were now being made for the great river crossing and the advance through Burma.

A few miles outside Kandy in Ceylon, on the once green lawns of the botanical gardens of Peridrinia, amongst the pepper and the nutmeg, the cinnamon and the clove, the vanilla and the flowering trees and the pools of great water lilies, Mountbatten had set up his headquarters of neat green wooden huts. Down in a hollow a large brick cinema had been built, where the daily briefings were given to all the staff on the progress of the South-East Asia campaign. It was a peaceful and exotic spot from which to direct a war.

It was not until I got to Kandy that I had first met Captain Inzer Wyatt. He belonged to the United States Special Security and had been learning the Ultra business at Bletchley. Inzer's job was to look after the Ultra needs of Generals Stilwell and Chennault, who commanded the United States Army and Air Forces operating with Chiang Kai-shek in South China. Inzer was a welcome addition to the SLU set-up, more especially as he was able to get Japanese army and air signals relayed direct from Washington.

He and John Stripe soon became firm friends and their close co-operation enabled me to sort out a rather bizarre situation.

John was getting Japanese army and air signals both from Bletchley and Brisbane, but he was not getting the Japanese naval information which contained valuable intelligence about Japanese supply convoys that operated around the Dutch East Indies; this was of the utmost interest to South-East Asia Command and Slim. The Japanese naval signals concerning these convoys did, however, reach London and British Naval Headquarters, Colombo, from Washington. Inzer Wyatt, for his part, was getting Japanese army and air signals direct from Washington, which he duly passed to Stilwell and Chennault, but he, too, was not given Japanese naval Ultra, which meant that the United States bomber force in Kunming had no information regarding the Japanese convoys. It seemed to be the same old story. I was able to make arrangements with London that Japanese naval Ultra dealing with convoy and supply traffic should now be made available to the SLU at Kandy, where John could also give it to Inzer who, in turn, was able to send it on to Chennault in China. It was rather a roundabout way of doing things, but it worked, and I believe Chennault had considerable success with his aircraft against these coastal convoys which so vitally affected the Japanese supply position in our Burma campaign.

Admiral Lord Mountbatten, the Supreme Commander of South-East Asia Command, was more relaxed in his cool tropical uniform than when I had last seen him in his immaculate blue and gold and starched white cuffs at a chiefs of staff meeting in London, before the unhappy Dieppe raid of 1942. He was then commanding the experimental combined force which undertook that operation. Now he told me he was well satisfied with the arrangements I had made, as he was, in fact, with all the Intelligence he was receiving from Ultra. He also fell in with my suggestion that Ultra should not go from his headquarters to the SEAC Liaison officer with the Chinese, since General Stilwell was already getting it from Wyatt and passing on to Chiang Kai-shek such information as he considered he ought to have. I explained to the Supreme Commander that, for security reasons, the same information should not go out to two different people on two different channels.

In Colombo I was able to meet Admiral Sir Bruce Fraser who was on his way to Australia to take up his Command of the British Eastern Fleet now operating with the United States Fleet in the Pacific. With him was Commander Alan Hilgarth, his Intelligence officer, whom I'd known when he was naval attaché in Madrid. He was, characteristically, very co-operative.

The flight between Colombo and Perth was one of the wonders of World War II. Twice on that long flight eastward did the sun rise in your eyes. I had known many parts of Australia as a teenager and I was looking forward now to meeting old friends, but first of all I wanted to make my number with the Australian Chief of Air Staff, Air Commodore Jones. I found him unhappy about the amount of information that was being passed to him from Brisbane. He certainly wasn't getting all that he should have, so I decided to look into the Brisbane distribution as soon as possible.

The SIS post in Brisbane had managed to get me a room at that excellent institution, the Queensland Club.

I found the Ultra set-up in Brisbane was most efficient, but it suffered a little from restrictions imposed by General MacArthur, on 'who should have what'. Nevertheless I was able, with the co-operation of Colonel Sandford, the young Australian officer in charge whom I had known in London when we were teaching him the job, to sort out some of the distribution problems so that both Melbourne and Stripe's SLUs in Delhi and Kandy should get more of what they needed.

But now the Australian and American forces were moving north again, distances were great and security in the 'island hopping' was going to be dicey.

The new SLUs I had collected from Italy had arrived after a long trip by way of Canada and USA only to be sent up from Brisbane, some three thousand miles to Morotai. They took a Typex machine and their one-time cypher pads in a weighted bag which also had a thermite bomb for self-destruction in case of trouble.

They had few clothes as their baggage hadn't arrived from Italy and it was not an ideal security spot since the Japanese occupied most of the island. Flying-Officer Reynolds told me the story:

'Our clients for Ultra were the Air Officer Commanding the First Tactical Air Force, Advanced Army Headquarters, General Blamey and later on the Advanced RAAF Command, A.V.-M Bostock. In addition we supplied Fifth US Bomber Command, also Commander of 31st US Infantry Division. So we kept pretty busy.

Unfortunately, the First TAF was some distance from the other units we had to serve and it took an hour or more to deliver signals over tracks that were axle deep in mud.

The information on Ultra consisted of Japanese shipping, aircraft and troop movements, prior to the Allied landings in Borneo, Tarakan on 1 May 1945, Labuan on the tenth of June, and Balik Pafan on 1 July 1945.

There were also Ultra reports of German submarines in the vicinity of Morotai carrying strategic material to Japan.

Our SLU was entirely dependent on the RAAF for everything, but they looked after us. Tents, food, etc., were in short supply. There were a lot of troops on the island, some 17,000 with TAF as well as the I Australian Corps.

We only had the one RAAF signals link and often poor radio conditions with heavy rain and high humidity, which caused problems with our only machine. Power, too, was difficult.

Our office was made of tree-trunk poles, hessian and a roof of palm leaves. We commandeered it from the Wing-Commander (Engineers), much to his disgust. We had to make it secure with wire netting and a door and I slept in this office with revolver and thermite bombs ready in case of Jap visitors; I also rigged up a trip wire. Being RAF we were rather conspicuous, and everyone was a bit curious to know what we did.

Luckily, my Sergeant Rosenberg used to go to

the synagogue at the US naval base and was able to get hold of American 'K' rations, cigarettes, milk, tea, sugar and finally a jeep.

Some time later another SLU joined me at Morotai and was allotted to look after Land Forces Headquarters and RAAF Command.

In June 1945 I flew back to Brisbane to sort out some of the problems of encyphering, which had bothered us at the other end.

In Brisbane many of our main signals now came from Delhi, but radio blackouts were frequent. Sometimes signals came via the Australian Post Office cable, or even by radio from Bletchley, and Japanese weather reports came up from Melbourne by teleprinter, so the SLU at Brisbane had a bit of a job sorting out what was to go on up to Morotai, but one way and another there was a pretty complete coverage of all the Japanese activities, and the urgent demand for two SLUs at Morotai was a measure of the anxiety by the Australian air and land forces for the information.

In fact the SLUs were being so successful, despite their difficulties, that the Australians asked for more and at the end of June 1945 there were, in addition to the SLUs at Morotai, one in Lae, New Guinea to feed the Australian First Army, and another at NW Area, RAAF.

SLU9 moved from Morotai with First TAF, RAAF, to Labuan in July.'

Just before the atom bomb was dropped, Reynolds was organized to take another SLU up to Manila, but luckily the flight was cancelled in time.

It is a simple account of one of those small bands of men whose proud boast was that Ultra always got through one way or another. Their responsibilities far outweighed their numbers or their modest ranks. I cannot finish the story of the SLUs without a full appreciation of Girl Friday, as WAAF Flight-Officer Dawkes was called. She worked under my own Administration officer, Group-Captain Sofino and, together with Flight Lieutenant Gibson who had been the first of the original members of my Hut 3 team, they recruited, trained, screened, nursed and tied up the myriad loose ends for the SLUs right across the world. I think the story of Flying-Officer Reynolds shows just how many and varied these loose ends were.

I can only hope that the satisfaction of knowing they had done one of the most fascinating jobs of the war was some compensation for their lowly ranks to these dedicated men and women of the Special Liaison Units.

It was while I was watching the output of the Ultra centre in Brisbane and the Ultra traffic moving between Bletchley, Brisbane, Delhi and Washington, that I began to realize more than ever just how we had achieved the ultimate in world-wide intelligence against our enemies. Before I came to this other side of the world, I had been almost wholly occupied looking after my own parish and, as I have already pointed out, this took little account of the important German naval Ultra which was almost wholly dealt with at the Admiralty in London. In Brisbane for the first time I was told something of the part that this information had played in the Pacific. No history of naval warfare in World War II can now be regarded as complete without mention of the information which was available to the Allied admirals. It was this information which in fact created the sea air battles in the Pacific.

Admiral Nimitz had to fight two decisive actions in the first three months after his appointment. The first was when intercepted signals gave him the Japanese plan for the capture of Port Moresby in New Guinea, which was designed to give them a base for further attacks on Australia itself. The Japanese plan aimed to outflank New Guinea by going far to the east to the Coral Sea before closing on Port Moresby. The plan was received on 17 April 1942 and passed to Admiral Nimitz. It gave him time to move his ships to meet the threat and, in fact, fight the Battle of the Coral Sea in early May. The Battle of the Coral Sea was not a decisive victory but it did stop the Japanese moving southwards, and the threat to Port Moresby was averted. The battle also showed the Americans the future pattern that battles in the Pacific would take; fought by aircraft from carriers and not by ship to ship.

Later in May intercepted signals showed that a great Japanese fleet would move to try and capture Midway Island, known as the sentry for Hawaii itself. The instructions in the signal were 'to provoke action with the main American fleet and to destroy it piecemeal' and finally it disclosed that an attack on the Aleutian islands would be made which was intended to draw off the Americans to the north and leave the way open to Midway. The Japanese fleet included a powerful carrier-borne striking force under Admiral Chinchi Nagumo. Admiral Nimitz knew that he was going to have to fight a considerably superior enemy.

The Japanese fleet moved out towards Midway on the twenty-seventh of May, just three weeks after Nimitz had received the information of the Japanese intentions. As a result, he was able to avoid the trap of allowing his ships to be drawn off to the north. The battle for Midway was to be the turning point in the Pacific war. It was fought almost entirely by aircraft; in fact the American dive bombers won for Nimitz a victory which, by destroying Nagumo's entire carrier force, destroyed the offensive power of the Japanese fleet.

It was this most important signal of the Pacific naval

war which caused a breach of security which nearly wrecked the whole secret. Somehow a journalist got hold of the story and published the fact that the Japanese coded signal had been broken. There was immediate reaction by Churchill; it was a sharp lesson, and security of this top cypher, which was one of the Enigma variations used by the Japanese Navy, was tightened to stop any recurrence.

There was to be another protest from London to Washington over the shooting down by the Americans of the Commander-in-Chief of the Japanese Navy, Admiral Yamamoto. Ultra had revealed precisely when he would arrive by air to inspect an island base. The brilliant timing by the Americans killed Yamamoto at a moment when his death had a tremendous effect on Japanese morale, but it was all carried out without an adequate cover plan. Like Admiral Doenitz in Germany, the Japanese fortunately did not believe their top cyphers had been broken, and these security lapses did no harm, but if the Japanese had had any more causes to doubt the security of their cyphers we should have been in trouble.

In 1944 it was still a long way by air from Sydney via Honolulu, and San Francisco to Washington, where I was able to meet my opposite numbers in the Ultra business and was able to tell them the arrangements I had made in Australia. At the Pentagon I got the first news of the apparent failure of Ultra to warn either Eisenhower, Bradley or Montgomery of Hitler's offensive through the Ardennes.

CHAPTER TWENTY

Hitler's Ardennes Offensive

When I got back to London in December I learned that von Rundstedt had grouped together all his remaining troops for a massive retaliatory battle in the Ardennes, which had taken the Americans completely by surprise and had led to much bitter fighting with heavy losses. I also found that there had been some serious disagreement between Eisenhower and Montgomery and that the American chiefs of staff had ordered Eisenhower to bring the matter to a head.

It was at this point that Tedder sent me a signal, over my SLU, asking me to take a 'personal only' message from Eisenhower to Churchill. It has been reliably stated that Eisenhower was prepared to tell General Marshall that it was either 'him or Montgomery'. I doubt if Montgomery really realized the seriousness of his position, or that he had put his own Prime Minister in the position of having to go to the Americans in order to get him off the hook.

This was obviously not the best atmosphere for me to go round the commands. However, when I did finally go in March, I needn't have worried. I found both the people at SHAEF and at Bradley's, Patton's, Simpson's and Hodges' headquarters were as welcoming as ever, despite the rough time that they had had. At Supreme Headquarters Tedder quietly thanked me for handling the Eisenhower/Churchill signals, but, in reply to his questions, I had no definite explanation for the failure of Ultra to warn us of Rundstedt's attack, except that apparently we simply had not been able either to intercept or break high-grade Ultra during the critical weeks before the attack. I told Tedder that since Ultra had again become available as soon as the attack opened, the tremendous secrecy which Rundstedt managed to impose before the operation began was obviously intentional, and the fact that lower-grade signals on Ultra had continued reinforced the assumption that the Germans still believed we didn't know the difference, and that this particular security measure was as much for security in the German armed forces as it was for us. I did point out that we had received the original orders from Hitler setting up the new panzer army and ordering the attack by Rundstedt, which admittedly at the time had seemed like another Hitlerian dream.

The extent of the German security precautions was later discovered when we got information from prisoners-of-war, about how all the troops and tank movements up to the front had been done at night without lights and that signals had been delivered by hand by motor-cyclists. I think Tedder agreed with me that Ultra had been so helpful during the previous year that some Intelligence staffs had begun to rely on it almost entirely.

After the rapid Allied advance in the west, Eisenhower and his staff had moved to Versailles, whilst Montgomery had gone to Brussels and Bradley had settled in Luxembourg. At Gore-Brown's request for more personnel, I had sent a bevy of WAAF officers to 'man' the headquarters at SHAEF which would allow a reserve for any additional SLUs that might now be required. And now that life in France was getting back to normal, I reckoned the girls had earned a little gaiety after the tough days in the London office. I left Mrs Owen to train some more whilst I was away.

What I really wanted to do was to get down and see Monk Dickson and find out from him the real story of the Battle of the Bulge. It was good to see Monk again; he had grown in mental stature from that rather nervous, but efficient, G2 that I had first met in Bradley's headquarters soon after D-Day, to the war veteran that he now was and with, as he put it, thanks to Ultra, the whole situation pretty clear in his mind. He told me of the most extraordinary precautions which had been taken by Rundstedt and his panzer army generals to attain absolute secrecy. Analyses of the varying estimates, forecasts and appreciations put out by the separate G2s before the Battle of the Bulge, have been made in great detail, but to me, probably the most pertinent cause of the surprise of von Rundstedt's offensive was the absence of high-grade Ultra before the battle.

There is no doubt in my own mind that the Intelligence staffs and the commanders at SHAEF army groups and army headquarters who had, for the past two and a half years, and in the case of the British, for four and a half years, had the enemy's intentions handed to them on a plate, had perhaps come to rely on Ultra to such an extent that when it gave no positive indication of the coming counter-attack, all the other indications were not taken seriously enough. Had I been in England I believe that the very absence of Ultra would have aroused my strong suspicions.

In the Intelligence appreciations put out by the G2, in the month before the battle started, it appears that there were, in fact, abundant clues from the statements of prisoners-of-war, from captured documents, from photo reconnaissance and from logistical Ultra for one man (Monk Dickson) at least to reach the right conclusion. It was Monk who told me the story of the battle and showed me the Intelligence appreciation which he issued on December the tenth.

I quote:

> (1) It is notable that morale among PW's freshly captured, both in the Army cage and at Communication Zone cage, recently achieved a new high. . . . It is apparent that von Rundstedt, who obviously is conducting military operations without the benefit of intuition, has skilfully defended and husbanded his forces and is preparing for his part in the all-out application of every weapon at the focal point and the correct time to achieve defence of the Reich west of the Rhine by inflicting as great a defeat on the Allies as possible. Indications to date point to the location of this focal point as being between Roermond and Schleiden [in the Aachen area, north of the VIII Corps front, where the German attack was actually made].
>
> (2) The enemy is capable of a concentrated counter-attack with air, armour, infantry and secret weapons at a selected focal point at a time of his own choosing.

Dickson concluded the famous 'Estimate No. 37' with a prophetic statement: 'The continual building up of forces to the west of the Rhine points consistently to his staking all on the counter-offensive as stated in capability 2'.

Patton's G2 with the Third Army, Colonel Oscar Koch, had that mixture of flair and enthusiasm which must have fitted in well with Patton's temperament. Koch's appreciation of the situation on December the ninth and December the tenth stated that enemy rail movements indicated a definite build-up of enemy troops and supplies opposite the north flank of the Third Army and that the massive armoured force gave him the definite capability of launching a spoiling offensive.

I think that these two old timers, even without the high-level signals from Hitler and the OKW that they were used to, had put their bits and pieces together correctly despite the extraordinary security precautions that Rundstedt had taken to cover up his troops' movements. Nor had they been lulled into a state of complacency by the Allied victories into thinking that the Germans had no more fight left in them. Once the battle had started, Ultra had confirmed the presence of our old enemies the Fifth and Seventh Panzer Armies as well as the SS divisions, and there had been enough Ultra to follow the lines the attack was taking.

The day after Christmas, the three generals, Rundstedt, Model and Manteuffel, who had commanded the spearhead of the attack, sent an Ultra signal to Hitler stating baldly that it was no longer possible to reach Antwerp, and that the only hope of a victory was to move northward across the Meuse with the Fifth and Sixth Panzer Armies in order to capture Liège and then to hold the line back from there to Aachen. This was a vital signal for Eisenhower who now knew at last that the attack had shot its bolt or, as Monk Dickson put it, 'we knew we had got them'. Hitler, as usual, wouldn't have any of it, and in a signal to his generals remarked that 'we have had unexpected setbacks because my plan was not followed to the letter'. Poor old Rundstedt, was he going to have to follow von Kluge? From experience we had learned that as soon as Hitler started refusing to do what the generals recommended, things started to go very wrong, and this was to be no exception.

Hitler now ordered a second counter-offensive to be launched on New Year's Day down in Alsace, in order to draw the Third American Army away from the north. This, too, was a vital signal both for Eisenhower and Bradley, and in it Hitler went on to say that he still believed that Antwerp could be taken, but both to Eisenhower and Bradley the above signals were a clear indication that the time had come for the Americans to counter-attack. I was to learn a short while later, at Bradley's headquarters, that Hitler's signal ordering the second attack in Alsace, by Blaskowitz's Army Group G, against the United States Seventh Army, under Lieutenant-General Patch, had enabled Eisenhower to make some quick moves to straighten out and reduce the Seventh Army front where a salient might have enabled the Germans to cut it off, and General Patch, due to the warning, was able to hold the German attack.

The American armies were now winning the second battle in the Ardennes. Manteuffel signalled to Model for permission to withdraw his line to a position east of Bastogne. This meant giving up more than half the ground that the offensive had won. Both Model and Rundstedt gave permission for this move; once again the Fuehrer refused, but by January the eighth Hitler had no option but to signal his approval to Model for a partial withdrawal, to the west of the line that Model had asked for. The withdrawal procedure had, as usual, developed into a sort of bargaining game between Hitler and his generals. Now the Fuehrer, having given his permission to withdraw, took charge and his next signal ordered the amalgamation of the Sixth and Fifth Panzer Armies under Manteuffel to guard the shoulders of the salient against any American attempt to cut it off. Monk Dickson told me that Eisenhower had already decided to squeeze the salient out rather than cut it off,

so he and Hitler were now working on the same plan.
The whole operation had been considerably hastened
by a panic signal from Hitler ordering the whole Fifth
Panzer Army to go to the Eastern Front.

In February Ultra gave the composition and the
strength of all three army groups how facing us and
from Rundstedt we had a valuable appreciation, which
he made to Hitler, of the new situation. In this he anticipated that the main Allied attack on the Siegfried
position would come opposite the Ruhr, the orthodox
direct route.

Rundstedt's signal was responsible for two operations by the Allies. First of all there was a deception
plan, which was put across to the enemy, and which fitted with Rundstedt's appreciation and no doubt helped
convince him he was right. Secondly, Eisenhower took
advantage of the German view and decided to give
Montgomery the job of turning the flank of the Siegfried line further north than the Ruhr. The result was
that when Montgomery opened his attack with the Canadian Army on February the eighth, it achieved complete surprise. General Simpson had now come fully
into the picture, his Ninth US Army was attached to
Montgomery's Twenty-First Army Group, and I was
able to feed Simpson direct with Ultra information.

As the Canadian and the British attacks developed
in the north, Ultra showed that nine German divisions
from further south were drawn up to the northern front
and Rundstedt sent a signal to Hitler on February the
tenth that the British attack in the north had threatened
the whole German front and the Ruhr. His mistaken
appreciation as to where the attack would take place
was eventually to prove fatal. Finally Rundstedt sent
the usual signal to Hitler asking permission to withdraw
since the Siegfried line was burst wide open. For the
first time Hitler gave his permission without arguing.

Perhaps Rundstedt knew all along what a hopeless position his armies were in and this time he had waited until the situation was such that the reply to his request must be yes.

CHAPTER TWENTY-ONE

Gotterdammerung

At the beginning of March I went over to the continent and called to see General Simpson who had established his HQ in a schoolhouse in a small village. He had been given a number of extra divisions by Bradley to counter the move of nine German divisions towards the north, which Ultra had told us about. Simpson was well pleased with the way things were going.

It was about the middle of the afternoon on March the seventh that Simpson got news by telephone of the capture of the Remagen Bridge by Hodges' army further south. There was, naturally, terrific excitement. Simpson wanted to move forward across the Rhine as quickly as possible to try and bounce the Germans before they were really ready for it. I believe he put this proposal up to Montgomery, but the latter had been making such massive preparations for the Rhine crossing for some months that he didn't accept Simpson's proposals for a change of plan.

Model's signals to his desperate army commanders who wanted to save their troops and retire over the Rhine were 'No retreat'. Hitler's writ still ran at this stage, to disobey it might mean a firing party; however, the west bank of the Rhine was finally cleared a week later, and on Ultra the German armies began to count the cost in men and materials, doleful signals to the OKW helping us to assess the enemy's losses.

In Luxembourg I found Bradley in a hotel which was now his Twelfth Army Group headquarters. His office was not large, but the long windows looked out over the park-like square, with its trees and flower beds just beginning to welcome the spring and the fountains adding a touch of gaiety. He, too, was almost gay; I had been rather expecting a rocket over the Ardennes business, but he brushed it all aside; as he said, once it had started the signals from Hitler himself had been invaluable in telling him all he wanted to know. This confirmed Tedder's story, especially the one which gave Ike time to prepare for the unexpected attack in Alsace. Whilst I was there signals started to come in from Rundstedt, and indeed from army groups and armies as well, which read like some sort of unrealistic war game. Bradley was puzzled, but I suggested that these were really for Hitler's personal consumption; they would doubtless all go back to him and he would be satisfied with the way in which his generals were handling the situation. Meanwhile German soldiers were dying for their fatherland and a Fuehrer who was now quite obviously unbalanced.

As I looked at the whole position with Bradley, in his office late that afternoon, even the Rhine could not hold us back when we were ready to cross it. But Hitler was still in command and there was no one now to get rid of him and to sue for peace.

Bradley told me how Patton had made a characteristic dash with his armour to the Rhine, which he accomplished in something like two and a half days. Ultra had told him just where the German forces were and he had worked his way around them.

This had evoked a panic signal from General Hausser of Army Group G, who warned Rundstedt that failure to withdraw might very well entail the envelopment and annihiliation of the First Army. Poor Hausser was being surrounded again.

At this critical stage Hitler had finally dismissed Rundstedt and put in Albert Kesselring as Commander-in-Chief of all the Armies for the defence of Germany in the west. So Albert had got to the top of the ladder at last, only to find it wasn't leaning against anything. On taking up his job he had ordered a quick inventory of the troops that he had got left, and it was these returns which I was able to give Bradley before I left. A single shaded light on Bradley's desk cast only a dim glow on the face I had got to know well. His eyes smiling behind his glasses, he paid Ultra a very nice compliment: he asked me to remain while he called in the principal staff officers of his Twelfth Army Group and I was presented to each of them.

Ultra, whether from Hitler, or Kesselring, or the army group commanders, was now of little help to us strategically except to show how completely unrealistic the whole command structure in the west had become. The German war machine had been built and geared for victory, and now in defeat it just didn't work.

Montgomery's build up of forces for the Rhine crossing rivalled the invasion of Normandy itself. We knew from Ultra that opposite them were what remained of the First Parachute Army and the Fifth Panzer Army, possibly the toughest fighters still left to the enemy in the west, but the river crossing assault was a mighty success.

Meantime, further to the south, George Patton, determined not to be outdone by his old rival Montgomery, crossed the Rhine north of the city of Mainz —knowing from Ultra there was little opposition—with a small force in rowing boats, without any preparation at all, the day before Montgomery's attack. He took the thin line of defenders completely by surprise.

This was so typical of the two men who were diametrically opposed both in character and in their methods of waging war. Montgomery always required his absolute superiority over the enemy in men and materials before he would move. Patton studied every Ultra signal and, knowing where every enemy soldier was in his path, would thread his way round or through them and find the undefended spot. He had done it in Sicily and then all the way from Brittany to the Rhine and yet he could swing his whole army at a right angle northward to deal with the German attack in the Ardennes at a speed which surprised Eisenhower as much as the Germans.

Kesselring signalled Hitler in Berlin 'the Rhine has been crossed from Wesel in the north to Mainz in the south and further resistance to the Allied armies is now doubtful'. It was more, it was the end.

At Rheims I found SHAEF very concerned about the Russian advance and a little disgusted at the total disregard by them of the Yalta Conference agreements. 'Tooey' Spaatz was also there, with his enormous caravan parked in the driveway of a vast red brick mansion. I was greeted with a bottle of iced champagne of a very fine vintage and with a well-known label which, Tooey told me, with a twinkle in his eye, was gratefully supplied to him by the lady of the house who not only owned the well-known brand herself but kept it in large cellars which were, in fact, just underneath where his caravan was parked. It appeared a very satisfactory arrangement and, as we gossiped about the days in Algiers, a tall immaculate blonde secretary put another bottle on ice. It was the last time I met him, but there could not have been a more cheerful exit.

Back in London, I found that Hitler was in Berlin and still directing his armies, which in most cases had ceased to exist as such. Through Ultra came the cry of a desperate man: 'Why do you not do as I have ordered, why do you not answer?' I tried to envisage the scene in that tomb in Berlin with the Russian armies closing in, and the meaningless little flags of the German divisions still in places on the map that had long since been evacuated. It was about a week after I got home, April the fifteenth, that we received the last order of the day from Hitler. It read: 'Once again Bolshevism will suffer Asia's old fate, it will founder on the capital of the Reich. Berlin stays German, Vienna will be German again and Europe will never be Russian.' It was a cry from the heart of one tyrant to another, the wolf to the bear.

There was one last Ultra from Goering: 'My Fuehrer, in view of your decision to remain at your post in the fortress of Berlin, do you agree that I take over at once the total leadership of the Reich, with full freedom of action at home and abroad, as your deputy, in accordance with your decree of 29 June 1941. If no reply is received by ten o'clock tonight, I shall take it for granted that you have lost your freedom of action and shall consider the conditions of your decree as fulfilled and shall act to the best interests of our country and our people. You know what I feel for you in the gravest hour of your life, words fail me to express myself. May God protect you and speed you quickly here, in spite of all, your loyal Hermann Goering.' He should have known better. Hitler immediately ordered his arrest.

It was Ultra that gave us a picture of Hitler during those last days up to mid-April 1945. We know now that the final two days before he actually committed suicide his frenzy seemed to die down, he seemed to regain some sort of composure with the decision he had evidently taken to do away with himself, and that he was normal, rational, and quiet. Quiet, too, were the teleprinters in my office. Although Ultra in the west was finished, it lingered a little while longer in the east until the atom bomb finally put an end to that war also. I handed back to Stewart Menzies the key to those red boxes which had done so many journeys between my offices and No. 10, Downing Street.

CHAPTER TWENTY-TWO

Conclusion

'The knowledge not only of the enemy's precise strength and disposition but also how, when and where he intends to carry out his operations has brought a new dimension into the prosecution of the war.' So said General Alexander in Tunisia in 1943. He might well have added that surprise is the most valuable ingredient of modern warfare; the ability to deny it to an unsuspecting enemy and to achieve it oneself are the elements of victory.

Since Ultra provided these elements and dimensions was it not the real architect of the Allied victories of World War II? But Intelligence alone, however brilliant, cannot provide dramatic success where military strength or preparedness does not exist and so it was in those dark days of 1940, when Ultra was only just beginning to emerge from Bletchley, that Hitler, due to the stubborn disbelief of the French generals, achieved surprise at Sedan, and disaster came to the Allies. Yet it was Ultra which helped to save the BEF. Alone now against the vast victorious German war machine, it became a question of survival rather than victory, and during the Battle of Britain it was Ultra that helped our Fighter Command to outwit Goering's massive attempts to destroy the RAF.

During the long fighting withdrawal of our Middle East forces from El Agheila back to Egypt, pressed all the way by the relentless Rommel, it is doubtful whether, without Ultra, Wavell or Auchinleck could have so cleverly boxed him to a standstill.

In Crete Ultra denied surprise to Student's parachute invasion and, although the island was lost, our knowledge undoubtedly saved most of our forces from capture.

Before Alamein, one cannot help wondering what would have happened if Rommel had achieved surprise for his vicious attack round Montgomery's left flank. At best it would have totally disrupted the preparations for Alamein. With our exact knowledge from Ultra of just what Rommel was going to do, his attack was met and beaten off. Alamein became the turning point from bare survival to aggressive victories.

It was Ultra which denied all seaborne supplies to Rommel's retreating army and forced him to withdraw right into Tunisia.

As the story of Ultra unfolded, its potential was limited only by the number of times the oracle decided to speak. The fact that we were fortunate enough to get a large number of signals direct from Hitler and his principal generals, as well as those of lesser grade which told us the details of the enemy's strengths and dispositions, enabled Ultra to provide the 'elements and dimensions' so vital to the planners of our operations.

In North-West Africa we and our new allies, the Americans, were ensured by Ultra of both surprise and almost total lack of resistance for the seaborne operation, and the final battles in Tunisia were fought with full knowledge from Ultra of Rommel's and von Arnim's counter-attacks and the details of the positions held by the enemy.

It was just before our landings in Algeria that the negative role of Ultra first proved so valuable; by this I mean the objectives of our own preparations being so evidently unknown to the enemy, judging from the guessing games that went on in signals between their various commanders and Berlin. It was this negative role which told us that we should achieve surprise. The enemy never quite knew where the Allied landings in North Africa, Sicily and Italy would take place. It is true that our plans for these operations had been based on the information from Ultra as to where there would be least opposition, but if for a moment one reverses the roles of Ultra there would have been little chance of our amphibious invasions in the Mediterranean or in Normandy achieving the successes they did. It is, I think, true to say that on these counts Ultra was the vital factor.

Successes, yes, but what about the failures? This new dimension of war needed a new dimension of thinking on the part of our commanders, and the different ways in which they either used or misused these opportunities was a measure of the men themselves. Maybe with some it was the knowledge that their commander-in-chief, and even Churchill and Roosevelt, were getting the same information that made some adhere closely to orthodox military training, and only fight battles when they had superiority in men and machines, whilst others would use Ultra to outwit the enemy and take him in the rear. This of course was the classic difference between those two generals, Montgomery and Patton, that finally bred such a deadly rivalry.

It was after Rommel's attack, before Alamein, when he had been badly mauled, that Churchill pressed Montgomery to take the opportunity Ultra had given him to wade into Rommel's remaining forces without delay, but Montgomery waited until he was fully prepared to launch the attack according to the plans which had been carefully drawn up. The six-week delay gave Rommel time to construct a formidable defence line and the cost in lives before the breakthrough was considerable.

In Sicily, Patton, who was made aware by Ultra of the precise position of the German panzer units and the direction in which they were moving after the Allied landings, slipped round their flank and got to Messina almost before the Germans could get across to Italy.

It was Mark Clark who, in that dreary slogging match up through Italy, three times did not use the opportunities Ultra had provided, and which Alexander had planned for him: first at Anzio, then after the fall of Cassino and later north of Rome, to cut off and surround Kesselring's armies. It was Alexander who, knowing the precise distribution of German troops at Cassino, planned the surprise attack over the mountains and it was France's General Juin who so brilliantly carried it out.

Alexander was a supreme user of Ultra in the Mediterranean. As I came to know most of the commanders personally I found I was in a good position to assess their probable reaction to Ultra.

From where I sat I often wondered whether a more flexible approach might not have broken up Rommel's defeated Afrika Korps and hastened the fall of Tunis in consequence, and that more determination might have accomplished a more rapid defeat of Kesselring's armies in Italy.

Over the years of reading the signals of Hitler, Rundstedt, Rommel, Kesselring and other German commanders in Europe, most of us who were closely connected with this miracle source, as Winston Churchill called it, obtained a fairly complete insight into the way their minds worked, of the attitudes of the various generals towards Hitler, and of the reasons behind their various appreciations, which they sent to the OKW, as to when and where we were going to operate. These latter gave us the priceless opportunities to mis-guide them about our operations with our deception plans.

Perhaps the best example of this was Rundstedt's appreciation in 1943 that the Allied invasion of France would come across the Pas de Calais. This document alone led to a complete chain of events, dictating much of our planning for Overlord and the setting up of Patton's phantom army in Kent to fit in with Rundstedt's views, a deception which kept a complete German army around Calais and four panzer divisions away from our landing beaches.

Ultra told us, too, that as soon as things started to go wrong with enemy operations Hitler invariably took remote control, which was an extra bonus, since most of his signals went on the air.

Although neither Hitler nor his top generals ever gave any indication on Ultra that they had caught on to the fact that their cyphers were unsafe, they must have wondered why their carefully laid plans never came off.

It was for Operation Overlord, however, that Ultra had been saving itself, or rather had been saved by probably the most careful security network ever placed around secret Intelligence, and it was in Operation Overlord that Ultra reached its peak.

Planning the assault, which was dependent on the precise location, strength and equipment of the Germans in Normandy, would have been guesswork despite the bits of information which the French could send us. Once ashore, endless valuable time and lives might have been lost in raids and probing attacks to find out where and how strong were the enemy. The British Second Army might have battered themselves against the enemy tanks concentrated around Caen, but instead Dempsey knew just where and how many they were, and the precise knowledge of the massive reinforcement of German armour at Caen enabled Montgomery to reshape the main plans to allow Bradley to break out to Avranches, whilst Dempsey was able to select his points of attack to cause the utmost disruption and to pin down the panzers; for Rommel it was like fighting with one hand tied behind his back.

The ultimate triumph of Ultra was, to my mind, the trapping of the German armies in Normandy at Falaise. Our full pre-knowledge of the German plans as laid down by Hitler, coupled with our knowledge of the strength of all the German units involved, brought out the best in imaginative action by Eisenhower and the American generals. To Patton it gave the opportunity to employ his technique of high mobility. It was the beginning of the end of the war in the west.

After Falaise, Ultra shortened the war by giving all the Allied commanders details of the weak points and dwindling resources of the enemy so that they could go forward into Germany as quickly as natural hazards would let them. This was highly important in view of the advancing Russian armies. Without Ultra we might well have had to meet the Russians on the Rhine instead of the Elbe, and they would have stayed put.

I do not know all the details of Ultra's successes in South-East Asia and the Pacific, but I can suggest that Ultra played a leading role in the strategy of MacArthur and Nimitz.

Up at Comilla Slim was getting all he needed to know from London, Washington and Australia. Ultra certainly provided the information on which the battle of Imphal and Kohima was cunningly fought by General Slim and Admiral Mountbatten, the battle which was the turning point of the campaign.

Perhaps the cryptographers greatest naval triumph in the Pacific was the way in which Admiral Nimitz used it so skilfully at the Battle of Midway, the last great sea battle, where the big ships never saw each other and where the battle was entirely fought by aircraft.

Maybe some day much more will be told about Ultra in that half of the globe and also about the battle of the Atlantic U-boats.

To all those who have been brought up in the belief that the Allied victory over the Fascist powers was accomplished with some ease plus the will of Allah, perhaps the early chapters of this book will have provided the sobering thought that it almost didn't happen. Let them judge for themselves just how much the near miracle of Ultra helped to make our victory possible.

I believe that most of the senior commanders, both in Britain and America, would, together with Winston Churchill and President Roosevelt, have endorsed the views expressed by General Eisenhower that 'Ultra was decisive'.

Index

Aachen, 256–57
Abwehr, 46, 120–21
Adolf Hitler Line, 168, 171
Advanced Air Striking
    Force, 54
Afrika Korps, 101, 106, 109–
    11, 115, 118–19, 121–
    23, 140, 145, 149–53,
    270
Air Ministry Intelligence
    Branch, 43
Alam Halfa, 114
Alamein, 106, 107, 113,
    115–17, 125, 140, 209,
    268–69
Albert Line, 229
Alexander, Field-Marshal
    Honourable Sir Harold,
    R.L.C., 32, 105, 110–
    13, 148, 155, 156–57,
    164–74, 267, 270
Alexandria, 112, 113, 159
Allfrey, Lieutenant-General
    C. W., Commanding
    British 5 Corps, 147
Anderson, Major-General Sir
    Kenneth, Commanding
    General, Eastern Task
    Force, 135, 141–43
Anzio, 164, 167–69, 171,
    270
Ardennes, 57, 252–53, 262,
    264

Argentan, 222–26
Army and Royal Air Force
    Intelligence Unit, 40
Arnhem, 237–39
Arnim, General Juergen von,
    148, 151, 268
Atlantic Wall, 178, 182–85
Auchinleck, General Sir
    Claude John Eyre, 47,
    106–10, 112, 268
Avranches, 212–18, 220–21,
    223, 233, 272

Babbage, Charles, 32
Badoglio, Marshall Pietro,
    161
Baldwin, Stanley, 1st Earl
    of Bewdley, 21, 75
Barratt, Air Vice-Marshal
    Sir Arthur, 53–54, 57
Barry, Milner, 32
Battle of the Atlantic, 98,
    125–27
Battle of Britain, 32, 47, 65,
    81–98, 108, 112, 204,
    267
Battle of the Bulge, 255
Battle of the Coral Sea, 251
Battle of France, 49, 63–64,
    100, 107, 108, 112, 204,
    214
Battle of Midway Island,
    251, 272

Bayeux, 196–99, 204–05, 207

Benghazi, 106, 112, 118, 121

Berlin, 183, 209

Biggin Hill, 80–81, 84, 87, 204

Bismarck, 125–26

Bittrich, General Willi, 238

Bizerta, 140–41

Blackford, Air-Commodore Gerry, 70

Blamey, General Sir Thomas, 248

Blaskowitz, General Johannes, 258

Bletchley Park, 16, 28–29, 31–34, 40, 43–45, 56, 116, 129–30, 147, 163, 170–71, 176, 217, 223, 224, 227, 242, 245, 249–50, 267

Blitzkrieg, 50

Blount, Charles, Commander of the air component of the BEF, 52

Blumentritt, General Güenther, 193

Bock, General Fedor von, 59, 107

Bone, 143

Bostock, A. V.-M., 247

Boyle, Archie, 41

Bradley, General Omar, 180, 195, 197–203, 206–08, 209–12, 214–20, 224–27, 232, 234, 235–36, 252,–54, 258, 261–63, 272

Brauchitsch, General Walter von, 58–61, 156

Brereton, Major-General Lewis Hyde, 181

Brisbane, 242, 245–46, 249–50

British Expeditionary Force (BEF), 52, 60–62, 267

Britten, Benjamin, 33

Buerat, 145

Buerat Line, 148

Bushey Park, 179

Caen, 193–97, 201, 203, 206–07, 209–10, 214–16, 271–72

Caesar Line, 168, 171–72

Casablanca Conference, 146–48, 175

Cassino, 164, 168–71, 187, 270;
    Line, 167, 170–71

Casteau, 195

Chamberlain, Neville, 30, 44, 75

Chambois, 227

Chennault, Major-General Claire L., 245–46

Chiang Kai-shek, 245–46

Churchill, Sir Winston, 15–16, 22, 30, 49, 58–66, 68, 72–74, 76, 81, 85–86, 89–95, 99–100, 103–17, 121–22, 128–29, 131, 134, 140, 148, 150, 155, 157, 161, 164–67, 169–72, 177–79, 189, 193–94, 199, 201–02, 206, 211–14, 217–18, 221, 229, 239, 241, 252–53, 269, 271, 273

Clark, Lieutenant-General Mark W., Deputy Commander-in-Chief Allied Force, 134–35, 156,

Clark, (continued)
164, 167, 172–73, 229,
270

Coastal Command, 126

Comilla, 242–43, 272

Coningham, Air Marshal Sir
Arthur, 114

Constantine, 151–52

Cooper, 'Josh', 33

Coral Sea, Battle of, *see* Battle of the Coral Sea

Coryton, Air Vice-Marshal
(now Air Chief Marshal Sir) Alec, 243

'Coventry', code name, 94

Crerar, Lieutenant-General
Henry R. D. G., 181

Crete, 72, 102–05, 109, 268

'Cromwell', code name, 89,
92

Cunningham, Andrew, 1st
Viscount Cunningham
of Hyndhope, 101–02,
104, 113–14, 120, 143–
44, 156

Cyrenaica, 100–01, 105,
125, 145, 161

Darlan, Admiral Jean François, 148

Davidson, General, 40, 44

Dawkes, Flight-Officer, 250

De Gaulle, President
Charles, 54

De Guingand, Major-General Sir Francis W., 206

Delhi, 147, 250

Dempsey, General Sir Miles,
180, 195, 206–07, 218,
236, 271–72

Denning, Commander, 127

Denniston, Commander Alastair, 16n., 24–26, 28,
32, 137

Deuxième Bureau, Paris, 27,
53, 147

Dickson, Colonel Monk, 180,
200–03, 212, 215, 219,
255–58

Dieppe, 239, 246

Dietrich, General of the
Waffen SS Josef Sepp,
197

Dill, Field-Marshal Sir John,
Chief of Imperial General Staff, 93

Dixon, Colonel Palmer, 131,
135

Doenitz, Admiral Karl, 127–
29, 252

Doolittle, Major-General
J. H. (Jimmy), Commanding General
Twelfth Air Force, 134,
181

Dowding, Air Chief Marshal
Sir Hugh Caswell
Tremenhare, Air Officer
Commanding-in-Chief
Fighter Command, 47,
73–74, 76–85, 91, 96–
97

Dunderdale, Bill, 59

Dunkirk, 47, 62, 75

Eben Emael, 58

Eberbach, General Heinrich, 220–26

Eighth Army, 110–15, 148–
51, 163, 166

Eisenhower, General
Dwight D., 16–17, 130,
132, 134–35, 139–40,
141–46, 155, 167, 175,

Eisenhower, (continued) 179, 181, 192, 206, 212, 214–18, 222, 224, 235, 252–54, 257–59, 272, 273

El Agheila, 140, 145, 267

Enigma cypher machine, 27–28, 31–32, 33, 35, 37–42, 54, 71, 86, 129, 130, 241, 252

Falaise, 218–21, 225–27, 232, 237, 238, 272

Florence, 173

France, fall of, 63, 68

Fraser, Admiral Sir Bruce, 246

Freyberg, General Bernard C., Commanding General of New Zealand Division, 104–05

Futa Pass, 230

Gamelin, General Maurice, 57, 59

Georges, General Alphonse, French Commander-in-Chief of Northwest Front, 58

German(y), invasion of Belgium and France, 55–56

Gibson, Flight-Lieutenant, 250

Godfrey, John, Director Naval Intelligence, 40, 45

Goering, Reich Marschall, Hermann, Master German Luftwaffe, 47, 67–71, 73–80, 81–96, 104, 108, 188, 231, 265, 267

Gore-Brown, Robert, 114, 200, 231, 254

Gort, John, 1st Viscount Gort, Commander British Expeditionary Force in France (BEF), 52–53, 56, 60–62, 156

Gothic Line, 229–30

Government Code and Cypher School, 24

Graham, Major-General M. W. A. P., 205–06

Guderian, General Heinz, 107, 183–85

Guzzoni, General, 158–59

Haislip, Major-General Wade H., 219, 224

Halder, General Franz, Chief of German Army General Staff, 59

Halfaya Pass, 106

Halifax, Edward Frederick Lindley Wood, 1st Earl of Halifax, 30

Hausser, Generaloberst Paul, 197–98, 208, 212, 222–23, 225–26, 262–63

Heinemann, General Erich, 177

Hess, Rudolf, Hitler's Deputy, 19, 29

Hilgarth, Commander Alan, 246

Himmler, Heinrich, Commander of SS, 29

Hitler, Adolf, 17, 19, 24, 29, 32, 34, 46, 49–51, 57, 60–63, 65–72, 82, 89–92, 99–103, 106–08, 111–19, 134, 139–41, 145, 148–51, 157–60, 161–73, 178, 181–201,

Hitler, (continued)
    205, 209–30, 233–34,
    238, 239, 252, 257–72
Hodges, Lieutenant-General
    Courtney H., 218, 253,
    261
Hood, H.M.S., 125
Horton, Max, 128
Humphreys, 44–45, 56, 63,
    92, 131, 135

Imphal, 243–44, 272
Interpretation Centre for
    Aerial Photographs, 41
Ironside, General Sir Wil-
    liam Edmond, 97
Ismay, General Sir Hastings
    Lionel, Chief of Staff to
    Prime Minister, 72, 93,
    170
Italy, invasion of by Allies,
    163–64

Jodl, General Alfred, 187,
    193, 224, 225
Joint Intelligence Commit-
    tee, 137
Jones, Air Commodore,
    Chief of Royal Austra-
    lian Air Force Staff,
    247
Jones, Dr R. V., 23–24, 74,
    175–77
Joubert, Colonel Philip, 54
Juin, Alphonse Pierre, 270

Kahn, David, 26; Works,
    The Codebreakers, 26
Kandy, 244–45
Kasserine, 149
Keitel, Field-Marshal Wil-
    helm, 187, 193, 199,
    225

Kesselring, Field-Marshal
    Albert, 20, 56, 75, 85,
    100, 106, 108–09, 112–
    13, 118–20, 122, 136,
    139–44, 148–52, 157–
    74, 187, 209, 229–31,
    263–64, 270
Kleist, General Ewald von,
    58, 107
Kluge, General Günther von,
    60, 107, 199–201, 207–
    09, 212–28, 257;
    suicide of, 228
Knox, 'Dilly', 32
Koch, Erich, 19–20, 29
Koch, Colonel Oscar, 256–
    57
Kohima, 243–44, 272

La Marsa, 155–56, 166
Lae, 249
Lawson, Air Commodore
    George, liaison officer
    at General Anderson's
    headquarters with
    RAF, 147
Leese, Lieutenant-General
    Sir Oliver, 167
Leigh-Mallory, Air Vice-
    Marshal Sir Trafford,
    77, 83, 96–97
Lemelsen, General Joachim,
    166
Liège, 257
List, Field-Marshal Wil-
    helm, 103
Londonderry, Lord, 21
Long, Squadron-Leader
    'Tubby', 53–54
Luftwaffe, 34, 39, 44, 47,
    67–71, 81–85, 91, 96,
    100–02, 106, 108, 141,

Luftwaffe, (continued)
147, 160, 188, 189, 231;
Luftflotte 2, 56, 69, 75, 76–78;
Luftflotte 3, 56, 69, 75, 76–78;
Luftflotte 5, 69, 75, 76–78
Lutyens, Admiral, 125

MacArthur, General Douglas, 130, 272
Maginot Line, 50, 58
Mainz, 263
Maison Blanche, 142
Malan, Wing-Commander 'Sailor', 80
Maleme, 104
Malta, 156
Manstein, General Erich Fritz von, 50
Manteuffel, General Hasso von, 257–58
Mareth Line, 149–51
Marshall, General George, 253
Martin, John, Winston Churchill's Principal Secretary, 92
Masterman, Sir John, 189; *Double Cross System of the War of 1939–45*, 189
Matapan, 102
Medenine, 150–51
Medhurst, Charles, 37–38, 43–44, 92, 131
Medmenham, 41
Menzies, General Stewart, 16, 27, 30–31, 34, 37–45, 64, 92–93, 107, 112, 130–31, 134–35, 137,

Menzies, (continued)
147–48, 172, 216–17, 221–24, 243, 266
Messina, 160, 270
'Milchcows', 128–29
Mitchell, Reginald, 32
Model, Field-Marshal Walter, 227, 230–31, 236–38, 257–58, 261
Montgomery, General Sir Bernard Law, 110–14, 116–19, 121, 140, 145, 149–51, 160, 163–67, 179, 188–89, 194–95, 197–206, 209–10, 217–18, 221, 224–27, 234–36, 238, 252–54, 259–61, 263–64, 268–72
Monti Aurunci, 171
Morgan, Lieutenant-General Sir Frederick, 175, 178–79
Morotai, 248–49
Mortain, 218–23
Mountbatten of Burma, Louis Mountbatten, 1st Earl, 241, 244–46, 272
Mussolini, Benito, 101, 161

Nagumo, Vice-Admiral Chuichi, 251
Naples, 119–21, 163–66
Naval Intelligence Division, 126
Nehring, Lieutenant-General Walter, 145
Newall, Air Marshal Sir Cyril Louis, Chief of Air Staff, 93, 96
Nimitz, Admiral Chester, 130, 250–51, 272
Normandy, 182, 184, 188, 192–95, 199, 205–06,

Normandy, (continued) 221, 233, 235, 263, 269, 271

Observer Corps, 78–80, 84
O'Connor, Lieutenant-General Richard, Commanding Western Desert Force, 99–101
Operation Anvil, 227
Operation Avalanche, 163–73
Operation Barbarossa, 20, 106
Operation Cobra, 208, 211–12
Operation Dynamo, 61
Operation Eagle, 76, 80
Operation Husky, 155, 157, 161
Operation Market Garden, 238
Operation Overlord, 166, 169, 172–73, 177–79, 182–84, 185–89, 209, 224, 229, 236–37, 271
Operation Sea Lion, 47, 68–71, 80–82, 90, 93
Operation Torch, 136, 144, 175
Orfordness, 74
Owen, Mrs, 89, 164, 170, 223, 255

Palermo, 158, 160
Park, Air Vice-Marshal Keith R., 73, 81, 83, 97
Pas de Calais, 178, 183, 187–88, 190, 192, 198–99, 213, 271
Patch, Lieutenant-General Alexander, 258

Patton, Major-General George S., Commanding General Western Task Force, 134, 146, 156, 160, 180, 186, 198, 203, 213, 215–19, 225–27, 232–34, 253, 256, 262–64, 269–70, 271, 272
Paul, Prince of Yugoslavia, 102
Pearl Harbour, 129, 242
Peenemunde, 176–77
Pettigrew, Miss (secretary to General Menzies), 38
Philby, Kim, 46
Photo Reconnaissance Unit, 89
Plowden, Major Humphrey, 53
Port Moresby, 250–51
Pound, First Sea Lord Admiral of the Fleet Sir Alfred Dudley, 45
Pritchard, Dick, 33

Quebec Conference, 179
Quesada, Major-General Elwood R., 203–04, 212, 219

Ramsay, Admiral Sir Bertram, 113, 156, 189
Rastenburg, 192, 211;
attempt on Hitler's life at, 211
Reichenau, General Walther von, 20, 24, 55, 57–59, 107
Reynolds, Flying-Officer, 152, 247–50

Rivet, Colonel, 148

Roermond, 256

Rome, 157, 161–64, 167–68, 172–74, 229

Rommel, Field-Marshal Erwin, 47, 100–01, 105–22, 136, 140, 144–45, 148–51, 162, 165–66, 178, 182–88, 191–99, 201, 207–08, 268–72

Ronin, Georges, 53–54, 147

Roosevelt, President Franklin Delano, 89, 129, 161, 166, 173, 179, 241, 269, 273

Roper, Professor Hugh Trevor, 46

Rosenberg, Alfred, official National Party philosopher and Foreign Affairs expert, 19, 22, 29, 67, 71, 108

Rosenberg, Sergeant, 248

Runstedt, Field-Marshal Karl von, 60–61, 107, 178, 183–88, 192–98, 201, 205, 207–09, 234, 237, 253–60, 262–63, 270, 271

Salerno, 162, 164

Sandford, Colonel, 247

Saul, Air Vice-Marshal, Richard E., 77

Saunders, Lieutenant-Commander, 45, 128

Schleiden, 256

Schlieben, General Carl Wilhelm von, garrison commander, 196–97

Schweppenburg, General Freiherr Geyr von, 183–86, 198

Sedan, 56, 58, 267

Shadow OKW, 63–64, 101, 106, 109, 116, 130–31, 136, 144, 148, 152, 157–60, 163, 167–68, 173, 178, 183, 186–87, 190, 192–94, 196–97, 207, 209, 211–13, 217–20, 222–24, 226, 230–31, 257, 261, 270

SHAEF (Supreme Headquarters Allied Expeditionary Force), 179–80, 182, 189, 191, 199, 201, 215–17, 222, 253–55, 264

Sibert, Brigadier-General Edwin L., 215, 232

Sicily, 139, 155, 157–60, 174, 264, 269

Sidi Birani, 99

Siegfried Line, 233, 259

Simmonds, General, 181

Simonds, Lieutenant-General G. C., CC II Canadian Corps, 218, 221

Simpson, Lieutenant-General William H., 180, 253, 259–61

Singapore, 72

Sinclair, Sir Archibald, _see_ Thurso, Archibald Sinclair, Viscount

Sinclair, Admiral Sir Hugh, 21, 27, 29, 65

SIS (Secret Intelligence Service), 23, 31, 40, 237

Slessor, Air Marshal Sir John, Command-in-Chief Coastal Command, 74, 129

Slim, General Sir William, 243, 272

Smith, Major-General Walter Bedell, Chief of Staff Allied Force, 135, 214

SOE (Special Operations Executive), 237

Sofino, Group-Captain, 250

Sollum, 106

Spaatz, Major-General Carl, Commanding General Eighth Air Force, 131, 135–37, 146–47, 181–82, 264

Special Liaison Units (SLU), 42–44, 46, 52, 54, 73, 111, 113–14, 119, 127, 129, 132–33, 136–39, 144, 146–48, 151–57, 167, 182, 189–90, 199–201, 202, 203, 205–06, 219, 232, 241–42, 245–50, 253–54

Speidel, General Hans, 193

Sperrle, Field-Marshal Hugo, 56, 75, 187

St Lo, 197–98, 207–08, 209

Stalin, Joseph, 107, 109, 111

Stanmore, 73, 78, 98

Stilwell, Lieutenant-General Joseph, 245–46

Strachey, Oliver, 33

Stratemeyer, Lieutenant-General George E., 244

Stripe, Squadron-Leader John, 241, 245, 247

Strong, Major-General Sir Kenneth, 191

Student, General Kurt, 104, 238, 268

Swinton, Lord, 21

Tactical Air Force, 114

Taranto, 119

Tedder, Arthur William, 1st Baron, 145, 155–56, 179–81, 187, 190–92, 215, 253–54, 262

Teheran Conference, 166–67, 179

Termoli, 166

Thurso, Archibald Sinclair, Viscount Thurso, 97

Tiltman, J. H., 32

Tizard, Sir Henry, 23

Tobruk, 105–06, 118

Todt, Dr Fritz, 213

Toulon, 141

Travis, Sir Edward, 16, 137

Tripoli, 100, 106, 112, 148

Truman, President Harry S., 167

Truscott, Major-General Lucian K., 166

Tunis, 121, 140–43, 147, 150–51, 158

Trun, 227

U Boats, 126–29, 144, 273

Ultra signal, 46–49, 52, 55, 58–60, 63–66, 68–72, 73–77, 80–85, 89, 91–92, 94–106, 108–13, 117–21, 125, 127–33, 135–36, 139–42, 144–60, 163–64, 166–67, 172–83, 189–91, 195–203, 205, 206, 213–14, 222–23, 230–32, 236, 239–47, 248, 250–59, 262–68, 271;

achievements of, 267–69, 271–73;

failures of, 269–70

V1 flying bomb, 175–77, 213

V2 flying bomb, 213

Vansittart, Sir Robert, 30

Vietinghoff, General Heinrich von, 163–66, 168, 170–72, 229

Wachines, 53

Wachtel, Colonel Siegfried Freiherr von, 177

Watson-Watt, Sir Robert, 23, 74

Wavell, General Sir Archibald, Commander of Middle East Command, 100–01, 104, 106–07, 112, 268

Weich, General Maximilian von, 103

Welsh, Air Marshal Sir William 'Sinbad', British

Welsh, (continued) Air Forces Eastern Air Command, 135, 142–44

Weygand, General Maxime, 59–61

Williams, Brigadier E. T., 113, 189, 205

Wycombe Abbey Girls' School, 137, 181

Wyatt, Captain Inzer, 245

Wynn, Roger, 128

Yalta Conference, 264

Yamamoto, Admiral Isoroku, Japanese Commander in Chief Combined Fleet, 252

Yellow Plan, 50, 55

Zempin, 177

DECEMBER 11, 1944 . . . U.S.S. *Candlefish*, submarine on wartime patrol, mysteriously lost at Latitude 30 in the Pacific. All hands perish, except for one survivor.

OCTOBER 5, 1974 . . . Six hundred miles northwest of Pearl Harbor, a submarine surfaces in front of a Japanese freighter. It is the *Candlefish*, in perfect working order fully outfitted down to steaks in the freezer yet without a trace of life aboard.

In Washington, D.C., a naval intelligence officer is convinced that the *Candlefish* was the victim of another Devil's Triangle, and convinces his superiors to send it on a voyage retracing her route of thirty years before in the hope of uncovering whatever fearful force lies in wait at Latitude 30.

Only when the sub is well out to sea, with no turning back, do he and the rest of the crew begin to suspect why the *Candlefish* has come back from a watery grave, and what that means to every living soul aboard.

GHOSTBOAT

by George E. Simpson and Neal R. Burger

BESTSELLERS
FROM DELL

fiction